Miss Priss

and the

Con Man

For Marilyn
and Vern,
with love,

Jill
11/12/11

Miss Priss

and the

Con Man

Jill Breckenridge

Jill Breckenridge

NODIN PRESS

Design: John Toren
ISBN:978-1-935666-29-5
Library of Congress Control Number: 2011941249

Nodin Press
530 N 3rd St
Suite 120
Minneapolis, MN
55401

This book is dedicated to my brother,
Chad Breckenridge, to my grown children
and growing grandchildren,
and, as ever, to John.

Except for specific historical dates and data, the truth in this memoir is my truth. My brother remembers quite a different father than I do. We will never know how my parents would have voted on the matter. They're resting, far beyond these concerns.

CONTENTS

*The stories people tell have a way of taking care of them...
Sometimes a person needs a story more than food to stay alive.
That's why we put these stories in each other's memory.*

– Barry Lopez
Crow and Weasel

*Willy was a salesman. And for a salesman, there is no rock
bottom to the life...He's a man way out there in the blue riding
on a smile and a shoeshine...A salesman is got to dream, boy. It
comes with the territory.*

– Uncle Charley in
Death of a Salesman by Arthur Miller

*"Truth," said the Traveler, "is a Breath, a Wind, a Shadow,
a Phantom."*

– Barbara Robinette Moss
Change Me Into Zeus's Daughter

Prologue

I read Mother's letter once, then twice more. She wrote that my father had been arrested. He was being held awaiting trial in The Tombs jail in New York City. I folded the letter, returned it to its envelope, and placed the envelope at the back of my desk drawer in the sorority house. It was 1954, my sophomore year of college in Boulder, Colorado. After the initial shock passed, I thought, "There must be some mistake—this can't be true."

Two years later, after my father had been tried, found guilty, and served his prison time, I still believed in his innocence. For much of my adult life, that is what I believed. Only when I entered my sixties, after forty-five years of attempting to forget my past, did I have the courage and sustained will to try and find out what had actually happened before my father's arrest and sentencing.

I was determined to uncover who he was as a person, this man I knew as my father. Moreover, I wanted to fully comprehend who he was to me and who he was under the law. This quest would not have been possible without the SEC and the Freedom of Information Act (FOIA) that allows Americans to request and examine past prosecution and court records of family members.

I've also been forced to examine my combative relationship with my mother during my father's frequent absences, and to look hard at what she and I became—because of who we were as individuals and because of the effect my father had on our lives.

But remembering was not enough. My own pursuit of forgiveness and repentance became part of the search for a deeper understanding of my family's turbulent history—of the way we were then—living in the West, where a dream was so close to reality, it simply waited for someone to call it by name, halter it, and lead it home.

1

Where I Come From

"It was still the Wild West, in those days, the far West. We knew toil and hardship and hunger and thirst; and we saw men die violent deaths as they worked among the horses and cattle..."

– President Theodore Roosevelt

"And please let Dad's deal go through." That's how my childhood prayers always ended. It seemed like his deals often didn't go through or did go through only to end in disaster. But Mother and I were always hopeful. At least I was. Over time, Mother tired of being hopeful, but I thought my dad was perfect.

Well, not perfect, perhaps, but I thought Charlie Breckenridge was the handsomest man in the world, without exaggeration. Mother said he spent so much time in the shower, she was afraid he'd melt like bar soap and wash down the drain. After combing his gray-streaked hair back into waves, he came out of the bathroom and saw me.

"Hello, Princess," he said. "How's my pride and joy today?"

Sometimes I'd catch him studying me, comparing me to his mother. He said I looked like her. Talked like her. Had her strong will. After staring at me a little longer, he'd shake his head in disbelief.

One thing different about me was that she and my parents had dark hair, but my hair was red. The only other trace of red hair in our entire family was my grandfather's red beard. I was the first redhead. That made me special. Mother and Dad said my hair was a beautiful, golden red color—and wavy—not that carroty, frizzy kind of red.

Dad's sister, Aunt Jo, told me that after I was born, she was in

Mother's hospital room, full of fall bouquets that raised fistfuls of maroon, orange, and gold blossoms into afternoon sunlight. When the nurse brought me in, she handed me to Mother, who put up her hand to signal, Stop! Then she instructed Aunt Jo, "Count her fingers and toes."

"But she's beautiful," Aunt Jo said, who'd always wanted a daughter. "Look at her coloring. And her features are perfect."

"I won't touch her until you count her fingers and toes," Mother said, turning her face away from me.

Aunt Jo did as she was told. Counted out loud, she was so mad at Mother, "One, two, three..." Luckily, the count added up to ten— and ten again.

"That's a relief!" Mother said, as Aunt Jo handed me over to her. It was quiet for a moment as Mother scrutinized me. Then she said, "Look at that pursed little mouth. She's going to be prissy."

The first thing close relatives say about the newborn-you becomes a blessing or a curse, foretelling their relationship with you, and shaping your life as well.

My mother in riding outfit, 1926.

"When I found out I was pregnant, I rode horseback nonstop," Mother told me once, laughing. "That just goes to show you how desperate I was. You know how I hate horses."

But nothing she tried worked. When I picture myself in her womb, I'm floating around in that stormy sea, arms and legs outstretched, holding on for dear life. Just like that striped cat in the cartoons, the one whose tail the mouse plugged into the electric socket. My eyes are as big as saucers and my red hair stands up straight as I hold on with all the strength I have in my baby arms and legs. I must have been hungry too because Mother starved during her entire pregnancy.

She never wanted a baby. Never thought she'd have one. My parent's friend, Dr. Budge, had examined her and said her uterus was so tipped, she didn't even have to use birth control. She'd never get pregnant.

Nine years later, I was conceived on the very day my father's mother, Anna Corder Breckenridge, died.

Mother may not have been able to end her pregnancy, but she wasn't about to lose her figure. She ate little, avoided milk, which she'd always hated, and drank as much gin as she needed to steady her nerves. When she was eight months along, she still wore khaki English jodhpurs that fit her like a leather glove. Nobody believed she was pregnant.

The author's baby picture, 1938.

I jumped ship a month early, and was born on October 23, 1938. At birth, sopping wet and bloody, I weighed five pounds, which is pretty good when you consider my starvation diet of the previous eight months.

"You slipped out so fast," Mother said, "like a little kitten." No wonder.

After we came home from the hospital, I got back at Mother right away. She said I cried nonstop for over four months. Only rocking made me stop. I guess I'd gotten used to the motion.

In those days, you weren't supposed to hold a baby much, so she put me in my crib at night and rocked that. She had to rock it so hard, my head flopped back and forth. Otherwise, I wouldn't stop crying.

Night after night, she rocked my crib until she got so tired she lay down on the floor and continued rocking from there. After what felt like hours, I'd stop bawling. She gradually let her hand slip down the leg of my crib and began to fall asleep. Just as she dozed off, my head popped up, and I began howling again.

"I almost forgot what sleep was during those months," she said. "I got so tired, I just lay there on the cold floor, rocking and weeping, both of us going at it!"

I realized later I wasn't just the child of a mother who drank gin instead of milk, who drank gin instead of eating solid food. I was also a child of the thirties, born at the end of a terrible Depression, when Roosevelt's New Deal had barely put the shaky economy back on its feet; born just before Hitler thundered his tanks into Poland and tipped the already insecure world my parents had known upside down and sideways.

Mother's hands always shook. They trembled and fluttered like small birds frightened into open air where they could be brought down by any stick or stone. Shielding each other in her lap, one or the other broke cover and fluttered, frozen in confusion, finding no hiding place under sun or cloud.

By nature, Mother was nervous—a word that, in those days, had a wealth of meanings. It could mean: anxious, scared, worried—even drunk. It didn't necessarily mean crazy; it just meant not quite on top of things. Whenever I asked her if she was feeling nervous, though, she'd say, no, she just had a headache, or she was just a little tired.

Mother hid somewhere deep inside herself where she felt safe, seldom betraying her thoughts or feelings by attaching words to them. When forced to speak, her words were often the empty ones like, How are you today? I'm fine, how are you? I'm fine, how are you? I'm fine...and on...and on, crooked circles of meaningless words collapsing in on themselves...

That's why, from the time I was a small child, I collected words, fitted them together like intricate rings, bracelets, and necklaces of prized and precious jewels, each gem aglitter, sparkling with meaning. Mother gave me many gifts by example, but her examples were often negative, so I avoided the shadow of who she was and stepped into the open space of who she wasn't.

I understand now why she never wanted children. She knew Dad had more charm than stability, knew her world was balanced on a fragile dollar sign that kept tipping over. Dad started cheating on her the first year of their marriage and by the time she got pregnant at twenty-nine, his running around was habitual. She was thirty when I was born. In those days, thirty was considered old to have a baby.

Mother knew she wasn't up to raising a child alone, so she called in reinforcements. She taught me to pray. As soon as I could talk, she sat on the edge of my bed and placed my small palms together. I repeated after her, line by line, a long childhood prayer asking for strength, health, guidance, and protection. Then I prayed for our family, ending with, "And please let Dad's deal go through."

For much of my life, I said that prayer.

Prayer has always seemed like a story to me, a story that begins with gratitude and ends with entreaty. The Breckenridge family fed on stories. They were as necessary to us as butter to warm bread. Stories, like prayers, could give you hope. They could even keep you alive.

Dad, Aunt Jo, and their father, whom I called Baba, loved telling stories about the Breckenridge family. Although I'd heard those stories many times, I always wanted to hear them again. Dad's were the best. They were usually told without many details, but I saw the scenes in my mind like a Technicolor movie.

My father, Charles Corder Breckenridge, was born in 1902, which made him too young to enlist in the First World War in 1917. At fifteen, Dad thought war was preferable to the sheep ranch he'd grown up on outside Boise. He'd always been a wanderer. His earliest memory, when he was three years old, was following the horse and wagon of Tommy Chung, the Chinese vegetable vendor, from house to house all over town.

Tommy couldn't send the little boy home because he refused to leave. So the vendor lifted Dad up into the wagon where he sat surrounded by somber onions, green-flagged carrots, and soil-frosted radishes. Behind him, tangles of string beans nested beside mountains of Idaho potatoes. My father gaily handed out fresh vegetables to aproned housewives. Whenever Dad's family couldn't find him, they went searching for Tommy Chung, guided by the song of his bell ringing at every stop.

As Dad got older, he was drafted into the ranch's daily chores. He always hated the endless work a ranch demanded, hated how little return you got back for your labor. A towheaded, blue-eyed charmer, he learned early—or maybe he was born with the knowledge—that winning people over with an earnest smile and a quick wit paid higher dividends than physical labor.

Men admired and trusted him, and every woman who still had blood running in her veins fell in love with him. His first pushover was his mother; she could deny him nothing. But she couldn't protect him from doing his share of the ranch work.

Raising sheep was always hard work, especially in late winter or early spring when the ewes dropped their lambs.

"That was the right word," Dad said, "*dropped*. We had to stay up all night and watch them constantly, or they'd walk away from their newborns. Even after we caught them, some ewes wouldn't feed their own lambs. There were always a few rejected orphans we had to attach to other mothers."

It was boom and bust for farm prices. One month, the price for sheep was high; the next month, prices fell off the cliff. Raising sheep wasn't glamorous like raising cattle, but it was often more profitable. Sheep were cheaper, needed less water, and one herder could drive more than a thousand head, although their constant bleating often drove herders crazy.

Word had it that before the sheep were brought in, Idaho was covered with waving green bunch grass as far as the eye could see. Sheep ate that grass clear down to the ground, and then cut up the ground with their sharp hooves. The scant grass remaining turned yellow and died with no new shoots till the next spring. Some said that because of sheep, southern Idaho was no longer carpeted with green grass but linoleumed with pistachio-colored sagebrush, dusty weeds, cheat grass, and lava rock. The only green places left were huddled next to rivers.

Dad said that story about the original grassland was nothing but *bushwa*, a dirty rumor started by cattlemen, who wanted the good grazing land for themselves. Cattlemen called sheep *wooly-monsters*. They said their cattle wouldn't drink from water holes used by sheep because their smell so fouled the water that cattle would rather dry down to leather than drink it. Raising sheep was a risky, unpopular business.

In those harsh days, whipping was the preferred form of discipline, and Dad said he spent most of his early years in the woodshed getting one beating after another. Aunt Jo said my grandfather, Baba, was a kind and gentle man who taught her the name of every wildflower. He could even tell desert paintbrush, with its red flower clusters, from narrow-leaf paintbrush, which also has red flowers, but a purple stem and leaves.

All Dad remembered was his father's beatings—too many to count. But no amount of beating could stop him. He ran away over and over again. Got into trouble at every opportunity. When he was nine, he disappeared after the Ringling Brothers Circus passed through Boise. His father tracked him to the next town on the circus schedule.

He found Dad inside the circus tent sitting on one of the round blue stands with white stars that elephants use in their balancing act. Preparing for his future career, Dad was raptly watching the trainer in the ring work four elephants through their routines. He was set on being an elephant trainer or a lion tamer. Over the boy's loud protests, Baba brought him home.

Dad read all the dime novels, but he loved best the *Fame and Fortune Weekly: Stories of Boys Who Make Money*. The weeklies had new stories in every issue, different variations of boys starting from nothing and winning the jackpot. Dad vowed to make at least a million dollars.

What he didn't get from those books—one of their stated main purposes—were the virtues of Honesty and Character. Somehow those lessons never stuck. If he didn't have the nickel or dime to buy the weekly, which he usually didn't, he stole it. Occasionally, he got caught, which meant another visit by the storeowner to his father, and another trip to the woodshed for my dad.

Aunt Jo told me that one summer, the four kids had to pick straw-berries and take them into town to sell. They all disliked picking berries, but Dad hated the chore most. It was a hot day. The sun hammered down on them, and the children were forbidden to eat a single one of those sun-warmed sirens. Although Dad complained the whole morning, surprisingly he ended up with the most boxes to sell. His were the biggest berries of all—plump, red, and irresistible.

Pulling their boxes of berries in wagons, the four kids walked to town and sold the fruit of their labor. The delighted grocer was al-ways happy to buy Baba's juicy berries. A few days later the upset man met my grandfather in church and told him that Dad's boxes of beautiful berries sold immediately. His customers were delighted until they discovered the boxes had berries only on top. Under that layer were clods of dirt.

My grandfather was embarrassed beyond words that his son had hoodwinked the grocer and his customers. Grandfather was honest and hard working. He was president of The Sons and Daughters of the Idaho Pioneers, and he worked to preserve historic sites and he-roic stories about early Idaho settlers. Silently, he paid the grocer for Dad's boxes of dirt, and it was back to the woodshed for my father.

"That woodshed was my second home," Dad said, laughing. "Maybe my first." But I knew how he really felt, and his eyes weren't laughing.

Whenever his eyes fell on me, they grew soft and kind. Dad said he treasured me from the moment I was born. He was thirty-six years old and had given up on having offspring. As the youngest of three boys born too close together, he hadn't been expected—or wanted. If that wasn't bad enough, when Aunt Jo came along, she stole his place at the end of the line. She always thought that was one of his problems.

When they were boys, Dad and his two brothers had to spend sum-mers far away from home alone with the sheep. Each boy, on differ-ent parts of the large ranch, grazed the sheep in mountain pastures accessible only in summer. They lived in sheep wagons, pulled out to their sites by cowboys on horseback. The wagons were outfitted with good beds, cooking utensils, wood-burning stoves, and windows that could be opened to let smoke escape and to welcome in a cool evening breeze.

Although his brothers were older, Dad started herding at twelve, still young enough to be afraid of the dark. For months at a time, the only living breathing sounds he heard were the bleating of sheep all day and the wails of mountain lions and wolves all night. The only human being he saw during those long summers was a camp tender who occasionally rode up with a packhorse and provisions—mainly beans and rice. For someone as sociable as Dad, this isolation was pure torture.

His black-and-white sheepdog, named Jennie, provided some comfort. She was the smartest dog Dad ever owned. Under her care, the sheep couldn't scatter from the flock and mindlessly wander away. Barking fiercely, she ran off any bold coyotes or cougars hunting newborn lambs.

In late spring, Dad and Jennie drove the flock back to the ranch for shearing. Dad's Uncle Grover could easily shear one hundred and fifty sheep a day. After the sheep were shorn, they were dipped to get rid of bugs. The new lambs' tails were docked short, and they were branded.

Grover was the first horse thief in the family. Good-looking, always surrounded by adoring women, he wasn't much respected by Grandfather and Grandmother Breckenridge, but he was my father's hero.

Dad said he'd never forget how Grover looked when he was castrating the ten-day-old male lambs. Grover did it the best way—the only respected way according to the expert Basques and Mexicans who taught him—with his teeth. This technique allowed him to bite off the testicles, and, at the same time, to pull out most of the connected inside apparatus, which prevented later infections.

Another herder held the lamb's legs and sat it down in his lap. Then, Grover cleanly bit off the testicles, spit them into a bucket, and laughed as he stood above the castrated lamb, blood running over his bottom lip and through his dark beard.

Dad also remembered visiting Grover in the fifties, when he was an old man. Driving way out of town on rutted dirt roads, past sagebrush and the startled eyes of jackrabbits, Dad found Grover living in a sheep wagon with his current Indian companion. Five or six little kids—all his—played in the dusty expanse around the wagon.

"He was just the same," Dad said, laughing, "hardly changed at all. Still good-looking. And all those kids! He must have been over eighty!"

The last time Dad went out with the sheep, he caught rheumatic fever. Too sick to stand or walk, he began crawling toward the ranch on his hands and knees. At night, he was too weak to find shelter, so he just put his head down on his arms and slept. Jennie curled up beside him, scaring off any predators.

The dog never left his side. During the day, she licked his face to encourage him on. Whenever he put his head down, resigned to give up and bake like a potato in the fierce Idaho sun, she nudged his shoulder with her head or nipped his arm until he started crawling again.

After several days, they finally made it home. But that was the end of sheepherding for Dad. In spite of the beatings, he refused to go out again. Many Basque families lived around Boise; they'd grown up herding sheep in northern Spain.

"I let the Basques do it," he said.

Dad swore he'd never be a sheep rancher. He wanted more. Mother embodied everything he aspired to. He first saw her in Boise when she was sixteen and he was twenty-two. She was driving down Warm Springs Avenue in her white convertible with white upholstery. The top was down. New leaves draped naked tree branches in bright green lace, and every capable pink and purple blossom was flinging whatever fragrance it could find into the spring air.

Mother wore a white dress with pink ribbons woven through the collar. Everything around her was white except for her blue-black hair, dark eyes, and those pink ribbons.

Dad said to himself, "That's the woman I'm going to marry!"

"Your mother was the most beautiful girl I've ever seen," people always said. Josephine St. Clair was born in 1908 in Silver City, Idaho. Her father, president of the town bank, had grown rich on silver booms. The St. Clair family owned the only car in town, a Model T Ford, called a flivver. Mother was an only child, so spoiled her bedroom floor was carpeted with real black fur. Ordered from the Sears Roebuck Catalog, the carpet was hauled by horse and wagon up the steep and curving roads to Silver City.

Curled up on that silky carpet, Mother spent hours dressing and undressing her beautiful dolls. The sun, reflecting off her silver wallpaper, made the gems on their ball gowns glitter. She walked her dolls across black fur to elegant castles where they met and married their Princes, all of them charming. After that first magical meeting, the Princess dolls never wanted for anything again.

Beyond Mother's imaginings was a world that wasn't fur-carpeted. But the price of silver went up and down—it was boom or bust. In one silver bust, her father's bank went broke. That day, when he walked through the front door of their house, no matter how Mother danced around him, curtsied and smiled, she couldn't make him laugh.

He managed to hold onto much of his money, but without a bank, the town was doomed. Everyone salvaged what few belongings they could pack on horses and mules or pull in horse-drawn wagons. Then, they slowly wound down twenty-three miles of torturous mountain roads.

Mother and her family rode down that mountain in their Model T, packed with whatever they could strap on top. Several mounted men—former bank employees—led pack mules carrying canvas bags of St. Clair clothing, bedding, and silver.

Dad said the Model T Ford was built to put the horse out of business. It could plow a field or pump water, and it could do up to forty miles an hour on a smooth road. But its brakes weren't up to the steep downward slope of those mountain roads.

As Grandfather St. Clair drove down the mountain, crawling around switchbacks and hairpin turns, Mother cried about leaving her beautiful bedroom that smelled of pine and sage. When she remembered how she put on her wool clothing every winter, then stepped out her front door and skied down the mountain, she cried even harder.

Down the easy grades the car brakes held, but every time the road got steeper, the brakes began to slip and the car picked up speed.

"All hands to! Out, girls!" her father yelled, and the hands ran toward the car as the child and her mother jumped out. Sometimes they didn't jump fast enough, and the car's speed increased so quickly, they tumbled out the open doors into the dirt as the Model T careened down the hill.

During these often-repeated episodes, Mother's father sat rigidly behind the wheel, his foot heavy on the useless brake pedal as the hands ran ahead to find big rocks along the road. The car continued to pick up speed until the hands threw rocks under its wheels and the car jerked abruptly to a stop.

After every close call, Mother and my grandmother, their faces streaked with dust and tears, took to walking, too frightened to climb back in the car immediately. When Mother got tired and couldn't keep up, they reluctantly climbed back in, their long dresses soiled and torn. All too soon, they repeated the whole tumbling sequence of events.

Carrying their few belongings, the exhausted group finally made it down the mountain. By that time, my mother carried a heavy fear of riding in cars that she could never set down.

They'd left almost everything behind. The houses were empty of people but still full of furniture and memories. The dusty beds were still made, ready for someone to climb into them. The children's rooms were occupied by dolls leaning against headboard pillows, while parked wagons stood by, ready to be pulled, and colorful balls waited to be picked up and thrown.

Mother grew up in Boise and went to high school there. Her parents continued to buy her all the beautiful clothes she'd come to expect. Dad didn't actually meet her until a year or so after he'd seen her driving the white convertible on Warm Springs Avenue. That first meeting took place when Mother was a senior in high school.

She and her date had driven out of town to pick up liquor for a party. During Prohibition, people bought liquor from a runner, the man who delivered bootleg for a distiller. Like today's drug dealer, the runner didn't produce the product, only sold it.

That night, the runner was my father. He and my mother fell in love at first sight.

Her parents were not in love with him, however. My grandfather was well aware of Dad's bad reputation. By then, he'd been in jail several times, but he never stayed long. His mother always rescued him with the combined force of her egg money and the goodwill of the jailer, who knew her husband and respected the family.

Mother's father tried everything to talk her out of him.

"Josephine," he said, "Charlie's got a terrible reputation. He's a common criminal. A crook!"

"He is not!" Mother said, "He's just helping people get bootleg. You and Mother drink every weekend. You don't go dry just because it's against the law. So how can you condemn him for making money by selling it?"

"I know," her father said," but that's not the best way to make money, and he's been in so much trouble..."

Mother interrupted him to say, " Well, isn't the law unjust, and isn't it a free country? You've always said that, Daddy. You've made your money. Why won't you give him a chance to make his?"

My grandfather loved his daughter, had never been able to say no to her. But this time, he didn't bend. After Mother graduated from high school, her parents sent her away to Westlake School for Girls, a finishing school in Southern California.

I was never sure why she went. She probably had some misgivings, herself, about marrying my father.

In Southern California, Mother was in her element. It was 1920, and Hollywood was still a dusty little retirement community. Horace Wilcox had bought the land to begin a Christian community. His wife called it Hollywood after the name of a friend's Iowa farm. Religion had not yet been eclipsed by dreamers willing to risk everything in their quest for fortune fed by fame.

But the film industry was beginning to take off. Harry Chandler, owner of the *Los Angeles Times,* gradually bought up most of the land in Hollywood and the San Fernando Valley. He wasn't sure how water could be brought into the Valley, but he knew it could be done.

He'd figure that out later.

Nor was the Hollywood sign in place when my mother arrived. A realty company engaged by Chandler to sell lots put it up as a promotion gimmick a year after she left. The sign, lighted by four thousand bulbs, originally read HOLLYWOOD LAND. Each letter was fifty feet high, and the light bulbs burned out so often that a caretaker whose only job was to change the bulbs lived in a cottage nearby.

Mother's Westlake roommate, Lucille Hosking, told me about the first time they met. Lucille had arrived a few hours earlier and had already put her clothing away in her dresser and closet. She'd gone out for a moment, and when she came back, "There was Josephine," she said, "in all her splendor. She had her gorgeous dresses scattered everywhere—all over her bed and all over my bed too. After a while, I said, 'Josephine, I'm going to need a place to sleep. What are you going to do with all these clothes?'"

Mother looked stricken. "I don't know," she said. "There doesn't seem to be enough room for them in the closet. I can't bear to be without my clothes!"

Evidently, the two girls figured it out because they became best friends. Later, Lucille lived in San Marino, and when my family moved to Pasadena in the fifties, the two old friends took up their friendship where they'd left off.

The curriculum at Westlake School For Girls couldn't have been very hard. It was a two-year "finishing school" with the stated purpose of teaching proper young ladies the secretarial skills of typing and bookkeeping. Mother never thought she'd need those skills. She didn't aspire to a menial career. All Westlake girls, Mother included, knew the unstated goal of the school was to introduce eligible young girls to wealthy men—the girls' charmed keys to the golden door of a secure, carefree future.

At first, Mother didn't date. She missed Dad so much, she wasn't in the mood. Then she received a letter from home bearing unwelcome news. A week or two after she'd left town, Dad had gone out to a local bar. The story was sketchy, but it seems he was angry about

Mother leaving, got drunk with a barmaid—a fiery brunette known for her small waist and large thirst—and woke up the next morning with a raging headache and a wedding ring on his finger.

Lucille said Mother cried for two days. Then she blew her nose, gathered herself together, and threw the ring Dad had given her out the second-story window of the dormitory. A bundle of his love letters followed. Mother hastened down into the yard herself and burned the letters, leaving a smoking rectangle in the lawn of the school as a memorial, crowned by the hot gold circle of Dad's ring.

By the time Mother entered Westlake, she was a flapper: pale white skin, rosebud mouth, and coal-black hair curving around her face like a tulip. She always darkened a tiny mole beneath her left eyebrow with black eyebrow pencil, her beauty mark.

In those days, almost anything could be bought for a price in Southern California, but Mother was not for sale. Never promiscuous, she didn't even like to kiss a date—and she didn't have to. She made her own rules. On a dare, she once danced the Charleston on top of a small round cocktail table. She smoked cigarettes, drank gin, attended parties on elegant yachts, and remained a good girl. Her inaccessibility made her all the more appealing.

Among Mother's many dates were Lance Darlington, an aspiring film star who looked like F. Scott Fitzgerald; Douglas Fairbanks Jr., an elegant movie star; and J. Paul Getty, one of the richest men in the world. The first two she found appealing. But she thought Getty was homely. Besides, he was thirty-three—an old man to her.

My mother wasn't much interested in J. Paul *or* his money. She was sure she'd marry for love and have plenty of money too. But Mr. Getty was smitten by her—and relentless. Mother laid out her conditions: The only way she'd go out with him was if her best friend, Lucille, could come along.

The two girls, dressed in silks and furs, sat in the back seat while J. Paul sat in the front with his chauffeur. Attempting to engage them, the older man awkwardly twisted around, while the girls whispered and giggled. He took them to parties around lighted swimming pools where champagne erupted like Old Faithful from huge silver bowls and a few ounces of beluga caviar cost as much as a diamond.

Soon, Mother grew tired of J. Paul and refused his invitations, but he sent birthday cards to her every year. The cards continued to arrive for five years after she was married.

Mother said no to a long list of bad fathers I might have had, graduated from Westlake, and came back to Boise. She'd erased Dad from her mind, and began to date again. One of the men she went out with was Uncle Jim, Dad's older brother.

Jim, the middle boy, was short and stocky like my grandfather Baba. He didn't have Dad's height or good looks, but he was honest and hard working. Although he was just a friend to Mother, he'd always had a crush on her.

Dad didn't stay married long—only a couple of months. Aunt Jo said the woman he married was a tough cookie with an even hotter temper than his.

"He started running around right away," Aunt Jo said, "and she wouldn't take any of his nonsense. He was lucky to get out of that marriage alive!"

One day, when Mother was at Dad's parents' ranch with Uncle Jim, Dad stopped by, and he and Mother saw each other for the first time in four years. Mother was twenty-one, Dad was twenty-seven. They took one look at each other and that was it.

My parents' wedding picture, 1929.

Over her parents' protests, they were married as soon as it could be arranged. Mother's wedding pictures were taken on what's called The Rim, overlooking Boise. She's standing on the lawn of their friends, Dr. Bruce Budge and his wife, Mary. He's the doctor who told Mother she'd never get pregnant.

Mother's wearing her long, white lace wedding dress. A white veil flows across her shoulders to adorn the ground behind her. Below her feet, the town of Boise stretches out toward the Rocky Mountains. A cloudy sky arches over her as she enters her new life with my dad, the young couple supported by three fragile words—love, honor, and obey—three words propped up by a repeated, rubber-kneed "I do."

Mother and Dad spent their honeymoon in Seattle, part of that time on a cruise. A family photograph shows her wearing a cloche hat and a slim, black, twenties-style coat with a fur collar framing her face. The newlyweds stand in front of a silver smoke-stack. Mother looks glamorous, jauntily holding a cigarette. Dad's wearing a hat with a brim, and the collar of his overcoat is turned up. He looks like a handsome gangster.

Nine years later, I was born in Boise, Idaho, at St. Luke's Hospital. Mother and Dad probably lived in an apartment there because Dad worked for the Standard Oil Company as a representative. He traveled around the state visiting gas stations and selling Standard Oil products.

The company liked him and he was well paid. Mother loved having a steady paycheck, something she yearned for her entire married life. Although Dad was a brilliant salesman, he had poor judgment, was a dismal manager, and had difficulty taking orders. One day he had an argument with one of his superiors at Standard Oil, walked out mad, and never returned.

From Boise my parents moved to Portland, where they worked at a restaurant and bar called The Azalea. We lived there from the time I was one until I was a little over two. Maybe it's only from photographs I've seen, but I remember a yellow playsuit Mother made me. Its bib front was the head of Ferdinand, the flower-smelling bull. My best friend was Ernie Bernie, as we called him. He was shy and sweet, and I was smitten by him.

Until we found a house to rent, we stayed at the old Benson Hotel. Built by a lumberman, it even had drinking fountains on the street out in front. Mother said I loved drinking from those fountains.

Mother had been taken on as the hostess at The Azalea; Dad

was the manager. The restaurant had good food and a busy bar. Like many food-and-drink establishments after Prohibition, The Azalea was in a building that once housed a speakeasy, so its location was well known.

We had picnics in the parks beside the Willamette River, and enjoyed the purple crocus, yellow daffodils, and rainbows of tulips that appeared toward the end of the hazy, wet winters. Dogwood, cherry, and apple trees, arrayed in white or pink, also blossomed early to greet the new season.

My parents were happy there. They liked working together. During hard times, Mother always said if things got really bad, she and Dad could manage a hotel or dude ranch together.

Business began to improve as the Depression eased, but German tanks invaded Poland in 1939, and, after the Pearl Harbor attack two years later, America declared war on Germany, Japan, and Italy. Rumors of impending attacks by undercover German squads somewhere along the West Coast terrified Mother, and she convinced Dad we'd be safer living in Idaho, close to family and friends during an uncertain time. So we moved back to Boise.

2

Sweet Deals in War Time

After we came back to Boise, the Second World War cast dark clouds over everything. It not only destroyed many lives, families, and cities, but the destruction it wrought continued long after the declared war ended.

Dad wanted to serve in the Navy, but only men from eighteen to thirty-six were eligible for the draft, and he was five years too old. His father sat on the Draft Board and listened to stories from boys who didn't want to go to war: their mothers needed them; their fathers needed them; they didn't believe in killing. Dad was never tempted to join their ranks. He was dead-set on enlisting. Mother was dead-set against it.

From the time the war began, Dad raptly listened to Edward R. Murrow, who began every broadcast with "This...is London." Pulling his chair close to the tall, standing radio, Dad leaned forward toward the cloth-covered speaker and shushed anyone who peeped until the broadcast was over.

The war in Europe caused dissension in our house. At first, my parents engaged in what the radio newscasters called skirmishes. Mother said Dad was too old—he had no business leaving a wife and young child to fight a war he didn't have to fight. Dad said protecting our country was his duty—everyone would think his father kept him out because he had pull with the Draft Board. Mother said that was baloney—he just wanted to escape his family responsibilities and have an adventure. His running off had nothing to do with patriotism. At that point Dad would often stalk out, slamming the front door, and drive around in his car to cool off.

Late in 1942, America got beaten in Guam, Wake, Hong Kong,

Borneo, Singapore, the Netherlands' Indies, and worst of all, the Philippines. We watched these locales go up in flames one after another on the Saturday night newsreels. People screamed and ran across the huge screen as everything behind them was reduced to rubble, smoke, and ash.

That destruction was the push Dad needed. Whether he lied about his age or the Navy didn't care, he walked in the front door one day and proudly announced he'd enlisted in the Navy. Mother, sobbing, screamed at him, "Damn you! Damn you! You're going to put us through that? And you don't even have to go!"

He shouted back, "This isn't about you, Josephine. It's about our world! Can't you see, goddamnit, they're trying to take over the world!"

Mother, still sobbing, said, "It is too about me. It's about your family, your wife and daughter. Why can't you let the younger boys do it?"

"I can't Josephine," he said, "I just can't," and he put his arms around her, around me too, because I'd run up and was holding onto their legs, crying, trying to keep them together.

Mother's words were muted by Dad's shirt as he held her against him, "You're just going for the adventure. I know it. There's probably some scheme you've thought up..."

Dad pushed us away and walked out of the room.

When he got his assignment, Dad found he'd be stationed on New Caledonia, in the southwest Pacific about eight hundred miles east of Australia. Quite a coincidence, Dad thought, with our Scottish last name, that Caledonia was the poetic name for Scotland. It was the island where warships refueled, and Dad would be in charge of all the fueling operations. By that time, carriers had replaced battleships because they could move the fighter planes close to any target and easily refuel them. New Caledonia was a crucial base for our war offensive, so it was ripe for an enemy attack at any time. Mother and Dad knew that, but I didn't.

Before Dad left, Bob and Edith Campbell had us over for dinner. I dreaded going to the Campbell's house because, since the war began, everyone got drunk, and I got stuck with their daughter,

Susan. A year older than I, Susan was a skinny little bigmouth who blabbed, long before I was ready to hear it, that there was no Santa Claus. The Campbell's sad farewell party was made more difficult because Bob, who was Dad's age, hadn't enlisted.

After Dad left, Mother and I moved into Baba's house at 3213 Crescent Rim Drive. It was a small house, and cozy. When we first moved in, I loved everything about that house except for the basement, where there were spiders. I still remember the phone number, 899R, because Mother drilled our new phone number and address indelibly into my memory.

"In case you ever get lost," she coached me, "you must find a policeman. Don't ever ever talk to strangers. Find a policeman in uniform, just like the ones I've pointed out to you. Okay? And what would you say to him?"

"I'd tell him my name, Josephine Ann Breckenridge. Or can I say Jill?"

"Say Jill. That's what we've always called you. What then?" she asked.

"I'd tell him my address."

"And what is the address?"

After I told her, she said, "And your phone number?"

"899R," I said.

Then, she relaxed for a while, though it wasn't long before she was nervously running me through the drill again.

She worried, too, that we were going to be too much trouble for Baba, since he hadn't been feeling well. But he said it cheered him up to have us there.

"During these hard times," he said, "we have to stick together. That's what a family is for."

I didn't know Baba very well before we moved in. I only knew he'd spanked my dad a lot, but both Mother and Aunt Jo thought Dad deserved it. I liked Baba, but he teased me in ways that made me mad. Being a tomboy, I loved being outside where I could explore every tree and hideaway in the neighborhood. Sitting down for meals took too much time, so I snacked whenever I got hungry and never had any appetite for lunch or dinner.

Mother and Baba thought I was too skinny. Baba would say, "Finish up that nice sandwich, Jill. It'll make you fight your grandmother."

That comment flared up my redhead temper and flushed my cheeks. I said I wasn't about to fight my grandmother. I was conceived the day she died, and I loved her. I couldn't understand why he said that awful thing about her when he loved her beyond reason.

The first time they met, my grandmother was searching for her younger brother who was always late. It irritated her that she was always the one sent out to round him up. In order to get a better look around, she rode her roan high up on the ridge. That's when she caught sight of him.

Furious, she galloped her horse straight-legged down the slope, dislodging stones into small rock slides and startling the sunning diamondbacks into raising their rattle tails and shaking them. Galloping up to him, she reigned in her horse and yelled, "Where the hell have you been?!" only to find out it wasn't her brother at all, but my grandfather, her future husband, whom she'd never met.

Raised Presbyterian, Baba was straight-laced. His religion prohibited dancing, but my grandmother loved to dance, so he played the fiddle at all the local gatherings. He said it made him happy just to watch her dance. She often wore a long dress of red and yellow plaid that melted his heart.

Just when I thought I'd die from missing Dad, he came home on furlough before shipping out to the Pacific. I was outside playing, so he came into the backyard and called me. He looked handsome in his white Navy suit trimmed with blue stripes, and his stiff white hat with a dark brim. A small irrigation ditch cut straight across the middle of the yard. As I ran toward his open arms, neither of us realized that water had flooded into the grass and made it wet and slippery. We ran toward one another, laughing with delight, until we both slipped at the same time, and our feet flew out from under us.

I landed first, one of my legs stretched across the irrigation ditch. An eye blink later, Dad fell with his full weight upon my leg. I screamed, the pain like nothing I'd known before. My parents rushed me to the hospital for an x-ray to find out what they already knew. My leg was broken, and the doctor put a large white cast on it. Dad felt terrible, but after it stopped hurting it was fun.

The cast was heavy and my leg itched under it, but I was a small four-year-old, so Mother wheeled me around in a baby carriage until the leg healed. People peeked in expecting a little baby, and there I was, ready to tell them the whole story.

"You and your little baby bird bones," Mother said.

The doctor told her I had a calcium deficiency and my bones were brittle. Every morning I heard the hand-held eggbeater whirring in the kitchen as Mother made me an eggnog. After beating the egg and milk together, she stirred in two teaspoons of sugar, a teaspoon of vanilla, and topped it with a sprinkling of nutmeg. She called me into the kitchen, a guilty look on her face, trying to make up for all the milk she didn't drink when she was pregnant. I never protested because I loved her eggnogs.

Baba kept a map of the South Pacific on the kitchen wall. He marked, with round-headed silver pins, all the locations mentioned in the *Idaho Statesman* newspaper he poured over every morning, or heard on his evening CBS radio broadcasts reported by H.V. Kaltenborn.

I was learning to read, and as we fought back against Japan and won a few victories in the Pacific, Baba wrote down the names of the islands for me and helped me form the unfamiliar syllables with my mouth. I loved the sound and spelling of those words, but I was too young to understand what it all meant—that many people were dying, and my father was in danger.

The Joe Palooka comic strips in the newspaper scared me, but I always tried to read Little Orphan Annie. Baba helped me with the words I didn't understand. With Dad gone, I often felt like an orphan myself. How I missed his hugs and kisses, his "Hello Princess!" every time he came home and laid eyes on me.

I was cold all the time too. I don't know if it was because I didn't have enough meat on my bones, or if Mother couldn't afford to buy me a heavy coat. I froze outside in Idaho's winter wind, and I was cold inside the house, too. Maybe it was because of wartime rationing, but Baba's house was always freezing—almost unbearable in the morning. Every night, Mother put a chair beside the heating grate in the living room floor and hung my next day's clothes over it. When she dressed me the next morning, shivering by the grate, warm air surrounded us as she helped me slip my skinny, goose-pimpled arms and legs into my warm clothes.

Baba was Aunt Jo's father too, and she often visited us. Sometimes she brought her son, Breck, who was two years younger than I. When Aunt Jo, Mother, and Baba had coffee together in the living room, Breck and I played at their feet.

That was my chance to get Baba to tell one of his stories. He loved to tell stories as much as his children, Dad and Aunt Jo, did. These family stories and my resemblance to my grandmother later helped to save my life.

"Tell about the wagon train," I said.

"You want to hear that story again?" he asked, teasing.

"Yes! Yes!" Breck and I called out together.

"Okay," he said, acting put upon, but we knew he was teasing.

Directing his story to Breck and me, he said it was way back in 1874 when he came over the Oregon Trail in a wagon train from Missouri.

"I was just about the age you are now, Jilly," he said.

His family was bound for Oregon, following the Western dream of better land, the dream of plentiful rain and tall green grass. Day after day for over two thousand miles, a hundred wagons bumped along on old fur-trapper roads through sagebrush stretching for as far as you could see. Often you couldn't see very far because the wind blew so much dust in your face, you had to tie a kerchief over everything except your eyes, slit almost shut.

He said they didn't welcome night because of possible Indian attacks. The Pawnees were angry because the wagon train's livestock ate down their grazing land. But wagon train scouts also kept an eye out for daytime Indian war parties or buffalo hunters.

Looking at us and smiling, Baba said he still remembered riding in the wagon next to his stepfather, behind the dusty rumps of the mules. He liked it best when the wagons stopped in late afternoon.

"We children had to gather enough firewood to cook the evening meal and keep the fire going all night."

After the children delivered their wood back to camp, they hunted horny toads and played with them. The toads often refused to play anything but dead until the children were called back to the circled wagons for dinner. Set free, the spiny toads came to life and scuttled away.

Baba sat back, preparing to end the story.

"You didn't tell about the campfires," I said.

"Oh, yes," he said. "I know you like that part. Well, after the evening dishes were done and the livestock tended, we sat around a blazing campfire. Someone always had a guitar or a harmonica and someone always had songs to sing. When the songs ended, someone told a good story or two. How we children hated going to bed!"

They didn't sleep long, because the adults had their sights set on Oregon's valleys of lush grass and fat livestock. Baba said they weren't poor emigrants. In order to come, every family had saved several thousand dollars—a lot of money in those days—to pay for the trip, and still have money left to replace livestock and buy tools on the other end.

I knew, from other stories he'd told, that Baba's mother and stepfather were in one wagon, and his stepfather's brother and his family were in the one just ahead of them. They crossed into Idaho from Wyoming, passed through Bear Valley, turned north toward Fort Hall, and followed the Snake River until it reached the Boise River. They planned to follow the south side of that river as it wound through the town of Boise.

While the two wagons were crossing the roiling Snake River, they foundered and nearly tipped over. After much shouting, splashing, and urging on the mules, they made it across. But they lost one mule to the river. It took six mules to pull a wagon, so one of the brothers couldn't go on. They reluctantly flipped a coin. Baba's stepfather lost the flip and said good-bye to his dream of an easier life. He stayed behind and settled on arid Idaho land, while his luckier brother forged ahead to the greener fields of Oregon.

Baba continued to help me with spelling as our war victories in the Pacific mounted. The names rolled off my tongue as I wrote them down: Guadalcanal, Tarawa, Eniwetok, Saipan, Ulithi, Iwo Jima, and Okinawa. I was in love with the sound and sight of those names. There were over one hundred island invasions, and most of them I laboriously wrote down with my pencil on a fat-lined pad of paper while Baba helped me sound them out.

He explained that our previous victories all occurred in the air, but the Allies had begun to fight on the ground. Then, he reminded me that my father fueled every carrier in the Pacific Ocean. Since carriers fueled both ground and air fights, I was sure our victories were because of Dad.

We rationed now, and also saved our bacon grease, cans, and empty toothpaste tubes for the war effort. Women were urged to donate their nylons.

"Never!" said Mother. "I already have to use a stupid 'A' card that limits our gas to three gallons a week, and on top of that, I have to try and figure out those damned food stamps some idiot designed. Enough is enough! I'm not about to give up my nylons too!" Some stores were offering rayons to replace nylons, but she wouldn't hear of it.

Baba decided to put a Victory garden in his large back yard, which already gave us summer raspberries and fall apples. He plowed up some grass and grew tomatoes, cabbage, squash, peas, beans, carrots, onions, and lettuce. He said the only thing wrong with his garden was that he hadn't figured out yet how to grow beef, cheese, coffee, and butter in the ground.

All those items were strictly rationed; many were so dear we had to cut them out of our diet entirely. A Porterhouse steak cost twelve points. Mother loved sardines, and a little tin of sardines also cost twelve points. Pineapple juice, which I liked, was one of the most expensive items on the rationing list at twenty-two points a can. Only pineapple juice or pineapple inner-tube rings might have disguised the terrible taste of Spam, which we often ate. Even catsup, also a good Spam disguiser, was ridiculously high.

If either Mother or I complained, Baba rolled out one of his many statistics. He said at least we didn't have to crouch in bomb shelters for fifty-seven straight nights of uninterrupted bombings like they'd done in London during the Blitz. If that didn't shut us up, he mentioned that four hundred thousand people in London alone had put their cats and dogs to sleep because they feared they wouldn't be able to care for them.

Mother and I glanced at Smoky, Baba's black and white cat, sleeping peacefully under the kitchen table, and quit complaining. Mother's two cocker spaniels, Mickey and Puppy, were outside on the driveway dozing in the sun. Although they were safe for now, Mother worried that the only dog food available had no nutrition. She said it was nothing but hooves and horns. But we had to settle for what we could get.

The first Christmas Dad was away, Baba said, "Jill, have you heard there won't be any Christmas this year?"

"Why?" I asked, alarmed, but guarded against his teasing.

"Because the Japs got Santa Claus," he said. "They mistook his sleigh for one of our fighter planes and shot the old boy down."

Stamping my foot, my face reddening with fury, I said I'd heard no such thing. On Christmas Eve, Baba, dressed up like Santa Claus, arrived with my presents. He rubbed his pillow-stuffed stomach and gave out a "Ho, ho, ho!" but his laugh wasn't all that good, and I knew it was he in the red suit.

Even though that blabbermouth, Susan, had told me months before that Santa didn't exist, I played along. It meant a lot to him and Mother. When I should have been happy, I smiled a fake smile and hated Susan for making me pretend.

Baba gave me a doll I named Princess Helena. She had a beautiful porcelain face and cloth skin. Her white lace dress was tied at the waist with a lavender ribbon. I never liked the Shirley Temple dolls, all the rage with their silly blonde curls and cutesy outfits. But I loved my elegant Princess Helena. Sitting in Baba's platform rocker,

I held and rocked her. The Nelks, an old couple next door that I dearly loved, said they always knew when I was home. They could see the back of Baba's platform rocker swaying back and forth across the window on their side of our house as I rocked my doll.

During the day, unless the weather was bad, I played outside. Polio was a big scare then. Since no vaccine had been found yet, the doctors thought short naps helped kids resist the disease. I hated those afternoon naps because I was never tired.

In my favorite snapshot of me, I'm sitting outside in the back yard on a chair covered with green, red, and yellow-striped canvas, my hands resting on my bare knees. It's summer, and I have on shorts but no shirt. Mother let me play in shorts, like a boy, for as long as she could. Clothes just slowed me down.

Unlike Katharine Hepburn, who cut her hair short and asked to be called Jimmy, I never wanted to look like a boy or to be a boy. I liked being a girl. I just wanted to be able to do the things boys got to do.

I was the fastest runner for my age in the neighborhood, and I was the only girl who played football with the boys. Although I was too small to tackle them, once I got hold of the football, nothing could stop me. Whenever I got the hand-off, I dodged and darted past boys twice my size as I flew toward the goal line.

My best friend in the neighborhood was Rosie Dedman, who lived across from us in the biggest, most beautiful house on the street. Our house was plastered with stucco, a fake stone, but hers was made of real stone. Her father, Dr. Dedman, was a gynecologist. Mother called him "a woman's doctor." He delivered all the babies in Boise during the war. That's why he wasn't drafted.

Mrs. Dedman had been an English teacher before she married. Rosie and Roger, her older brother, learned a vocabulary word every day. Early in the morning, before the children got up, Mrs. Dedman wrote a new word in her beautiful block letters and taped it on the refrigerator. The children had their very own dictionaries, which they kept in their rooms and used to complete the assignment. By the end of the day, they had to know how to pronounce the word, spell it, and use it in a sentence. At dinner, they took turns showing off the new word for their father.

I couldn't wait to get over there every day and write down the day's word, learn how to spell it, memorize its meaning, and make up a sentence using it. Baba let me use his dictionary, and when I got stuck, he helped me look up the word.

Rosie and me on the first day of kindergarten, 1944.

"*Comprehend:* c-o-m-p-r-e-h-e-n-d …to grasp the meaning. I comprehend why we're at war with Germany."

"*Pastoral:* p-a-s-t-o-r-a-l…relating to shepherds or country life. My father had a pastoral childhood."

Mrs. Dedman thought I was going to have a splendid vocabulary, and she complimented me on my singing voice too. Almost every day, she made pies, and with the leftover dough she fashioned crescent-shaped tarts sprinkled with cinnamon-sugar. In the afternoons, she called us in for milk and a crisp cinnamon tart. Her kitchen smelled like a spicy heaven.

I worshipped Mrs. Dedman. Rosie and Roger had brown hair because they were both adopted, but Mrs. Dedman had red hair like mine, and the softest, sweetest voice I'd ever heard. She and Mother joked that Rosie and I must have gotten mixed up in the hospital.

Evidently Mother heard from Baba about the vocabulary words at the Dedman's house. One day, when I came in from playing, Mother was wearing the first pair of slacks she'd ever owned to prove she was her own boss. They were black, and she looked slim and elegant. Slacks had become fashionable because of Rosie the Riveter. For the first time in our nation's history, women worked in factories and served in the military. Mrs. Dedman said they were helping us win the war.

That night, when I came in from playing, I not only noticed the slacks. I also noticed that Mother had been drinking. It wasn't the first time. Since Dad was in New Caledonia and Baba's religion prohibited alcohol, Mother had started drinking alone.

My plate of food was waiting on the table. Even though she'd fixed dinner for me, she hadn't fixed anything for herself. I sat down. Then I noticed there was a word taped up on the refrigerator. We were going to play the word game at our house too! I felt a flush of pleasure.

Mother said the word out loud to me. She spelled it, gave the definition, and used it in a sentence.

"*Bullshit:* B-u-l-l-s-h-i-t...What bulls do after they eat. Don't fall for that bullshit."

She laughed at her own joke.

I didn't think it was funny and told her so.

"What's wrong? Can't take a joke, Miss Priss?" she said. "Come on, have a little sense of humor."

"It's not funny."

Getting up from the table, I went to my room and shut the door. I wasn't hungry. How I missed Dad. Mother wouldn't have acted that way if he'd been home. I never understood why she called me Miss Priss. I wasn't a bit prissy, like Shirley Temple. Maybe it meant a know-it-all who loved to learn new words. Maybe it meant she didn't like me.

No matter how sad I felt, my bedroom always comforted me. I had bunk beds with matching brown cowboy spreads. Across those brown spreads, cowboys wearing red or yellow shirts roped calves and rode bucking broncos. I also owned Hopalong Cassidy cowboy boots and a Lone Ranger ring that glowed in the dark. I'd ordered it with a Wheaties coupon. The ring sat on my dresser. It glowed with a blue light all night long.

After climbing the wooden ladder on the side of my bunk beds, I slept on the top bunk. If I was feeling scared in the dark or really sad, I looked at the ring. Its blue light made me feel better. I turned over on my stomach and slid down under the covers until my feet rested flat against the footboards. By moving my feet forward and back, I could rock the bed. I rocked hard. That's how I fell asleep every night.

In time I found it easy to tell if Mother had had even one drink, not only by the smell on her breath (vodka does have an odor), but by her slightly bloodshot and watery eyes. And I could guess how many drinks she'd had by how slurred her speech had become and how mean she was.

During the day one of Mother's dogs kept me company. She'd brought two Cocker Spaniels—a father and his son—into her marriage. Mickey, the father, was an old red cocker. He snapped, Mother said, because he had sore ears. He was so cranky, he'd snap at you when you least expected it. Mother was the only person he didn't try to bite. If I'd lived in wartime London, when people put their dogs and cats to sleep, I'd have been first in line with Mickey.

But I'd have hidden his son, Puppy. A blonde cocker, Puppy was good-natured but dumb, fat, and lazy. He was stubborn, but patient. I dressed him up in cowboy hats and red kerchiefs. When I got a little older, I imagined saddling him and mounting. I tried to teach him to gallop, but he was stubborn.

When I slapped his reins—his leash—on his back and said, "Giddy up!" he barely roused himself from his sluggish overweight walk. With enough coaxing and slapping of the reins, he lumbered into an awkward gallop as I followed, horse-style, my right foot leading, then my left foot catching up.

Rosie had a black and white Boston terrier named Trixie. The two dogs together looked like Mutt and Jeff. Besides their differences in size and girth, the most glaring difference was that Trixie was smart and fast. She learned how to gallop right away, seemed to enjoy it, and made Puppy look like a clumsy plow horse in comparison.

I was crazy for horses, begging Mother to let me take riding lessons. Rosie was already signed up, and I wanted to take lessons with her. Mother got very nervous when I mentioned it. She was terrified of horses and rode only when she had to (like when she was trying to get rid of me). Otherwise, she said she'd rather walk, no matter how far the distance.

When I asked why horses scared her, she said that when she was a girl in Silver City, a friend of her parents had disappeared while riding her horse in the hills. Although people were worried when she didn't come back, they thought she was fine because her horse was calm and reliable.

The men formed a search party and combed the hills around Silver City. For several days they turned up nothing, but eventually one of the men tracking her horse came to a spot where it had obviously shied away from something and reared—probably a rattler. On the ground they found the woman's gold locket, and they also found pieces of her brain on nearby lava rocks and further off in the brush. They deduced that when the horse reared, her foot went through the stirrup, and as she fell toward the ground she was still attached to the horse, which dragged her head-down across the rocks as he bolted away. Mother said she was still haunted by the image of that woman's skeleton bouncing alongside her horse as it galloped through the hills.

Over the years Mother told me that story at least five times, and in time Dad grew weary of it. He wanted me to love horses like he did, and he came up with a story of his own. Uncle Grover had told it to him when he was little.

Grover was with a group of men heading out to hunt some lamb-killing coyotes. The men had to ride their horses across the treacherous Snake River during spring thaw, and they didn't realize they'd ridden into strong currents forming an undertow.

I asked Dad what an undertow was, and he said it was a current that pulled you underwater as if some giant had grabbed you by the ankles and jerked you down. The horses swam hard, struggling against the current. All of them except one made it to the other side with their riders on their backs. One horse had been pulled into the middle of the river. He and his rider were floating quickly downstream.

Eventually the rider was swept off his horse's back into the swiftly moving river, and began floundering and shouting for help. He couldn't swim. His friends were powerless to do anything, but as he started floating away the horse swam after him, caught his shirt in his teeth, and tried to pull him ashore. When the shirt was ripped from the horse's teeth he grabbed it a second time, holding his rider up for a moment longer. But the man finally slipped underwater and didn't surface again. The horse swam after him, turning his head back and forth, scanning the surface of the water. When he found nothing, he swam toward the bank. After a hard struggle, he made it to shore.

Mother was unconvinced. She said, "I don't plan on riding *any* horse, thank you, especially not one crossing the Snake River."

She hated water even more than she hated horses. If forced to swim, she dog paddled, her head rearing up out of the water like a cat thrown into an ice-bath. I inherited her fear of water.

With Dad off at war, the responsibility fell to Mother to raise me alone. She didn't feel up to the job, so she gave me prayer. Then, collecting what money she could spare, she signed me up for any class she thought would develop my talent and prepare me for what was very likely to be an uncertain future.

My first classes were summer swimming lessons in the town pool. Because I didn't have an ounce of fat on me, I was a sinker. No matter how hard I tried to float, on my stomach or on my back, I sank like a stone. The pool must have been one part water and four parts chlorine. Floundering down toward certain death, I always got water up my nose. It stung like fury. After every swimming lesson, my nose was stuffed-up and my eyes looked like red coals. I took swimming lessons for one summer, complaining bitterly. The next summer, I refused to submit to the torture.

Today, if water from the shower sprays my face, I still gasp and suck in my breath. Nor do I like boating on or flying over any liquid. In my opinion, water is what you drink, wash your hands in, or contemplate from a distance while sitting in a comfortable chair like I do now from inside a little cabin on the North Shore of Lake Superior.

However, I loved to go exploring. One beautiful summer day, I suggested to Rosie that we explore over the hill. She looked scared at first, but I could see her weakening. We lived up on Crescent Rim Drive, and it was a long drop to the wild, overgrown land below. The Dedmans didn't even know who owned it. We were dying to see what it was like down there, but our mothers strictly forbade going over the hill.

We decided not to take the dogs because they might bark and scare away wild animals we wanted to spy on. To give us strength and courage, we began our adventure by sucking the sweetness out of two honeysuckle blossoms from the bushes in Rosie's back yard. We waited until her mother was in the kitchen, at the front of the house. Then, we began our descent.

When our zigzagging path wasn't too narrow, we held hands as we picked our way down to the bottom of the hill. Rosie was braver on our trips to town, but I was braver on such adventures into the unknown. To keep our spirits up, we encouraged each other. At steep places, I turned over on my stomach and went down feet first, while Rosie squatted above me and held onto my arms. Then she came down on her stomach as I put my hands on her legs, then on her rump and back to steady her. We sat and slid down the steepest, most slippery places.

Once we reached the bottom, we found another path and followed it, carefully noticing the way we went so we wouldn't get lost. Everything was overgrown, just like the jungles far away in the Pacific we'd seen in newsreels. All around us, it was green green everywhere except for the blue sky way up between the treetops. We found branches, stripped off the leaves, put the sticks over our shoulders and marched, left right, left right, left right, just like our soldiers overseas.

Then we got tired and sat down on the path beside a line of black ants carrying little white bundles. Using our sticks, we messed up their line and watched them run around in a frenzy trying to find their little bundles again. Once they found them, we'd mess them up again.

We marched on until we came upon a baby bird, helpless and ugly, that had fallen out of its nest. It was red and naked except for a few tufts of dark feathers, with bulging eyes and a yellow beak that opened when we bent over it. The poor little thing thought we were its mother.

Turning the bird over and over, we studied it like scientists. One of us poked it with a stick. The other one did too. We knew we'd hurt it when blood oozed from its yellow beak. Now we'd have to kill it and put it out of its misery. We jabbed it hard with our sticks until it stopped moving. Then, we swept it off the path into the underbrush. A dark wet spot remained behind on the dirt—evidence of our crime.

We walked back on the same path without speaking, and climbed silently up the hill. It was a little easier going up than coming down. Still, it was slippery and scary. Even in the steepest places, we scrambled up alone, lost in our private thoughts. We didn't encourage or help one another. The excitement about disobeying our mothers had vanished, and we never spoke of the adventure again.

The next day, we both broke out in poison ivy that covered every inch of our bodies, even inside our noses, mouths, and every other private place we owned. In light of such damning evidence, we had to confess to our expedition. The itching was ferocious. Nothing made it stop. Twice a day our mothers carried us back and forth between the two houses to share a lukewarm bath enriched with Gentian Violet that colored both the water in the tub and the tub itself a bright purple. In the morning, we bathed at my house; in the afternoon at Rosie's. Those baths only soothed, for a short while, the ravaging itch.

Neither of us got punished because our mothers thought the terrible itching we endured was punishment enough. For over two weeks, they carried us back and forth without once complaining. Both their tubs turned the color of violet Easter eggs. The two mothers scrubbed and scrubbed them with cleansing powder and bleach, trying unsuccessfully to return their violet tubs to whiteness, while our bumpy, scratched-raw skin turned as red as that baby bird's.

The longer Dad was overseas, the more sullen and despondent my mother grew, and the madder she got at him. Although he was an officer, made a reasonable salary, and sent home a little money every month, it wasn't enough to pay our few bills and help Baba with the joint expenses. Mother didn't want to work, never thought she'd have to, but she knew if Dad had his way, he'd happily let Baba support us. That didn't feel right to her.

From the time I was a little girl, Mother told me more than I ever wanted to know about Dad's affairs—business and personal. She was sure he made plenty of money. As head of the fueling operations for New Caledonia, he met everyone who came or left the island. That put him in a perfect position to wheel and deal. Mother guessed this was the reason he enlisted. If he didn't become a war hero, he'd at least escape the burdens of family life for a while and make a little profit off the war.

Mother was also convinced Dad was wine-women-and-songing. No doubt, that's where most of his paycheck was going. The enlisted men, who expected to be bombed by the Japanese any moment, would have paid exorbitant prices for an occasional escape. Mother knew Dad was probably providing the whole island with their liquor—that was the wine part—and providing God knows what else. He'd find ways to offer them what they wanted.

From painful experience, Mother knew about Dad's other women. That was the women-and-song part. She'd end every story about his affairs by saying wistfully, "If he just wouldn't spend so much money on them."

She imagined Dad, tan and handsome, living in a tropical paradise, leading the life of a wealthy sugar plantation owner, while she worried about money, scrubbed purple bathtubs, and took care of his father and me. On top of everything else, her old cocker spaniel, Mickey, died. I couldn't pretend to be sorry, but she was bereft.

When I finally stopped itching and the rash went away, Mother decided she had to get a job. We needed the money. With the labor shortage, finding a job was easy. She worked as a secretary, exercising the skills she'd learned at Westlake School For Girls—the skills she thought she'd never use. She did the typing and bookkeeping for a realty company, and she was good at it. The owners were an older couple named Jean and Larry Brown. They were generous people, and even bought her a new IBM electric typewriter, a device which had just come on the market.

The Browns loved Mother and gave her time off whenever she needed to take me someplace, or, when Baba got sicker, to take him to the doctor. Diagnosed with prostate cancer, he stayed in his room most of the time now. The doctor said he wouldn't get any better.

Mother hoped he could last until my father got home. She wanted my Dad to make peace with him before he died.

"Your father was an absolute devil," Mother said. "Nothing made
him behave."

She told me that one Saturday night, when Dad was a teenager,
he asked his father for some cash for a night out. Baba, tightfisted by
nature, wouldn't part with any of his money. Dad stormed out, but
after his parents were asleep, he came back and stole his father's black
Model T Ford.

The next morning, my grandfather and grandmother got dressed
in their Sunday finery to go to church. Baba was a deacon in the
church, and very devout. When they went out to get in the car, it
was gone. Someone gave them a ride to church, where they found
the Model T.

After stealing the car, Dad picked up some friends and they rode
around for a while. When the car was almost out of gas, Dad drove it
up on the church lawn. There it sat, a ghostly reminder of secular life,
as churchgoers arrived for the Sunday service. And there it remained
for several days, because it had no tires. Dad had sold them to get
money for bootleg so he and his friends could continue their party.

"Was he sorry about what he'd done?" I asked Mother.

"No," she said. "He thought it was funny."

Since my summer swimming lessons hadn't gone well, Mother en-
rolled me in a summer watercolor class taught by Helen Hart. Miss
Hart picked us girls up in her yellow jeep every Saturday morning
and took us to Julia Davis Park for our lessons. In Boise, Miss Hart
was what we called "a character." She wore long red scarves that sailed
out behind her as she zipped around in her yellow jeep. I was fasci-
nated by her dramatically mascaraed eyelashes, black arched brows,
red tulip lips, and gold hoop earrings as big as bracelets. People in
Boise called her "Artsy Fartsy," but she didn't care.

At the park, we set up our easels and painted the lake and the
massive weeping willow trees growing around it. We learned how to
dampen our watercolor paper to make a rainstorm over the lake, dark

blues and grays running down the wet pages and dripping onto our bare feet. I loved the color so much, I could have eaten it raw.

Mother hung up my paintings all over the house. When friends like Edith Campbell commented on them, Mother said, "Yes, aren't they wonderful? I don't know where that child came from. Not from us, I can tell you...with that brain of hers."

I guess she meant that as a compliment, she said it often enough, but it made me feel lonely. I was beginning to wonder where I *had* come from. Looking in the mirror, I saw an Ugly Duckling. I hated my pale eyebrows and eyelashes, my freckles, when my parents' eyes were dark and their skin spot-free and beautiful.

At five years old, I adored my mother. I obeyed her and did my best to make her happy. The older I got, though, the meaner she became when she drank. I began to wonder if I might be happier living with Aunt Jo or Mrs. Dedman. But when I really thought about it, I knew that even though I longed for many of the things they had, I would have been miserable living in either of their houses.

Aunt Jo's husband, Uncle Am, didn't like me. He called me "Jelly," saying it with an evil little smirk. I didn't understand why he disliked me, because I'd never done anything to him. Maybe he was jealous because Aunt Jo loved me. He sneered at me, saying things like, "Had any toast today, Jelly?" His comments were stupid, but mean. I stayed as far away from him as possible.

I would have been miserable at Rosie's house, too, because everything wonderful there changed at night and on weekends when her father came home. I sometimes had dinner with them, and those dinners were awful. Not that the food wasn't good. We sat in their dining room eating delicious food off china plates with beautiful silverware. But Dr. Dedman must have been tired when he came home from delivering all those babies. His face was drawn and grim, and he almost never talked. When he did say something, it was to criticize Roger, whose eyes had a nervous blink. Rosie got by okay because she did most things right, but Roger seemed to irritate the doctor. Those dinners went on forever.

I loved sleeping overnight at Rosie's house, though. She had a beautiful all-white bedroom and a white four-poster bed with a white canopy. After being in Rosie's room, I'd have gladly sent my cowboys off to some other rodeo.

Although Mother was mad at Dad, she wrote to him often and looked forward to his replies. For security reasons, he couldn't talk about the war effort, but he could talk about the island of New Caledonia. He said it was beautiful. In the pictures he sent, it looked like Mother imagined—a tropical island movie set.

One day I went into her bedroom and found her sitting on the bed staring at one of the New Caledonia snapshots. It was a picture of Dad. He was naked to the waist, wearing only his white Navy shorts and brown sandals. His chest and arms were tanned, and he was smiling as he held a green parrot on one arm. He looked healthy, happy, and handsome.

On either side of him was a native girl wearing only a grass skirt and a necklace of white flowers that almost covered her breasts. The girls were smiling too. After staring at the picture for a while, Mother took her fingernail scissors and cut the girls away from either side of him. With her silver cigarette lighter, one at a time, she set them on fire in the ashtray. After the girls burned down to ashes, she put the picture of my father and his parrot in a silver frame and set the frame on her dresser.

Mother always left her pack of cigarettes on the living room table. When Susan was playing at my house one day, I stole two cigarettes from the pack and some matches from the kitchen. Susan and I snuck out and hid in the weeds bordering the canal behind Baba's house.

The wind was blowing hard but we got both cigarettes lit. The smoke choked us and made us cough. We hated the taste too, and snuffed out the cigarettes right away.

It was the first "grown-up" thing I'd ever done. I was five at the time. I didn't put going over the hill with Rosie in that category because it ended so badly with the poison ivy attack. Susan and I made a solemn pledge never to tell our mothers, but she went home, walked in the front door, and tattle-taled it right out of her big mouth.

At the time, a painter was doing some work in Baba's bedroom. When Mother, looking very serious, pulled me over to the living room couch and sat me down next to her, I knew I was in trouble.

"I understand you've been smoking."

"No I haven't," I lied.

"Jilly, I don't think that's true." She looked hard at me.

"How do you know?" I remembered my promise to Susan, and vowed to remain true to her and our secret.

"Oh a little bird told me," Mother said, "and I want you to tell the truth. I think you smoked with Susan."

I looked her right in the eye and lied.

"Well, I haven't been, and we didn't."

Mother, sighing, said, "Jill, go take a look at your eyelashes and eyebrows in the bathroom mirror."

"Why?" I stalled for time, knowing this was some kind of trap, but not sure how to get out of it.

She took my hand and we walked into the bathroom together. I leaned toward the mirror and looked closely at my eyelashes and eyebrows. They'd been long lashes—blonde and thick. Now they were hardly more than black stumps. Suddenly, I remembered how windy it was the day we smoked, and how the wind kept blowing the flames from the matches back into our faces as we struggled to get the cigarettes lit. I'd singed off every hair in my eyebrows and eyelashes.

As punishment, I had to stay in my room for two whole days. Mother didn't spank me; she just looked hurt. I felt terrible. I worshipped her and would never have done anything to hurt her. I was also embarrassed because I thought the painter must know I'd been a bad girl. Contrite, I promised I'd never lie to her again. Privately, I vowed I'd never confide in Susan again either.

One night, Mother seemed happier than I'd seen her in a long time. She was going out with friends to have some fun. Sitting in her black slip, she put on her make-up at her dressing table with its three-part mirror. She started with her face cream—a lighter cream than the thick cream she wore at night. Then she applied her black mascara, wetting the little brush with her tongue, then rubbing it back and forth on the strip of black color and stroking it carefully up the top lashes, then down the bottom ones.

After stroking on the mascara, she put her upper eyelashes into an eyelash curler that looked like half a birdcage. She put two fingers through the handles and then closed the soft rubber down on her lashes. When she opened the half-cage, her eyelashes curled so high, you'd think they were birds flying up to perch on her eyebrows.

I watched her in awe, thinking she looked a bit more like Lillian Gish, the silent film star with her darling rosebud mouth, than like Vivian Leigh. Or at least some combination of the two. Finally, she put on the face make-up that she ordered from out of town, the color mixed especially for her. After wiping any cream and make-up off her eyelids and eyebrows, she darkened her eyebrows with a black pencil into two little arches, dotted on her black beauty spot under her left eyebrow, and put a drop of Evening in Paris perfume on her neck under both ears.

She slipped her nylons over each foot very carefully because she couldn't buy any more stockings until the war ended. After she pulled them up over her knees and thighs, and caught them with the fox-nose holders of her garter belt, she straightened the dark seams in back.

Finally, she slipped into her black suede, thick-platform high heels with open toes and ankle straps. They made her wobble a little when she walked, but she didn't care because she said high heels made your legs look good.

After she put on red lipstick from a tube, she dropped a black dress over her head, careful to hold it away from her face so she wouldn't get any make-up on it. The dress was black crepe with lightly padded shoulders and a white polka dot pattern. She turned away from the mirror and leaned back, looking over her shoulder at herself.

"How do I look?" she asked, admiring herself in the mirror.

"You look the best!" I said.

Earlier, she had fixed dinner for Baba and me. It was hard for Baba to get up now, so she brought meals on a tray to him in bed. About six o'clock, the doorbell rang and Mother introduced me to a man I'd never met. A good-looking man. His name was Rodney Davidson. I knew there were lots of Davidsons in Boise, and they were all rich.

Mr. Davidson leaned toward me, reached out, and shook my hand. While Mother made him a drink, he sat on the couch and tried to make conversation with me. I knew immediately that something wrong was going on, and I didn't like it. I knew Dad wouldn't like it either.

He was trying to be friendly, asking me questions I'd have to answer like, "How old are you?" but I just glared at him, my arms folded in front of me, and didn't say a word. Even if he'd sat on me with all his weight, he wouldn't have gotten the word, "Five," out of me.

I was so impolite, he looked uncomfortable, but he tried one more time: "Do you go to school yet?" When I didn't respond, we held our standoff in strained silence. Soon Mother came back with the highballs and I glared at her too. They quickly finished their drinks and went out to dinner. I don't know when Mother got home.

But I did know that something bad had happened. Knew it was going to get worse, and nothing would ever be the same again. Mother only went out with Rodney Davidson once to get back at Dad, but evidently she told Edith Campbell, Susan's mother, about it. Edith told her husband, Bob, and he wrote to Dad in New Caledonia.

Dad was insanely jealous of Mother, and he must have sat on that tiny island and stewed about her one night out for the rest of the war. His code of ethics—a philanderer's twisted pride—demanded that you don't mess around in your own back yard. Dad made sure that his women were never from Boise. Mother had humiliated him in his own hometown. And with a Davidson, who was not only charming and attractive, but could have bought and sold Dad five times over. My father must have imagined that everyone in Boise was laughing at him, which intensified his anger and grief.

But everything went on at home as if nothing had changed. The next Christmas, Baba insisted on playing Santa Claus again. Only this time, even if I'd still been a believer, I would have guessed that no Santa could ever look that bad. His Santa suit hung off him like red living-room drapes, and his beard hung loosely around his emaciated face. Instead of a plump and jolly old elf, he looked like one of the survivors of the Bataan death march. He was so weak, when he tried to laugh, his "Ho, ho, ho" came out like a whisper.

He couldn't get back to bed without Mother's help.

By the time the war ended, Dad had built up so much anger, he came home crazy. His murderous state of mind might have been posttraumatic stress disorder (PTSD) from the strain of waiting day and night for bombs to drop on New Caledonia. Or it might have been Charlie Breckenridge's insane jealousy, or some poisonous combination of them both. Mother's date with Rodney Davidson lit the match that touched off the first stick of dynamite in our domestic World War III.

I was nearly six years old when Mother and I went to Long Beach and met Dad. Later, I wondered why she took me. You'd think they'd want time alone after being apart for so long. It occurred to me later that I was supposed to be her human shield.

We went to the amusement park in Long Beach called The Pike. Mother was terrified by most of the rides. I wanted to try every one, so Dad took me on the Ferris Wheel and the Merry-Go-Round. After much begging, Mother took me on the Tilt-A-Whirl. I was having a whee of a time, laughing and shouting, but she was totally silent.

Halfway through the ride, I noticed that her face was ashen and her knuckles were white as she gripped the bar. Before the ride, her hair had been swept up and held in place with combs, black curls swirling around on top of her head. The ride had whipped us around so much, all the combs had flown out of her hair. As we tilted and

Our family holiday at Long Beach.

whirled, her hair stuck straight out from her face. She looked like a crazy woman shooting electricity from her head.

Through clenched teeth, Mother said, "Get...me...out...of... here!"

"Stop!" I shouted, but we kept spinning around.

"Stop the ride!" I yelled every time we passed the operator. After several more spins around the circle, he heard me, and the ride groaned to a stop. Clutching the rail, Mother was frozen in her seat. The operator climbed on and unhooked her stiff fingers, one by one, from the rail. He helped her down, hair flying wildly around her ghostly white face.

An hour or so before that ride, we had a family picture taken. The backdrop of the picture is the tail-end of a trolley car. I'm sitting on the back rail. Mother and Dad are standing on either side of me. Dad looks furious. Mother looks hung over. I look scared. Not one of us is smiling.

Our private war had begun. The carefree life I'd known as a child was over and there was no calling it back. But the end of childhood as I'd known it wasn't the only casualty. After Long Beach, Dad stormed off somewhere and Mother and I came home alone. We were there when the ambulance came to take Baba to the hospital for what turned out to be his last trip. The same vehicle also served as the town hearse, and when it pulled up Baba said, "Aren't you a little early, Floyd?" We all laughed. As Floyd wheeled him into the ambulance, Mother and I began to cry. I was holding the beautiful doll Baba gave me, and in the emotion of the moment, I dropped her. She fell face down. When I picked her up and took her in my arms, her face remained on the asphalt in small porcelain pieces.

I held her as if she were a child wounded beyond medical help. But her faceless body made me so sad, I later stuffed her into the trashcan, white dress and all. I never played with dolls again. To this day, they remind me, not of something cute and cuddly, but of dead bodies preserved by stuffing instead of formaldehyde.

Baba died in the hospital a week later without ever saying goodbye to my father. He kept asking Mother, "Where's Charles, Josephine?" and she replied, "I don't know, Dad. He should be here any day now—he must have been held up."

After hearing the same answer several times, Baba looked at her skeptically, took her hand, squeezed it, closed his eyes, and died.

Mother didn't know where Dad was—out on a bender, somewhere, she guessed. He didn't come home until long after the funeral.

3

War's Collateral Damage

After my father came home and the family's war years began, I dreaded weekends only a little less than festive occasions. I remember four disastrous Christmas holidays (though looking back, there couldn't have been more than three) and violent weekends too many to count. Those war years are tangled together in my mind like strands of black pearls thrown together into a dark drawer.

In the beginning, when I was younger and the fights were less vicious, Mother tried to protect me from them. Late at night, she would bundle me up in a blanket and carry me next door to the Nelk's house. Such a sweet, older couple, they never asked questions. They held out their arms to accept me, carried me to their double bed, still warm from their sleeping bodies, and put me between them. With the Nelks' protective bodies on either side of me, all my nightmares would vanish—until I returned home the next morning.

As my parents' fights became more violent and erupted more suddenly, Mother no longer had time to take me to the Nelk's house, so she would take my hand and run with me out of the house to our car parked in the driveway. We'd lock ourselves in and fall asleep, Mother in the back seat and I in front—the shorter seat because of the steering wheel. As the sun rose, we woke, startled, and scurried into the house so our neighbors wouldn't see us.

The best evenings of those bad times were when Dr. and Mrs. Budge brought their son, Bruce, to my house, and our parents ordered in Chinese food from Benny's. Bruce was a cute blonde boy, just my age, even naughtier than I was. Always protective and kind to me, he treated me like the little sister he never had. But he was so wild, he scared me.

Since there was no table in the kitchen, Mother pulled down the fold-up ironing board and covered it with a blue-checked cloth. That became our dinner table. While the grown-ups drank in the living room, we sat at our narrow table eating Chow Mein and Egg Foo Yung, saying mean things about our parents, standing up occasionally to imitate them stagger-ing around drunk. Giggling, we let the Chow Mein slip off our forks, and choked on our crisp noodles. I don't re-member any fights on those evenings, probably because we all ate dinner and the Budges went home early to put Bruce to bed.

The author with the Nelks.

After I turned six, my parents often went to the Campbell's house. Since Mother was so protective, it seems odd she would have left me alone, but I don't remember having a baby-sitter. My parents wouldn't have wanted anyone to see what was going on in our house.

I tried to wait up for them because being awakened from a deep sleep was terrifying. I'd rock in Baba's platform rocker until I fell asleep, wake up later with a twisted neck, and put myself to bed.

Saying the long prayer Mother so diligently taught me didn't help much. Even after repeating it several times, I was still wide-awake, terrified of what was to come. I couldn't lie still. Eventually, I turned over on my stomach, scooted down to the bottom of my bunk bed, and rocked myself to sleep.

Some time later, I was awakened by a man's shout, a woman's scream, a glass breaking, or the sound of my mother's body hitting the living room wall. Unlike the shatter of a drink glass or the razor edge of a scream, when Mother's body hit the wall, it made a sicken-ing thud.

From a deep sleep, I recoiled to wakefulness, lay frozen in terror for a minute, and then realized it was my parents. They were home. Putting on my green flannel bathrobe and fuzzy red slippers, I scuffed—shoo-she, shoo-she, shoo-she—into the living room.

When I started sitting in on those fights, I approached the melee empty handed. Over the months, and then years, I learned to read, and often brought a book along. I sat in the rocking chair and rocked furiously as I read, but I can't remember a word or even a title from any of those books.

Once I learned to draw, that was easier to do while my parents were fighting. I could draw and still keep track of what was being said. Since I'd started taking horseback riding lessons with Rosie, my infatuation with horses had increased. To every fight, I brought along my tablet and drawing pencils so I could work on a horse drawing. With practice, I learned to draw a steady line while rocking back and forth in Baba's chair.

My horses, no matter what color—white, bay, palomino, black, chestnut, appaloosa, or pinto—were always drawn in profile. They had one front and one back leg raised, the legs closest to me. And every one of the horses I drew was strong and fast enough to carry me safely away.

By the time I entered the ring, the fight had already been going on for a while, rising gradually in pitch until it finally had the volume to wake me. Sometimes my parents were dressed in the clothes they'd worn that night to a party. At other times, Mother might have changed into her white satin nightgown and white chenille bathrobe, while dad had put on his pajamas under his red plaid robe with the green lapels. No matter what they wore, they always had drinks in their hands. Through our parched house flowed a river of liquor that never ran dry.

During these frequent battles, my job was not to pay close attention. Their fights were too boring for that—a constant repetition of the same insults, with only slight variations, growled or shouted over and over again.

"You son-of-a-bitch, you and your other women!" Mother might say, launching the first volley.

"And you were playing around like an alley cat while I was trying to win a goddamned war!" Dad would shoot back.

The dialogue was often interrupted here, as Mother, who usually threw the first punch, flew at Dad, trying to scratch his eyes out. But he could easily knock her aside with one slap of his hand. She was five-foot-six inches tall, but slender, and she flew through the air like a tennis ball.

Then, the ugly narrative continued.

"Me playing around?! You bastard! You've always played around, and I never even looked at another man until..."

"Until I was a million miles away about to have the shit bombed out of me! Then you had to pick that bastard, Rodney Davidson!"

Mother took a slow deliberate sip of her drink.

"No, I didn't choose him," she said, forming each word slowly, as if speaking to the village idiot. "I've told you over and over again, he asked me out to dinner, and I went. That's all."

Now Dad took the slow sip, glaring at Mother.

"No matter what you say, Josephine," he said, using the same voice an adult uses to address the insane or children, "it isn't *all* that happened because you've made me the laughing stock of Boise. I've never embarrassed you with a woman who lives around here."

"Is that supposed to make me feel better?" Mother demanded. "You were sleeping around with those native girls--don't try to tell me you weren't! And you always spend money on *your women*, money we don't have. I get my nose rubbed in it when I balance the checkbook!" She took a sip of her drink.

"Then don't balance it!" he said, taking another sip of his drink.

"Oh sure! Then you bounce checks and the bank shuts down our account again."

Sometimes I interrupted the dialogue to say something like, "I've heard that about a thousand times," or, "Why don't you just drop it?"

They stopped, stunned, and looked at me as if they'd forgotten who I was and what I was doing there. Then, they started up again as if I'd said nothing. Dad might continue.

"Josephine, I've never embarrassed you in your own home town!"

Dad seldom called Mother by her full first name unless he was mad at her.

"Don't you think I'm embarrassed when I have to crawl into the bank and make up some shoddy excuse for you again?" she said. Then, she threw a low blow, "You're just jealous because Rodney has more money than you'll ever have!"

This comment brought about a pause in the dialogue as Dad lurched out of his chair toward Mother and she rose to take him on, hands slapping at him, until he punched her in the shoulder or arm, and Mother flew across the room again.

These repetitive dialogues, interrupted by violence, sometimes went on for several days at a time—until the liquor ran out, or sheer exhaustion put them to bed. My job was to listen, calculate, and watch them like I watched a pan of milk heating up on the stove for hot chocolate. The heat was turned up high, and I had to be vigilant so the milk didn't boil over, spill on the burner, sizzle down to a stinking brown crust, and ruin everything.

I needed to calculate how hot things were getting in order to keep my mother alive, because she didn't seem to be able to do it for herself.

In happier times, when I was three, I used to beg Mother over and over again to read my favorite book, *Scat! Scat!,* to me. The book was hopelessly sentimental and I loved it beyond reason. On the cover was a picture of a fluffy white kitten surrounded by a pastel pink and blue background. The pictures, all in pastel colors too, illustrated the tragedy of a little kitten that was trying to find a home. Throughout the story, one person after another said, *"Scat!"* to the kitten as they chased it away from their warm houses. My heart ached for that kitten. Mother read the story to me so many times, the pastel pages, marred by thumbprints, were dog-eared.

Although no one had literally chased me out of my house, our family warfare accomplished the same thing. I'd always loved playing outdoors, but from the time the violence started, I nearly lived outside. I never sat, I paced. I never walked, I ran. I began to hate the house I'd once loved, and came inside only when I had no other choice. As bereft with loss as that white kitten, I had no safe place to come home to.

The last time I visited my grandfather's house at 3213 Crescent Rim Drive in Boise, it seemed to have shrunk. A stucco house trimmed in green, it was a dwelling you'd find variations of in any small American town, a design as repetitive as images on a roll of stamps. That house became my first lesson in the difference between appearance and reality. Although it was an innocuous little house, it often masked terror. A house is just packaging for the human lives fluidly moving—or flailing around—inside it. The residents determine whether it's a house or a cage.

In my thirties, I saw a therapist in an effort to free myself from the anxious dread that had surrounded me like an unholy aura for most of my life. I asked her to help me revisit that house in memory. By entering it again, I hoped to disperse the ghosts that haunted me. Although my therapist was hesitant, after some coaxing, she agreed.

When I'd relaxed in my chair, I closed my eyes. With her prompting, I described what I saw as I visualized walking up the sidewalk toward the three front steps of the house. Halfway up the walk, I stopped, terrified.

I spent two long sessions in her office, standing frozen on the sidewalk of memory, crying quietly, as I attempted to escape my father's damage. But I couldn't get close enough to put a foot on the first step. Even now, the thought of it makes my shoulders tremble, and I have to shake the fear, like freezing rain, off my back.

Finally, my therapist asked, "Have you had enough?"

"Yes," I said.

It was silent for several minutes as I blew my nose and tried to gather my composure, struggling to return from that sidewalk to the safety of her office. In a soft voice, my therapist began to speak.

"Our unconscious protects us," she said. "It won't let us remember or return to anything we're not able to handle."

"Will it always be that way?"

"Probably," she said. "Many children with backgrounds like yours don't survive childhood. They're so traumatized, they commit suicide."

"Really?" I said, "I never felt like doing that."

"Often these suicides look like accidents. Some kids fall from high windows, or run out from between parked cars into a busy street. Others do crazy, daredevil things."

She paused. "Did you take any big risks as a child?"

Although I was confused by her question, I couldn't say no.

Because of our family warfare, at the age of six, I was no longer a child, and this dramatic change touched off a secondary war between Mother and me. Before the fights began, I'd been a compliant child, anxious to please. I would have done anything to make my mother happy. Now, my feelings about her were, at best, ambivalent. Usually they were hostile.

Mother always knew Dad was insanely jealous. By going out with Rodney Davidson, she had destroyed our paradise. She not only waved a red flag in front of a mad bull, she hit that bull over the head with it. I knew Dad's behavior was much worse than hers. He'd cheated on Mother for years. But I never *witnessed* his philandering. Although I knew it happened, it never felt personal. I *saw* what Mother did. I was there.

Since she was the one who got us into this mess, I blamed her totally for the nightmare we were caught up in. I hated her for what she'd done, hated having to save her life weekend after weekend. Mother and I fought almost every day now—sometimes more than once a day. The reason was that I had stopped minding her. Even when I tried to mind, I couldn't. Why should I behave when she didn't?

One day, I had done something wrong. I have no doubt it was my fault. Mother spanked me, put me in my room and told me to stay there. I deserved the punishment. But it was summer and the windows were open. Since my bedroom was on the first floor, I pushed the window up a little higher, unlatched the screen, and climbed out into the backyard.

Mother found me there and spanked me again. After she put me back in my room, she closed and latched the screen, then closed and locked the window. When she left, I pulled my chair over to the window and climbed up on it. It took me a while to make the lock turn, but I finally got it unlocked. Then I unlatched the screen and climbed out again.

Mother was in the yard waiting for me, and this time she spanked me, not with her hand, but with a wooden spoon. I refused to cry, so she hit me harder. Because I still wouldn't cry, she spanked me on my bare legs as well as my bottom. When she couldn't reduce me to tears, she put me in my room and we went through the same routine again.

This scene was repeated five or six times. I remember thinking to myself, " If she's going to keep me in this room, she'll have to kill me first." Nothing short of death would have kept me there.

Finally, Mother sat down on the chair in my room and began to cry. I know her tears were real because it was the first and last time I ever saw her cry. Maybe she thought I'd feel sorry and apologize to her, but that idea never entered my mind. I'd hardened my heart to her.

Walking through my bedroom door, I went outside to play. The welts on my legs and bottom stung, but I felt good. Everything was different now. She wasn't my boss any longer. There was no going back. She would never be my boss again. Without any discussion, negotiation, or contract, I'd made a deal with her: I'll be totally responsible for myself, and you simply stay out of my way.

I closed the door on that dark house and joined my real family outside—the animals in their more predictable natural world. Spring and summer were my favorite seasons. After galloping Puppy to my hideout in the bushes by the canal, I sat, curled up in a safe ball, my arms around my knees, chin resting on them.

Puppy lay on his stomach beside me, his nose on his front paws, his back legs stretched out behind him. Above us, green leaves like hands and others like fingers directed the sun falling across and around us in moving shafts of light. I traced the patterns with my finger.

The Western landscape was a table laden with food for the soul that I could return to again and again. I took the green in through my eyes until it fed me full. Color was the seasoning. I could always count on the red of tulips and the purple of crocus to make daffodils a more delicious yellow. Not far away, the Rocky Mountains were lined up exactly where they'd been for centuries, standing so tall that clouds draped around them like tablecloths.

I grew daring enough to begin exploring the cement-lined irrigation canal running through town. It crossed the end of my grandfather's long back yard. Rosie and I were not allowed to go there because the water flowed rapidly, and it was way over our heads. Rosie could swim, but I couldn't. Farther down the canal from Baba's house was a waterwheel, which was strictly forbidden. The bad boys often played there.

We called them the bad boys because they were older than we were—probably in junior high—and naughty. The forbidden things they did thrilled us. On dares, they rode one of the waterwheel's blades up over the top of the wheel. They had to jump off before the blade went down under water on the other side. One wrong move and the wheel blade would crush them against the canal's gray cement lining.

Rosie and I watched, openmouthed, as they risked their lives over and over again. The bad boys liked having an audience. They thought we were cute—Rosie with her short brown hair in braids on either side of her face, and me with my red hair swept up, coiled, and pinned on top of my head, so it would be out of the way.

Our biggest dare was to push the dogs off the canal bank into the water. We walked along beside them, still on their leashes, as they swam with the canal's swift current. After a while, we pulled them out and dried them. We risked this adventure every chance we got.

Over time, the fights between my parents got longer and more intense. In the beginning, Dad hit Mother mainly on the shoulder or arm. Later, he started hitting her in the face. Since I was her shield, she began keeping me out of school until the fights ended, which sometimes took several days or longer. I couldn't do much to protect her, but I did my best.

After a particularly bad fight that lasted three days, Mother ended up with a black eye. She held an ice pack over her puffed-up eye, as it turned from red to blue to yellow-green. Seeing her bruised eye really upset me. I needed to talk to someone about it, so I told Rosie.

I assumed she already knew about the fights, thought the Nelks had told the Dedmans; or maybe the Dedmans had seen Mother and me coming inside those mornings after we'd slept in our parked car in the driveway. But Rosie looked stricken, especially when I told her how my parents hit each other—about Mother's black eye. She loved my parents, and always wanted to play at my house because it was more fun than her own.

"Why do they do that?" she asked, baffled.

What could I say? They hit each other because they loved each other? They hit each other because they hated each other? Which one was it?

"I don't know."

"They really *hit* each other, *hurt* each other?" she asked, re-coiling in disbelief.

"Yes," I said, regretting I'd ever said a thing.

"Oh, no..."

Slowly, the look on her face changed from shock to fear. I felt

Mrs. Dedman and Rosie, 1945.

her physically pull away from me, knew that her shrinking back was about the hitting—like I was the one doing it. Just by being a part of my family, I was guilty too. Guilty of what, I wasn't sure.

A few days after our conversation, I noticed Mrs. Dedman looking at me oddly. It didn't feel like sympathy. It felt like pity, a sentiment I immediately loathed. Since my parents began fighting, I'd noticed other people looking at me that way too, and I hated them for it.

From then on, I felt less welcome at the Dedman's house. What's more, I sensed that if Mrs. Dedman had her way, Rosie would never play with me again. This knowledge was a burden of sadness almost beyond bearing. In my mind, I could hear Mrs. Dedman's sweet voice saying, *Scat! Scat!*

I knew I could be naughty, knew I didn't mind my mother. Although I wasn't hitting her like Dad was, I loved him more. But I was part of both of them, and they were part of me. I had Mother's temper—mine flared up even faster than hers. The Miss Priss part of me said to the Jill part, "If you're such a good person, why did this happen to you?"

Perhaps Mrs. Dedman's rejection meant that even by being my very best self, I couldn't earn and keep the love of a kind person like her, a person I admired. My heart felt clenched, as if by a giant fist that would surely squeeze it dry. After it dried, my heart would harden, crack, and shatter into a hundred pieces like the face of my beautiful doll.

Soon after this recognition, I began having a dream that recurred every night for years. Although it doesn't sound particularly scary now, at the time it terrified me. I was in a school bus, seemingly alone, except for the driver whose back was to me. Suddenly I felt eyes on my own back. When I turned around, I saw that a tall giraffe was following the bus. No matter what I did, he kept staring at me, so I tried to hide. Wherever I hid—under one of the seats or even beside the driver—the giraffe's gaze sought me out, and he fastened his huge eyes on me again. I tried everything to get away from him but nothing worked—I was powerless to escape. He continued to watch me no matter where I hid.

There were no other girls our age in the neighborhood, so Rosie and I still played together, but everything was different. Mrs. Dedman never told me I had a beautiful singing voice. She never encouraged me to learn her daily words, although they were taped up on the refrigerator every day. At first, I tried to catch a glimpse of them and learn them by myself, but it wasn't the same. The vocabulary words that once made me happy now made me sad. So I stopped looking at them.

I learned from the aftermath of sharing my secret with Rosie that no one would help me. Even if I told people who acted like friends, once they knew, they would turn against me. I was totally alone, and I had to figure it out by myself. Whatever happened to Mother was my problem. She was in danger, and I was the only one who could save her.

Aunt Jo tried to help. One morning, she happened over in the middle of a several-day fight. It was Tuesday, and my parents were still wearing the clothes they'd worn Saturday night. Mother's elegant cocktail dress looked like a rumpled, black gunnysack. There was a cigarette burn the size of a tack's head on the front of her skirt. Dad's impeccable dress shirt was wrinkled and untucked from his beltless trousers.

"What are you two up to?!" Aunt Jo said, as she stormed in the front door. "And Jill, what are you doing home from school?"

She didn't wait for answers, but simply glared at my parents. Her lips were drawn tight into a determined line, and above that line, her eyes narrowed into slits, like a mountain lion, crouched, preparing to attack.

That must have been her expression when her older brothers were taunting Jo, the youngest in the family. They teased, then out-ran her, leaving her far behind. All the boys ran away from her except my father. He was the second youngest, her favorite brother, who always slowed down to wait for her and wipe her nose with the tail of his flannel shirt. Now she looked at him and at my mother as if they were wet garbage spilled onto a clean kitchen floor.

"You're both disgusting!" she said. "Dump those damn drinks down the sink and get this place cleaned up!"

Mother and Dad, who only moments before had been shouting and thumping on one another like sumo wrestlers, wilted into shamed children. They scurried around picking up stale drink glasses and ashtrays full of cigarette butts, and carried them to the kitchen.

"Get out of those clothes!" she said. "You stink to high heaven of booze and cigarettes!"

"Now, Jo..." Dad said, trying for an authoritative tone.

"Don't 'now Jo' me!" she said. "I'm embarrassed to even be related to you, and what this is doing to Jill..."

Words failed her as Mother and Dad shuffled into their bedroom and soon reappeared in bathrobes. I helped Aunt Jo clean up the kitchen, dumping full ashtrays into the trash, and stacking the smelly ashtrays on the counter.

"I should call the police," Aunt Jo said, "and have you both arrested!"

"No!" I said, alarmed.

"Please don't," said Mother, "they'll take Jilly away from us."

"Please don't, Aunt Jo," I said.

After a pause, she said, "Well, the least I can do is get rid of this liquor."

Her mouth taut and furious, she emptied one bottle of liquor at a time down the drain, holding the bottle far away from her while she poured, as if the brown or white liquid might leap back up from the open mouth of hell and refill its bottle. When the last gurgle disappeared down the drain, she held the empty bottle by the neck and broke it in the sink.

When she'd finished smashing every emptied bottle, the sink was full of hundreds of tiny glass eyes blinking open and shut, open and shut, over what they had done and what they would do again.

After Aunt Jo made my parents promise they'd send me back to school the next day, she went home. I think she was afraid that if she stayed, she might kill them both with her bare hands.

The next day, I went back to school, and my parents packed in a new supply of liquor.

Our home had turned into a sizzling hell, but because I lived in hell didn't mean I'd lost the will to live. The worse my parents' fights became, the more I fought to survive. When I couldn't take any more, I rode my bike over to Aunt Jo's house to spend the night. She ran a hot tub and washed my hair. Then she dried me with a soft towel. I crawled into the bed in her guest room, curled up under the warm covers, and slept ten or fifteen hours at a stretch. When I woke up, I pedaled back home again.

One night, after I crawled into Aunt Jo's guest bed, I noticed a dictionary on the bedside table. I pulled the dictionary onto my lap and let it fall open. Closing my eyes, I let my second finger float like an eagle on the wings of chance over thousands of tasty words. Then, it dropped down to feast on one. I opened my eyes to see "*Pulverize: p-u-l-v-e-r-i-z-e...*To reduce or be reduced to a powder. Aunt Jo almost pulverized my parents." I laughed. Then, I had a sudden flash of insight.

There was a dictionary on the shelf in my bedroom at home—Baba's dictionary, which he'd given me before he died. All I had to do was open it to find hundreds of words, thousands of words. Nobody—not Mrs. Dedman or anybody else, for that matter—needed to give words to me, and nobody could take them away. Words belonged to the whole wide world. They were already mine.

After my parents died, I found some of my early report cards Mother had saved. I missed over a month of second grade, most of it in the second quarter. At that time, I'd just turned seven. After the first quarter, Mrs. Helen Disney, my second grade teacher, wrote, "Jill is a good worker and a fine leader." After third quarter, she wrote, "Jill has most of her work made up after her long absence"; and after forth quarter, "Jill is a very dependable worker."

While the other second grade children were learning their multiplication tables, I was learning how to survive a war. What was the lesson in this? I puzzled over it at the time. Perhaps war was the price adults paid when they strayed into a forbidden land. My parents' war didn't just wound and cripple them. It took down everything around them. Maybe I could learn the important lessons my parents had somehow missed.

I was sure of one thing: the few rules my parents knew had ceased to have any meaning or control over them. I needed to make up some rules for myself. Perhaps they would serve as a map to keep me from entering the forbidden country my parents had wandered into.

I'd explored, as much as possible, the countries where other people lived, especially Aunt Jo and Rosie's families. I knew those families wouldn't want me, and I didn't want to live in their countries either.

School was the first foreign land I'd entered where I thought I might find a home. It was the safest place I knew. I made a deal with school: I'll be a good girl, play the game by the rules you've set up;

and you give me a home—and hope for the future.

I began by learning the rules. The first rule was: Do well in school. That meant behaving and getting perfect grades. On every report card, after every school category, I had to get an S for Satisfactory or an E for Excellent. Even a single U for Unsatisfactory would be a personal discrace.

My deal cost me dearly. In some subjects, I had to perform beyond my ability. During our family war years, I was often absent, distracted, or exhausted when I was in school. I missed much of the early schoolwork that would have prepared me for later learning. In spite of this, I knew that only perfect grades could help me escape the nightmare land of my parents.

During this difficult time, besides Mrs. Disney's second grade class and Helen Hart's summer art classes, horses saved my life. I was taking riding lessons every Saturday morning with Rosie, and those rides left me delirious with delight. Our mothers took turns driving us to the old armory for our lessons. In summer, when it was nice, our lessons were outside. We walked, trotted, and cantered around in a circle, but for the first several lessons, we just walked.

Our riding instructor was Chet Keltner, who owned the stable. He taught us to kick the horses softly to make them go and to rein them in to make them stop. We also learned to neck-rein, turning the horses left and right.

I always rode Old Buck, a buckskin horse who was so fat, my short legs stuck almost straight out from his sides. He acted dumb but he'd been around the ring a few million times, and he'd developed his own strategies for having a little fun with new riders.

Although he was slow and gentle, he was stubborn as a square wheel. When I neck-reined him to turn left, he turned right. When I kicked him to go, he stopped. On those stops, he often peed, extending his long red thing farther than I believed possible. No amount of kicking made him hurry or start walking again. He peed for what seemed like hours, and when he was finally finished, we started around the ring again, leaving a steaming ammonia lake behind us on the dirt floor of the armory.

Mother tightening the cinch on Lucky.

After several lessons, I learned how to make Old Buck do almost what I wanted.

"Gentle, but firm," Chet said over and over again. "That's right, kids. Show those horses who's boss!"

Chet was tall and thin with skinny, slightly bowed legs. He wore a cowboy hat and owned a little bay mare he rode with a hackamore instead of a bridle. The horse didn't even need the hackamore because she turned from knee pressure or on voice commands. How I envied him that horse. Even though I knew she was too spirited for me, I wanted her for my own.

After those riding lessons, I hated to wash my clothes or my hands. I wanted the smell of horse and leather to be part of me always. When I was mounted on a horse, I wasn't just a puny little girl. I had power and speed. Well, not on Old Buck, but I could see how I was going to get power and speed when I had a better horse.

I learned fast. Soon I was trotting and cantering on better horses, leaving Old Buck behind. Chet rode a Western saddle. He taught us on English saddles so we could post, he said, and not jar our teeth out while we were learning. I wore my cowboy boots, and after Mother's story about the Silver City woman, I kept my heels down and my weight on the balls of my feet so my toes would stay in the stirrups.

I also wore the new cowboy shirt Mother made for me. It was two shades of brown separated by green piping. On the darker brown, fitting over my shoulders, Mother had embroidered red and yellow flowers attached to one another by curly green stems and leaves. I liked that shirt as much as the Ferdinand the Bull outfit she made for me when I was in love with Ernie Bernie.

After Rosie and I became better riders, we joined Chet's Equestrian Team and started riding in horse shows. I was never happier than when I was riding. If I wasn't riding, I was drawing horses. The refrigerator door and the walls of my bedroom were covered with them. I'd even learned to draw two stallions rearing up and pawing at each other with their front hooves as they fought over the mares. I loved *The Lone Ranger* on the radio and listened to every program.

It wasn't long before Rosie and I, at seven, were trusted enough to go together on the bus and see the movies downtown. The trip frightened me, but Rosie knew the way. She held my hand when I was scared. We saw every Gene Autrey, Roy Rogers, Hopalong Cassidy, and Lone Ranger movie that came to town.

One problem with both the cowboy movies and the radio programs was the women characters. All they got to do was stand in the door and wave goodbye as the cowboys rode off on beautiful horses toward exciting adventures. Dale Evens, Roy Rogers's wife, was the best woman. She got in on a little bit of the fun at least. Sometimes she sang "Don't Fence Me In" or "Happy Trails To You" along with Roy, but the adventures were just for the men.

When Rosie and I rode horseback or pretended to gallop around with Trixie and Puppy, we were always cowboys, never cowgirls. We knew where the fun was, and it wasn't wearing a skirt—even a cowgirl skirt.

Mother teased me more now. She hadn't signed on to the deal I'd made to fire her, and she got back at me every chance she got. When Rosie and I came home from the movies, Mother always asked me about them. I told her a little bit, but not a lot. She kept prying, but I wouldn't say much.

"Cat got your tongue?" she asked sarcastically.

"No," I said, protecting the privacy of my own thoughts, "I just can't remember."

"Like you can't remember how to get back and forth on the bus?" she asked, a mean smile on her face. "What a scaredy little Miss Priss you are."

I flushed with shame, but didn't let her pry another word out of me. The movies, my dreams about horses, and my plans for school were my business. Mine alone. Even though I asked her to stay out of my room, and shut the door to keep her out, I knew she went through my things when I wasn't home. She never got my clothes back in the drawers the way I'd folded them.

Mother and I became a mismatched planet and moon to Dad's sun. That would have been bad enough, but Dad, who was trying to set up a new car deal, was an unreliable sun, slipping out of orbit and disappearing for unexplained periods of time. When Dad was home, we behaved better. But when he was gone, without any gravitational center, we bumped into each other, recoiled, then exploded into shouts.

Alcohol played a big part in this space odyssey too. As Mother fell further and further into the bottle, our fights increased and intensified. Although the fights felt like warfare, they were more personal than war because we loved each other and hated each other, both at the same time.

Mother was always worried about money. No matter how hard she worked at her secretarial job, no matter how frugal she was, she could never earn enough money to pay our monthly bills and cover Dad's expenses. She was relieved when he finally got his Kaiser-Frazer car dealership. He was excited about selling the first American-made automobiles to come out since the war. The factory, in Willow Run, Michigan, began producing cars in the summer of 1946. Dad knew this was his chance to make it. He signed up right away and set up a dealership on Capital Boulevard. Mother and I thought they were beautiful cars. Stylish. In lovely, often two-tone shades of green, blue, salmon, and aqua.

Dad sold his Kaiser-Frazer cars for $1800 to $2500. Although they were more expensive than the established popular cars like Chevrolet, Ford, and Plymouth, Dad said his cars were made like Swiss watches. Not only would they challenge those Detroit carmakers, they'd sell better too.

Even though they had only 6-cylinder engines, Dad said they were so well designed, they had plenty of power to match the standard V-8s. Nobody would worry about that little difference in the engines. After the war, people were ready to invest in style and comfort, and they were damned well willing to pay a little more for it too.

Dad spent hours, stretching into days, on the phone getting the dealership up and running. Even after he accomplished that, we didn't see much of him. When he was home, he was either distracted or on the phone. Sometimes the calls were friendly; other times he was arguing about one thing or another with someone. But he always greeted me with, "How ya' doin', Princess?" and swept me up in a big bear hug.

He'd say, "Come along and keep me company, Jilly," when he went on errands or to the grocery store. I stood next to him on the front seat taking in the sights. It was fun watching the women clerks at the cash registers swoon when he called them "Dear." They blushed and gave him their most winning smiles.

When Dad was home, Mother not only had an occasional black eye, but her eyes were often swollen nearly shut. This swelling just happened on weekends—and just when Dad was home. She went to one doctor after another, but they were all baffled. Finally, one doctor said it must be an allergy. He had her try several salves and eye drops to eliminate the swelling, but nothing worked.

As a last resort, he decided to give her x-ray treatments. X-rays were new and all the rage in those days. I was familiar with them because every good shoe department had an x-ray machine called a Fluoroscope. Whenever I tried on new shoes, I had to step up on the machine so a salesman could see if my toes had enough room. Stripped of skin and flesh, my tiny foot bones didn't look big enough to hold me up, much less run around on.

I kept falling and breaking those brittle little bones, as the doctor called them. Besides my broken leg, I fell on the steps of the Campbell's house one night when we were going to dinner there. The toe of my black patent leather shoe caught on the top step and I fell flat on my face. I *would* have to bleed at their house on my new white dress with navy polka dots, while Susan stared in horrified fascination and her older brother, Bobbie, looked on.

Bobbie was the only one of the Campbells I liked, and he liked me too. He was four years older than I, and he disliked Susan as much as I did.

I soon paid for my delight in being Bobbie's favorite. My parents were away for the weekend and I was staying with the Campbell's. Bobbie, Susan and I were playing on the front lawn. He lay down on his back and bent his knees back to his chest, with his feet flat in the air. When he chose me to sit on his feet, I felt smug.

I reached back, and he held onto my hands for a moment to steady me. Then, he quickly straightened his legs and flew me up into the air. He must have miscalculated how light I was. I went up so high, I thought I might sail away beyond the treetops. When I stopped rising and came down, I landed hard on my left arm. It hurt even more than my leg had. I knew that I'd broken it. Bobbie felt terrible, but I told him it wasn't his fault. We were just playing.

I asked the Campbells to call Aunt Jo. She was the only person in the world I wanted to be with. Edith and Bob hesitated because Aunt Jo hated them, and they felt the same way about her. Crying in pain, I insisted.

Aunt Jo took me to the hospital, where they x-rayed my left arm. It was broken in two places. I was grateful to be right-handed, but my left arm hurt like fury.

After they put it in a cast, Aunt Jo took me to her house. She heated up hot chocolate, which we sipped while sitting at her kitchen table. Aunt Jo treated me like a grown-up. We had a wonderful talk. She was convinced my injury was due to the Campbell's neglect, but I said Bobbie and I were playing. It was an accident.

For consolation, she told me one of my favorite stories about my great-grandmother and the Indians. Aunt Jo said that outside of

Boise, the ranch house of my great-grandmother was pillaged and burned by angry Indians. She hid in the bottom of a dry creek bed, stretched out flat on her stomach. Her twins, no more than three years old, were hidden under her full skirt. One of the twins was a boy, the other, a girl—my Grandmother Breckenridge, whom I resemble.

My great-grandmother could smell her house and everything in it burning. All the family's dresses, shirts, and coats that she'd laboriously made; all the quilts she'd stitched by hand in front of the fireplace; all her wedding pictures, and the pictures of her twin babies went up in flames as she shushed her two children. If they'd cried, it would have been the end of them.

Aunt Jo said the Indians were mad because we took their land without giving them anything but trinkets in return. With the help of neighbors, the family rebuilt their ranch house. In those days, everyone helped because it was a community.

Soon after that disaster, the Chinese cook was stirring lye soap in a cast iron pot over the oven flames as the young twins played on the kitchen floor with their wooden horse and wagon. When the cook went outside to dump some dirty dishwater, the little boy climbed up on a chair with a spoon in his hand, dipped into the pot and swallowed a big tablespoon of lye soap. He died a slow and terrible death.

"Ranch families had it hard in those days," Aunt Jo said. "Here one day, gone the next. It was a tough life…" She paused, looking down sadly. Then she reached across the table and put her hand on my good arm. "A tough life," she said again, "like yours, Jill. But you're strong. You'll be okay."

When Mother and Dad got back from their trip, the doctor started the x-ray treatments for Mother's eye allergy. Every day for several weeks, the x-ray doctors shot her in the face with radiation. Because they had no idea about the damage radiation could do, they didn't protect the skin around her eyes or the rest of her face and neck.

By the end of the treatment, Mother's allergy was no better, but she'd begun to have side effects. The eyelid of her left eye—the eye with the darkened beauty spot above it—drooped, and the sensitive skin around her eyes, mouth, and the front of her neck was dead.

Without warning, Mother had lost her flawless skin, the skin she'd inherited from her mother and I'd inherited from her. Her exquisite eyes were off-kilter now, too. Premature wrinkles had formed around her mouth, eyes, and the front of her neck. She looked much older. Although she still had a slim figure and perfect legs, her lovely face was damaged beyond repair. Mother had lost her beauty, her most prized possession—what she loved best in the entire world.

The doctor gave her prescriptions for a greasy pancake make-up to cover the wrinkles during the day and a heavy moisturizing cream that smelled like rancid grease to put on at night. To divert attention from her wrinkled skin, she wore bright red lipstick all day every day—even to bed. Poor Mother, who could be so sweet or so mean. She didn't deserve this.

Later, she figured out that the rubber on her eyelash curler was what caused her allergy. Her eyes were swollen only on weekends when Dad was home. She used her curler after she'd put on her black mascara before they went out.

When she stopped using the eyelash curler the swelling went away and never returned. The radiation treatments were totally unnecessary, but it was too late to reverse the damage. At night, wearing her satin nightgown, she often sat before her three-sectioned mirror, her gray-streaked black hair swept up on top of her head. Looking quizzically at herself, trying to figure out why she had such bad luck, Mother applied the gooey night cream to her skin, studying her tragic new face.

I wondered who she was now that she wasn't beautiful. Wondered if the beautiful face she used to have was any more *her* than the disfigured one she now tried to mask. One problem with beauty is that it's all people see when they look at you. If that's all you can see in yourself too, once beauty leaves you, there's nothing to put in its place.

Mother once told me that she drank because, after a drink or two, she forgot herself and could be clever and witty, like Dad. Who was that self she needed to forgot in order to be entertaining? Liquor and her beautiful face had helped her hide who she was and avoid becoming who she might have been. They had both betrayed her.

Dad was having hard times too. The first year at his dealership had gone badly. For whatever reason, the cars weren't selling as he'd expected. One morning we found a huge billboard in our front yard that someone had dumped during the night. Dad was furious. He made some phone calls and by afternoon the sign had been hauled away. He wouldn't talk to me about it, but I wondered if he'd ordered the sign, then didn't have the money to pay for it. The sign maker, tired of waiting, dumped it in his front yard.

Summer was over. I dreaded seeing the orange, gold, and red leaves flame up and then drop like death threats from the coming season. Curled up in my hideout, I studied the brown skeletons of once-green trees as flocks of migrating birds fluttered and whirled on the wind. I wanted to live in the sky with them, to come and go as I pleased, to escape the frozen face of winter.

Holidays were the worst time at our house because there were always parties, and that meant more drinking. My parents' battles happened often now, and they were intense. The minute I saw Christmas decorations or heard a Christmas carol, my hair practically stood on end. "Jingle Bells" made me shiver, "Silent Night" made me want to scream, and "Angels We Have Heard On High" nearly made me throw up. Nothing would have inspired me to sing even one Glo-o-o-o-o-oria.

Many mornings, I woke to hear Mother retching into the toilet bowl. Booze and Mother just didn't get along. Although she loved and needed it, she was probably allergic to it. She didn't drink during the day on weekdays because she had to work, but she poured herself a drink the minute she got home at night, seldom eating dinner. "Drinking her dinner," as we always said. On weekends, all limits were off. Whether she was drinking iced tea, lemonade, or Seven-Up, it was always laced with vodka.

Dad used his glass pitcher, equipped with a slender glass stirring rod, to mix an entire pitcher of dry martinis every night. He drank them by himself, each cocktail served with a white onion rolling around on the bottom of a v-shaped, clear-stemmed glass. His drinks were accompanied by hors d'oeuvres of sharp smelly cheeses, crackers, little dill pickles, and hot peppers. He ate these alone, since they were too strong for Mother or me. His Limburger cheese smelled so putrid, I often ran from the room holding my nose. Dad never got sloppy drunk like Mother, but his mouth tightened with anger. There's nothing meaner than a gin drunk.

As Christmas ominously rolled closer, Mother's retching increased in intensity, as did Dad's martini meanness. The worse the fights became, the less I remember about them. Dad carried me back to my bedroom several times, and, with all his might, threw me onto my top bunk bed.

"Stay in bed!" he yelled in his mean voice. When he threw me that hard, I bounced up and nearly hit the ceiling. Refusing to stay put, I popped up, climbed down my ladder, and followed him into the living room again.

From the time he began throwing me into bed, I knew things had changed for the worse. Although he threw me hard, he never hit me. The most he did was grip my arm, sometimes tight enough to leave round finger bruises, when he marched me back to my bedroom.

He stared at me oddly sometimes, and I knew he was comparing me to his mother. He'd loved, respected—even feared her—because she was so strong-willed. Since the family story was that I'd been conceived the day she died, I knew he thought I might be her, returned for another go-round. I hoped that would save me.

But when I looked deep into his animal-angry eyes and studied the savage expression on his face, I knew, at any moment, he could snap and kill both Mother and me. Whenever I thought about this, I quickly put it out of my mind. Since there was nothing I could do about it, I didn't dwell on it.

I couldn't read or draw during these later fights, since the violence happened quickly now, and I was more actively engaged in keeping Mother alive. Several times, I got trapped between the two of them in the hall. I tried to protect Mother and separate them as they slapped and punched each other. They didn't even know I was there. Squashed between them, I could barely breathe as I tried to push them apart.

Then, Mother grabbed my hand, and we ran for the bathroom. With Dad thundering behind us, she slammed the door and locked it in the nick of time.

"Josephine, let me in!" he yelled, slamming both fists against the door. "I mean it! Let me in!" He pounded on the door again.

The door bent toward us creaking and groaning as he pounded and pushed. Mother, backed up to the door, pushed with all her might too, the curls on top of her head bobbing, as Dad pounded on her back through the thin door.

We spent one Christmas Eve barricaded in the bathroom, and the Eve stretched past midnight into Christmas itself. Finally, Dad's shouting, swearing, threatening, and pounding stopped, and it got quiet. He'd probably stalked away to pour himself another drink.

Mother and I glanced in relief at one another. When it stayed quiet, we prepared to get some sleep. Mother made a bed for me in the bathtub. She took off the pink toilet seat cover, rolled it up, and made me a little pillow. Taking the two pink bath towels from the towel racks, she put one under me and covered me up with another one. Then she wrapped her white robe tightly around herself and curled up on the bathroom rug. We both fell into exhausted sleep. I don't remember Christmas Day or any other holidays from that period. I'm sure there must have been presents, but I don't remember any.

However, I do remember other gifts that Mother gave me. In the winter, I took figure skating lessons. They were held on the frozen lake in Julia Davis Park. I'd taken watercolor lessons there in the summer, painting the blue water I now spun on top of. I practiced figure-eights for hours, and learned how to fly up in twirling leaps from the ice. Mother made several ice skating outfits for me with her new Singer sewing machine. On one, a brown velvet skirt, cap, and vest, she embroidered yellow flowers with green stems and leaves.

Because Dad was worried about his failing car dealership, he decided to go to Michigan and check into the outfit himself. After setting up appointments with Henry Kaiser and Joe Frazer, he drove out to meet them. If he didn't like what he saw, he planned to jump ship before he lost his shirt.

Dad was gone a week, and arrived home buoyed up by stories and high hopes. Although he'd left driving our modest green Kaiser Special, he arrived home in a new Frazer Manhattan. It was sleek and salmon-colored, with a visor over the front window and silver grill-work fancy enough to impress the King of Arabia.

Dad had been made the key dealer in the Western states. He loved both men who owned the company, and said talking to Henry Kaiser was like chatting with a friend at the hardware store. As a matter of fact, after Henry tired of being a portrait photographer, he worked in a hardware store as he launched his construction career. A German immigrant, he left school at thirteen, just like Dad did, and made it on his own. It was a good choice, Dad said, because he'd made a tidy fortune.

"Mother," he said, "Henry and his family often lived in their car, *in their car,* as he put down the first paved roads in Vancouver, British Columbia! Henry paved the whole West coast. By God, if he can make it, we can!"

Kaiser gradually started building his own machinery and diesel engines. He then turned to shipbuilding, and by the end of the war, he'd built Liberty ships, Victory cargo ships, and aircraft carriers. Dad had fueled these ships on New Caledonia and become familiar with Kaiser's impressive work. That was why he'd originally checked into his cars.

"He's a great man, Mother," he said, "a man who even started a health care plan for his employees—in the thirties, for God's sake! Plus," and he interrupted his story to laugh, "he told me some of the best off-color stories I've heard in a long time!" He dropped his voice too low for me to hear and told her one. They both laughed.

"Ha, ha," I said, walking out of the room.

Dad was impressed with Joe Frazer, as well, but he and Joe didn't have as much in common. Mr. Frazer was born wealthy, his mother a relative of George Washington. Dad said Frazer had gone to Hotch-kiss School, which was very prestigious—although none of us had heard of it. Then he went on to Yale's Sheffield Scientific School.

"In his favor," Dad said, "Joe's always been in the car business—Chrysler, as a matter of fact, for fifteen years. He's a great public speaker and he knows the market, whereas Kaiser has the money to back up his know-how."

Unconvinced, Mother asked, "What did they say about the fact that every month, we're going deeper and deeper into debt?"

"Josephine, for God's sake," Dad said, "it's going to work out! At least give me a chance to loosen my tie before you start in with your damned worrying!"

The next weekend, the two of them had the worst fight ever. They'd been with Bob and Edith Campbell, whom I'd grown to hate—Bob, with his greasy black hair and beaver teeth, yellow and jagged; and Edith, short and dumpy, with her high whiny voice and scarlet rosebud mouth.

That night, as usual, I woke to shouting and screaming. By the time I got to the living room, Mother was on the floor. Her cheek was bruised and her lip bleeding, but she scrambled to her feet, flew at Dad, and he punched her again. After that happened two more times, Mother and I tried to make it out the front door to the car, but Dad blocked us. Then we tried to make it to the bathroom, but he caught us and smashed us both against the wall.

Mother managed to break free and run, with him right after her. She ended up in my bedroom, trapped in the corner between the wall and my bunk beds. Dad had his hands around her neck, and her face began to turn dark. I screamed and pounded on his back with my stuffed palomino horse and then with my fists until he let her go. The next day, Mother had a black eye, a cut lip, and bruises in the shape of fingers around her neck.

What I saw clearly, and lay awake thinking about that night, was that the next time they fought, he'd probably kill her. What was I going to do? How could I stop him when he was so much bigger than I was?

My nightmares increased, although they took an odd turn. At school, I was in love with Carl Smith, a boy too tall for our grade, probably because he'd been held back. The story in school was that he'd lost his mother right after the war. She'd been waiting for his father to come home from the army. Standing on the train platform, she anxiously looked for him as his train pulled into the station. In her excitement, she stepped too close to the train and its wheels sucked her under. She was run over by the very train Carl's father was returning home on.

Carl looked like a boy without a mother. His hair was seldom combed, and he had dirt in the creases of his neck. He seemed sad, something I knew about and easily recognized. Carl was much bigger than I was because I was small for my age, and I'd started school a year early in order to begin first grade with Rosie. During school recess, the boys chased the girls, and tried to catch and kiss them. Usually the kiss was just a peck on the cheek. The chase was what it was all about.

We breathlessly played this game in back of the school in a U-shaped indentation made by the way the two buildings were joined together. This U was where trucks delivered supplies for the school. The trash cans were kept there too. Although scary, it provided lots of hiding places and open spaces to run across. Even though I ran fast, Carl was so much bigger, he usually caught me and made me his prisoner. I don't remember that he ever kissed me, but being caught and held tight in his arms was thrill enough.

When I fell asleep at night, after I dreamed about the giraffe, I had another dream about that space in back of school. It was always late afternoon, and I was always there alone when a big truck drove in. Two men wearing red bandana masks jumped out of the truck, chased me down, and caught me. They tied my arms and legs together, then stuffed me into an empty metal trash can.

After opening the back doors of the carrier on the truck, they rolled the can holding me inside. As they drove away, I could hear other children moving around in their trash cans and crying, so I knew I wasn't alone. We were being kidnapped, but where were they driving? What were they going to do with us?

Night after night, I had that same dream. I'd wake up, wide-eyed and shaking. It always took a few minutes for me to realize that it was just a dream. But as the fights between my parents got worse, I noticed that the chase and the kidnapping had become so familiar, they didn't frighten me as much any more.

During that summer, Rosie and I swam the dogs in the canal every chance we got. One weekend, Dad was supposed to baby-sit me while Mother worked at the real estate office, typing the closing papers on a house. He was raking the yard, and I knew he wouldn't notice where we were. This was the time to swim our dog horses. We galloped our steeds to the edge of the canal and prepared to push them in.

Trixie usually went in quite easily, but Puppy always needed a lot of pushing and shoving before he'd swim. I had the leash wrapped around my wrist when I began to shove him in. He surprised me, and quickly jumped in himself, pulling me in behind him. The leash slipped off my wrist right away and he swam back to the shore, where Rosie pulled him out.

I floated for a moment, then sank toward the bottom. Like I'd learned in swimming class, I tried to move my arms and legs, but they seemed trapped in a slow-motion dream. The water looked like green soup, with weeds and other blurred shapes floating along beside me. I was frightened and struggled to swim. Gulping down water, I made no headway. My movements became slower.

Warm and sleepy, I heard the water calling my name, and relaxed into my own drowning. At that moment, Rosie noticed the bad boys standing on the other side of the canal. They were watching me with interest, thinking I was just swimming underwater—impressed I could hold my breath for so long. It never occurred to them that I was drowning.

Rosie yelled to them, "It's Jill! She can't swim!"

The biggest one of the bad boys immediately dove in, swam down to where I was, pulled me up out of the soupy water, and deposited me at Rosie's feet. He turned me over on my stomach and pushed gently on my back, which started me vomiting up the murky water I'd swallowed. Then he disappeared.

When Rosie got Dad's attention, he came running. By the time he arrived, I was groggily sitting up, Puppy licking my face. The boy was long gone. We didn't know his name, so there was no way to thank him for saving my life.

When Mother got home, she was furious. She held Dad responsible, and didn't speak to him for three days.

Rocking myself to sleep at night, I worked out a plan for the next time Dad tried to kill Mother. I never considered calling the police, because I hadn't forgotten what Mother told Aunt Jo: if the police knew about their fights, they'd take me away. Where would they take me? Who would keep Mother alive if I wasn't with her? I couldn't talk to anyone about this. I had to figure it out by myself.

Maybe Dad wouldn't try to kill Mother again. But in case he did, I had to be ready. I thought of everything I might do—lock him outside, trip him, drop something on his head. But I knew none of those strategies would work. When he was gin drunk and enraged, he would just get up and come at her again like a grizzly bear gone loco.

If it happened again, in order to save Mother, I'd have to kill him. That was the only way I could stop him from strangling her. But how could I do it? He was so big...

I decided the only way I might be able to kill him was by using a butcher knife. His back would be to me as he was killing her. I felt my own rib cage and could tell how hard it would be to get a knife through an adult man's ribs. My only hope was to shove the knife between his ribs.

Then, I got a plan. First I'd try to get him away from Mother by pushing and hitting him, all the time screaming at the top of my lungs for him to stop. In case that didn't work, I'd hidden the longest, sharpest butcher knife from the kitchen in the most central place I could think of. It was under my grandmother's white lace tablecloth in the linen closet at the end of the hall by our bedrooms.

After trying everything else, I'd race to the closet and get the knife. Holding it over my head in both hands, I'd run at him fast. If I could run fast enough, my speed would help me shove the knife between his ribs and kill him, stop him, the way you stopped any crazed animal.

Having a plan made me feel better, but I couldn't sit still for a minute, rocking like one possessed, pacing around the house, and racing everyone I knew in the neighborhood. I was working up the courage and speed to act, and I was so charged up that no one, not even the older boys, could catch me.

I had the kidnapping dream every night, but it changed. Instead of ending with me in the trash can, terrified, the truck kept rolling along, and I began figuring out how to escape. I rocked the can back and forth, back and forth until it rolled against the back doors with such force that they opened. Inside the can, I bounced down onto the road, rolled into a little gully, and was able to kick the trash can open. Now I just had to figure out how to get untied, and I'd be free.

One day, a month later, Dad came home early from the dealership. He looked like he'd been punched in the stomach. Kaiser-Frazer was going down, leaving all its dealers holding the bag. The parts of my parents' conversation I overheard made it clear that Dad had lost everything. He was so deep in debt, the only recourse he had left was to declare bankruptcy.

"What will we do?" Mother asked, her voice quavering.

"I'll have to earn some money," Dad said, "so I'll convert the business into a used car dealership. I've always had used car trade-ins anyway."

Looking broken, he sat down on the sofa. Mother sat across from him staring down at her shaking hands.

A week later, they went to dinner at the Campbell's. I tried to stay awake, but couldn't. Soon I woke to shouts and screams. By the time I got to the living room, they were already locked in battle. After several insults thrown back and forth, Dad grabbed Mother's arm and she screamed in pain as he nearly twisted it off. Jerking away from him, she grabbed my hand and pulled me toward the bathroom, but Dad cut us off. Mother dropped my hand, got past him, and ran to my bedroom where they wrestled again, grunting and swearing, trying to hit one another.

Dad trapped her against my bunk beds. He started to strangle her as I hit him with my fists and screamed at him to stop. I saw Mother's face turn dark again, so I ran to the linen closet and got the butcher knife. Then, I raced back to the bedroom. By then, her face was even darker.

Holding the knife over my head with both hands, I ran toward him as fast as I could, working up speed and yelling, "I'm going to kill you, Daddy!"

At the last minute, he turned toward me, knocked the knife from my hands, and slumped to the floor at the foot of my bunk beds. Great wracking sobs came out of him from such a deep place they didn't even sound human. He sat slumped over like that, sobbing, for the rest of the night.

Mother and I left him there. We walked quietly across the hall to my parents' bedroom. After Mother locked the door behind us, she crawled into her twin bed, and I crawled into Dad's. I didn't feel sorry for him. I didn't feel anything except exhaustion. Turning over, I fell asleep on his pillow that smelled faintly of Old Spice cologne.

After that night, he never hit her again.

4

Horses and Accordions

I woke with a start. Mother, her hand on my back, was calling my name softly.

"Jilly, wake up, Honey. You're having one of those nightmares again. You've been screaming."

I turned onto my back, rubbed my eyes, and blinked through the gauze curtain of waking. She looked so sad, I knew I'd done it again. Night after night, I had terrible nightmares, and not just the ones about the giraffe and kidnappers. Those dreams weren't so bad anymore. If I crawled under the long back seat of the bus, the giraffe couldn't get his head inside the window, and his big eyes couldn't find me. Although he never went away, I was safe from him as long as I stayed hidden.

The kidnapping dreams weren't as terrifying anymore either. I'd figured out how to rock my trash can over on its side. It rolled out the back of the truck, bounced, and rested in a weed-filled ditch. After I pushed out of the barrel, I found a sharp rock and sawed through the ropes around my wrists. I was working on the ropes around my ankles. In time, I'd be able to cut through them and free myself.

Since the violence had stopped the nightmares were different, and much worse than before. I never remembered much about them except being smothered or dying some other terrible death. Mother said I screamed the swear words that she and Dad had yelled at one another.

Neither before nor after I ran at my father with the butcher knife did we speak about the warfare that ravaged our family. But in my dreams, as I tried to sort it out, I was clearly replaying those days, months, and years of violence.

The only way I could fall asleep at night was to reassure myself the fights wouldn't flare up again. When Dad was home, after I was in bed, I made Mother kiss him goodnight so I'd know everything was okay between them. She tried to make a joke of it, calling out in a syrupy singsong voice, "Now, I'm walking over to Daddy's bed and leaning over him. Now, I'm kissing your Daddy goodnight... kiss, kiss."

Only then could I go to sleep. But the nightmares didn't stop. They made every night a drawn-out horror and they made my waking life impossible too. Every morning, I felt limp and drugged. My head ached, and I was so exhausted I could barely stay awake at school. Even in classes with teachers I liked, all I wanted to do was put my forehead down on my arms and sleep.

Dad's used car dealership was in Boise, but he still traveled a lot. He was discouraged that Kaiser Frazer, the business he'd worked so hard at, had gone under. When he declared bankruptcy, he flushed the little left of his credit down the toilet, so money was in short supply.

I came to understand that when Dad started dealing used cars, it was never a good sign. Like a prizefighter who'd been sliced up and served on buns to the fans, it meant he'd crawled back to his corner to plot another improbable knockout. I never knew where he went on his trips. I don't know if Mother knew either.

Later, it became clear that he was making the slippery transition between above and under-the-table business. Wherever he was, whatever he was doing, he'd begun playing with a box of lighted matches in a dynamite factory. One night, he came home with his right eye black and swollen, his lip bruised, and his forehead bearing an ugly gash. Maybe he got into a barroom brawl over someone else's woman he'd taken a liking to. Maybe he owed money to someone unsavory enough to beat him up or kill him if he didn't pay it back. I asked him what happened.

"I got into a little altercation, Jilly. Don't worry about it—I'm fine." He smiled and patted me on the back, "Just that old liquor talking."

Although I was concerned about Dad, I was more absorbed in

my own problems. Third grade was almost over. After making up all the work I'd missed, I was still way behind the other kids. This reality was compounded because I had started school a year early to be in Rosie's class. My problem wasn't reading because I read well, although I didn't read at home anymore. Unless something was assigned for school, I couldn't sit still long enough to get through even one chapter of a book. But I'd built up a good vocabulary and I could read when I had to.

Being absent from school so much and often too distracted to take in the lessons when I was there, I'd missed much of my first three years. There were not just cracks but gaping holes in the foundation of my education. This was especially true in math, a subject that not only scared me, but never made any sense to me either. Learning the multiplication tables was a major endurance test. With great effort, I finally memorized them, only to find a few weeks later that without any warning, they had slipped from my memory like trout off a hook.

In doing simple addition and subtraction, I was erratic. To this day, when I'm under pressure, I can add up the smallest numbers like 2 + 2, which I know is 4, and get 5. I have to count on my fingers for more complex calculations like 8 + 6 or 7 + 5, which is not only embarrassing, but takes time.

I had to do something about my terrifying nightmares. They were making Mother sad, and I wasn't going to do well in school if I was exhausted and tortured all the time. So I stopped dreaming—or, at least, stopped remembering my dreams. I never woke Mother again at night, and I never had to lug a nightmare's exhausting baggage around with me the next day.

Once I asked Mother, "Did I change during the fights between you and Dad?"

She looked at me sadly. "Yes, completely," she said. "You were a totally different child." I wish I'd asked her how I was different, but she looked too sad to discuss it.

That summer after third grade, when I was eight, my parents tried to make up for the bad times we'd been through. They were drinking much less than usual, and we entered The Perfect Family phase. At least Dad and Mother did. Since I still refused to mind Mother, I wavered back and forth between perfect and bad. But my parents, who had been very very bad, became very very good.

I suspected it wouldn't last, knew that even the happiest Disney films ended after the princess sang her cheery song and the yellow birds flew around her carrying blue ribbons in their beaks. All the happiness vanished when the lights came on and the theater emptied, leaving you alone in your seat, filled with longing, holding an empty popcorn bag, and wearing pop-sticky shoes. But I enjoyed the singing and the birds while the magic spell lasted.

We took some family trips, which we'd never done before, driving way up into the Rockies where we had our very own lake, mountains, pine trees, and blue sky. The air was so clean and pure, you couldn't stop taking deep breaths of it. Mother and Dad complained if they saw even one other car drive along the road.

Dad and I got up early to fish for brook trout. I helped him pick green grass to line the wicker fishing creel he carried over his shoulder. He was an exquisite fly fisherman, striding into the middle of the stream wearing his hip-high waders. Casting out his fishing line, he flipped the rod back and forth, back and forth over his shoulder and behind him. The line flew up over his head, and with the fly on the end of it, sailed way across the stream and flicked the surface of the water. With a twist of the wrist, he snapped his fly-laden line back over his head, and then cast it out again, the line dancing in graceful curves and loops above and around him.

Because I didn't know how to cast yet, I used live angleworms, which I dug up and kept in a can of moist dirt. The worms got skinny and squirmed when I put them on my hook. I hated how the dirt oozed out of them, but I never complained. Dad said I'd be as good a fisherman as Aunt Jo. She regularly rented a private plane and flew with a pilot into the northern Idaho wilderness to catch steelhead trout.

Dad set me up on the bank beside a deep pool where the fish loved to hide. Sometimes I caught as many trout as he did. I carefully took each one off my hook and put it in the creel, then baited up to catch another one. When we each had four or five little brookies, Dad cleaned them right there on the bank.

We headed back to camp, where Mother had built a campfire, and fried up bacon and potatoes. We smelled the food cooking while

Aunt Jo with a steelhead trout.

we fished, and had worked up good appetites. After scraping the pan clean of potatoes, Dad rolled the fish in flour, added bacon grease to the pan, and fried the trout. We toasted bread on sticks over the fire and had a royal feast.

After breakfast, Dad and I hiked away from camp while Mother did the dishes in the stream. Dad taught me how to shoot with his .410 pistol. It was too heavy for an eight-year-old to aim and fire with one arm, so he had me balance my right wrist on my left arm for support. I practiced shooting at a pop can he'd set up on a stump. It sometimes took me more than one or two shots, but I always sent the can flying through the air eventually.

On another trip, we visited Mother's birthplace, Silver City— now a protected ghost town. All the houses were still standing, equipped with the furniture and clothing their owners had left behind. Mother's house wouldn't be considered big by current standards, but it was a beautiful wood frame structure with a porch stretching across the front. When she saw it again for the first time in decades, she wept.

It might have made her feel better if we could have gone inside, but the house was locked up tight, and protected by a guard armed to ward off looters. No one was allowed to enter the houses, even if they said they once lived there. The stiff-backed guard, wearing a cowboy hat bigger than he was, remained polite but unmovable.

Through dirt-splattered windows, we saw the once elegant tables, chairs, and couches covered with layers of dust and strung together by cobwebs. I wanted to see the black fur on Mother's bedroom floor, but the guard wouldn't let us go behind the house and look in her bedroom window.

That summer I was hungry for adventure. When exploring a building under construction with some neighborhood kids, I climbed to the top of the concrete shell. It was two stories high. My friends called me to come down but I loved balancing way up above the other neighborhood buildings. I could see far away and felt as free as a golden eagle floating among the clouds.

Carefully walking around the edge of the building, I caught my toe on a metal rod sticking up from the concrete, lost my balance, and suddenly fell down, down, down. It felt like I was in slow motion until I landed flat on my back on the concrete floor. Although I was still conscious, I couldn't breathe because the wind had been knocked out of me. Sure I was a goner, and trying to get my breath, I flopped around on the floor like a caught trout.

One of the kids ran to get Mother. She was dressing to have dinner out with Dad. Wearing her full white slip and nylon stockings, she came running. By that time, I was sitting up, groggy but breathing. She was so glad I was alive, she dropped to her knees on the cement floor, sobbing, and threw her arms around me, tearing the knees out of her best nylons. (The feet were already gone.)

Rosie and I had been taking riding lessons for some time, and we were no longer beginners. We rode good horses now, even on the trail by ourselves, and we'd done well in the group equestrian shows. It was time for something more challenging. Although we were younger than the other students, Chet suggested we enroll in an advanced class, and learn to ride for show, and to jump.

When I excitedly told Mother, the color drained from her face like the last seconds of a fast sunset. In that fading sunset glow I knew she was seeing brains spread across lava rocks.

"Mother, I'm a good rider, not like that Silver City woman."

"She was a good rider too—the best."

"Well, it won't happen to me."

"Riding is dangerous. It can happen to anyone."

"I'll be really careful."

"No," she said, loud and clear, *"never."*

Even though Rosie's mother thought it was a great idea, Mother wouldn't hear of it.

I brought it up over and over again, but Mother said I wasn't even nine yet and small for my age—much too small to jump a big thoroughbred. I said it was an advantage in jumping to be small because you put less weight on the horse. Mother said I wasn't strong enough to rein in a big horse. I said I already rode big horses and had no trouble handling them.

Finally, she said, "*No,* and I do mean *no,* Jill. I don't want you to bring it up again." She took me by the shoulders, looked me in both eyes, and said, "You can ride if you must, but I will never let you jump. *Never,* do you hear me? It's just...too...dangerous."

That ended my jumping career. I grieved because, fearless as I was, I knew I'd be good at it. No doubt her determination was based on anxiety about my safety, but the expense of those advanced lessons and the good horses they'd require might also have been at the back of her mind. That wouldn't have been a problem for the Dedmans, but it would have been for us.

From then on, Mother occasionally took me to the stable where I rode by myself, while Rosie took weekly lessons as she prepared to show and jump horses. When I saw Rosie with her class members, all of them going through their paces in the ring or gliding smoothly over low practice jumps, a lightning bolt of sadness slashed through my chest.

One day, I waited at the stable for Mother to pick me up. She was late because of a house closing. I heard a commotion, followed by someone swearing. A man was trying to load a beautiful chestnut mare into a trailer. The little mare was terrified of the trailer. She kept rearing back every time she got close to the loading ramp. I could see the whites of her eyes as she lunged back, trying to escape.

The man jerked on her halter and physically tried to pull her up the ramp, but she reared, then planted her hooves, stiffened her front legs, and refused to budge. Swearing and jerking on her halter, the man began to lash her with his riding crop, whipping her relentlessly.

He delivered each cutting blow with guttural grunts, accompanied by the mare's labored rasping breaths. She reared back away from him over and over again, frantically trying to escape like a bird thrashing its wings against the bars of a cage until the feathers are torn off and only the bloody bones remain. She was foaming at the mouth and her shoulders were mottled with sweat and bloody stripes. Exhausted, she toppled over and stretched out across the ramp, too weak and broken-spirited to move. I couldn't turn away, hypnotized by the horror before me.

Swearing and yelling, the man continued to beat her. When that didn't work, he started kicking her in the head and ribs, each curse punctuated by the dull thud of his boot.

"Get up, you son-of-a-bitch! Get up!"

The mare was bleeding from the nose and mouth, her eyes frenzied with fear. Then, she put her head down on the ramp and stopped fighting. The man, kicking her and swearing, kept inflicting his relentless damage.

When Mother's car pulled up, the battle was over. All had become quiet except for the dull thunk after thunk of the man's boot. Mother didn't notice what was going on. I climbed into the car without saying anything. It was my secret. She was the last person in the world I would have told about a man beating his beautiful mare to death.

Trying to fill the blank space from the loss of my riding classes, Mother signed me up for Girl Scouts. The first meeting I attended, we made a log cabin from Popsicle sticks. The second one, we made animals from marshmallows and toothpicks. I knew that Boy Scouts got to do fun things like learning to build a fire, use a compass, and explore the woods after dark. Evidently Girl Scouts did only silly things. I told Mother I wasn't going back.

About the same time, Dad decided to join the downtown Episcopal Church in Boise. Mother said he thought he'd meet people there who'd finance his business ventures. Even though Sunday school wasn't as bad as Girl Scouts, I hated it. Most of the Bible stories, like Noah and the Ark, were stupid. Nothing could make me believe that anyone would be dumb enough to get on a flimsy wooden Ark with all those wild animals. And what did Noah propose to feed them? Even if he managed to find some food during a heavy rain and flooding, how would he keep the meat fresh? In Bible times they didn't have refrigerators. After a day or two, those hungry lions would be nibbling away on the giraffes' legs.

But the most puzzling unanswered questions for me were: Where was Mrs. Noah? All the other animals came onto the Ark two by two. Was she left behind, like the cowgirls, to drown? If so, who chose the people and animals that got saved? And who took care of the babies that were left behind?

As if the flood weren't enough, Noah's ark was a floating disaster waiting to happen. I shared my thoughts in Sunday school one day. The other kids stared at me, openmouthed, like I'd taken off my Sunday dress and didn't have any white cotton panties on under it. The teacher glared at me, but she couldn't come up with any satisfactory answers to my questions. She muttered something about faith, but I knew it would take more than faith to keep that boat afloat.

From then on, if Mother and Dad wouldn't let me come to church with them, I acted like I was going to Sunday school, ducked out, and sat in a nearby restaurant until the service was over. The waitress, with a humped back and knotted-rope fingers, liked me. She served me a Coke for the quarter I hadn't put in the Sunday School offering. If the waitress prayed hard enough, I wondered, would Jesus come down, straighten her back, and untie her knots?

Whenever Mother and Dad let me, I came into the stone church with them. I marveled at the vaulted ceiling and stained-glass windows in vivid reds and cobalt blues. I loved the songs and language of the Episcopal service, rolling the words around in my mouth like Hershey's chocolate melting on my tongue.

During the singing, organ music, and prayers, I looked up at the empty cross, then above it to the light shining through the stained glass windows, each section of dazzling color framed by black. I was transported by the knowledge that Christ loved me just the way I was, no matter what I'd done or left undone, freckles or no freckles. Kneeling there, knowing He would always love me, I got tears in my eyes. I held onto the pew in front of me to keep from floating to the top of the nave or melting into one of the stained glass windows, joining the prophets and martyrs to become a character in the ongoing story.

I got a good look into the firmament of heaven and saw, glowing on every side of the dark lines of sorrow and shame, the beautiful reds and blues of stained glass. And the light—the light shining through. So much light infused me with pure joy.

Dad loved the accordion, and when he heard Dick Contino on *The Lawrence Welk Show*, that did it. Even though I had no interest in music lessons, he wanted me to play the accordion. Not above fighting dirty to avoid an accordion career, I mentioned that Mr. Contino was a conscientious objector during the Second World War. In those days, most people thought that men who refused to fight for America were cowards, if not downright traitors.

Dad looked uncomfortable, but just for a moment.

"He must have had a good reason," Dad said. "Your grandfather sat on the draft board during the war. He said many of those boys followed religions that prohibited killing, even in wartime, and others were badly needed at home."

So, I started taking accordion lessons. Practicing was the hardest part for me. I hated being trapped inside every day for a whole hour, an hour scant on music, but punctuated by tortured twisting, stretching, groaning, and frenzied foot tapping. Since Dad was gone so much, working on one deal or another, Mother took me to lessons and oversaw my practicing.

Thus began The Accordion Wars. On my treasured weekends, I fought against coming inside to practice because weekend time was my time. And I fought against practicing after school because I wanted to play outside. Short on both talent and patience, I hated repeatedly practicing the same songs, making the same mistakes over and over again. When I got frustrated, I would kick my music stand and watch, delighted, as the music books exploded into flight. Sailing that music around the room gave me the most pleasure in my entire accordion career.

After several kicking episodes, Mother couldn't help but notice that the silver skeleton of my music stand was bent and lopsided like a starved Tin Man. She listened at my door and quickly figured out what was going on. When she heard the sound of my shoe hitting the music stand, she burst into the room and witnessed the music books flying up in the air. That was our call to battle, and we shouldered our weapons, screaming like opposing armies.

Mother had the superior military force, but my guerilla tactics always scored some victories. I learned to kick the music stand and catch it before it hit the floor or the wall and made a racket, and I became adept at running around the room to pick up the music, often getting it back on the stand before Mother burst through the door.

If practicing was bad, playing for company was worse—though that's probably the reason my parents gave me lessons in the first place. Their idea of a good time was to throw a party where everyone got drunk, and have me stroll through the boozy crowd like a street musician.

After several months of wretched daily practice, I began to build up a repertoire that included "Beer Barrel Polka," "Tea for Two," and "Ghost Riders in the Sky." People asked me to play the same songs over and over again. Like an organ grinder's monkey on a chain, I compliantly did what I was told, but I never liked it. To add to my agony, the daughter of one of my parents' friends, a prim, Shirley Temple kind of girl named Carol, just *loved* to play for company.

Soon I was made a part of my teacher's Accordion Band. We played mainly in hospitals and nursing homes. It was grim work. Many audience members were already conked out when they were wheeled into the room. The few residents who *were* still able to hear and sit upright tended to drop off to sleep immediately. I expected

The author (back row, left) in her accordion band, 1949.

them to die by the roomful, especially during our group renditions of "Ghost Riders in the Sky."

Any pleasure I might have taken in my accordion career was further compromised by Susan's father, Bob Campbell. After he'd had a few drinks, he tried to corner me and put his hands on different locations of my small body. I used the dodging tricks I learned playing football with the boys, and spun away from him, but I hated his yellow teeth leering above me.

I finally told Aunt Jo about it. She got furious, and wondered if she should say something to Mother and Dad. I said no, I could take care of it myself. I just avoided him. That had worked so far.

Aunt Jo told me that Bob was always pawing her too—he wasn't picky about who he pawed. For a long time, she just glared at him and moved away, but she eventually got tired of the game. One Saturday night, they were both in the hosts' kitchen, when Bob put his hand on her behind. She flipped up her skirt and said, "There! Get a good look, you goddamn son-of-a-bitch!" Then she picked up an empty liquor bottle from the counter and said, "If you...ever...touch...me... again, I'll crack this bottle over your empty...bald...head!"

Looking terrified, Bob Campbell backed off.

After Aunt Jo finished her story, she laughed and said, "I don't think he'll bother me again. Your dad told me Bob said to him, 'Your sister is the meanest woman I've ever met!'"

"I don't care what he thinks," she added, "as long as he keeps his hands to himself."

Dad and Mother's good behavior didn't last long. We went to Sun Valley that summer after third grade because Dad had arranged a promotion for his car dealership with the popular radio and movie stars, Phil Harris and Alice Faye. The stars had different last names but they seemed to be married—or something. I was excited about meeting them and seeing Sun Valley, which I'd heard so much about from Mother.

As a girl, she'd spent summers there on the Martin Curran Ranch. Mr. Curran owned the whole valley. He and his wife, good friends of Mother's parents, didn't have any children. From the time Mother was little, she brought along a friend, and they stayed for the summer. The girls slept on the ranch's beautiful screened-in porch, rode along on cattle roundups, and watched cowboys brand the new calves.

The Currans had lots of company because Mr. Curran was a guide for hunting and fishing trips. One of the people Mother met there was Ernest Hemingway. She told me that some of his Nick Adams stories were based on experiences he'd had at Curran Ranch.

"Mother," I said, when I was older and had read Hemingway's fiction, "weren't you excited to meet him?"

"No," she said, "not particularly."

"Didn't you know he was famous?"

"Oh, I guess I knew he'd published a book or two."

"Didn't you want to get to know him better?"

"Not really. He seemed old. He'd already been married and divorced."

"Couldn't you have gotten together with him later?"

"No," she said, "I wasn't interested."

"Why?"

"Oh, he didn't appeal to me."

"Why?"

Jill and her parents with Phil Harris (second from left) and Alice Fay (in hat) at Sun Valley, Idaho.

Mother thought about it for a minute, then got a disapproving look on her face and said, "Because he was squat."

The Sun Valley resort was undiluted heaven, with beautiful hills, an outdoor skating rink (frozen even in the summer), horseback riding, and any food I wanted brought to me on a tray. The dining room was built around the skating rink so when you weren't skating, you could watch other people skate.

But Phil Harris and Alice Faye were a disappointment. The first night, we all sat down to dinner. Everyone ordered drinks, and I had a Shirley Temple. The adults had another round of drinks, and I drank another Shirley Temple. When it came time to order the third Shirley Temple, I said I was hungry.

They ordered dinner for me and kept drinking. Phil and Alice drank even more than my parents or any of their friends. I didn't think that was possible. Their alcohol consumption must have broken some kind of record. The four adults were drunk from morning to night for the whole weekend. Disgusted, I went off by myself, rode horseback in the hills all day and skated at night. By the end of the weekend, I was pink-cheeked and healthy looking. Phil and Alice looked like ghosts in gray sheets. Mother and Dad looked like left-over chicken gravy.

My parents' short period of good behavior had ended. I had made a new friend named Hope, but as my mom and dad reverted to their old patterns, she had stalked out. Although tiny, she'd been good company. Hope never called me Miss Priss, never talked or shouted on the phone for hours, and never traveled to unspecified locations to do undefined things for indeterminate periods of time.

I would miss her, sitting behind me when I rode horseback, her small arms circling my waist, her feet kicking my horse's side, encouraging us to challenge the wind. Or cheering for me when I crouched over my ice skates and spun into the air, jumping higher than I would have dared to by myself.

On the way home in the car, Mother and Dad talked, and I curled up on the window ledge behind the back seat. They thought I was asleep, so I kept my eyes closed and listened.

Mother said, "Those two really put it away!"

"You can say that again!" said Dad.

I thought, "You two should talk! You kept up with them every step of the way!"

Mother said, "I'm worried about Mary Budge. She's started drinking during the day now."

"No wonder," Dad said. "Bruce Budge is having an affair with his nurse. Since his office is connected to the house, that's pretty close to home."

Mother was quiet a minute. Then she said, "Well, you should talk."

"Josephine, you know I've never fouled my own nest. Since we've been married, I haven't even looked at another woman in Boise. You're the one who should talk!"

"Humph," Mother said, "well you've certainly made up for it out of town."

"*Josephine,* it's our vacation—let's not fight."

"An alley cat is an alley cat, no matter what alley it yowls in," said Mother, "And I blame Bruce for making Mary an alcoholic too."

"No one ever *made* anyone an alcoholic," Dad said. "You do that all by yourself."

"Mary didn't even like liquor at first," Mother said, "but Bruce kept pushing it on her. He knows she's allergic to it. You'd think a doctor would be smarter than that about alcoholism."

I felt sorry for their son, my friend, Bruce.

Mother and I went along on just one of Dad's mysterious business trips. In blistering August heat, we loaded up on bottled water and hung a full, wet, canvas water bag over the front bumper to fill up the car radiator if it boiled over. Which it did—often—hissing and steaming as if a dragon were trapped under the hood.

Driving across Idaho and Nevada, we stopped at every town we went through so Mother and Dad could get a drink. The bars in those little towns were dark and smoky, with neon beer signs the only lighting. Old men with nicotine-stained beards stood in front of the slot machines rhythmically pulling down the handles, as if they'd become machines themselves. Most of them had brown teeth, with gaps where teeth were missing. In between pulls, they squinted at the slots, searching the spinning fruit for sweet cherries, but bagging only sour lemons and oranges.

The old men asked me questions I answered in a perky Shirley Temple way. They laughed and slapped their denim-covered legs, then asked me another one. Even though I didn't like Shirley Temple, I understood why she acted so cutesy. Adults liked it. Some of the old men called me "Red." Others called me "Rusty."

Between the hissing radiator and the smoky bars, it was a stop-and-start trip. I got a firsthand look at nearly every small town bar in Idaho and Nevada. The best part about the trip was that either my parents or the patrons always gave me nickels to play the jukebox. We went all the way to Winnemucca, Nevada, and spent the night in the Sonoma Inn.

While we were there, Dad met with some shady-looking men wearing dark suits, as Mother nervously watched me float around on a plastic raft in the pool. The next morning, we turned around and retraced our route, mining again the same bars we had mined on the way out.

In one small town, I left the bar to scout around and see what was going on. I came across a small town carnival and foot races—part of a summer celebration. When I joined in, a few people glared at me. Maybe the races were just for local kids. But since there weren't any rules posted prohibiting outsiders and I didn't want to go back to the bar, I took off my Hopalong Cassidy cowboy boots and ran in my stocking feet.

I won every race in my age group and returned to the bar, triumphant. In my fist, I held the prize money—thirty-five dollars. The crinkly paper bills felt good in my hand. By that time, Mother and Dad were drunk and out of cash. They tried to bargain a loan for one more drink, but I considered them a bad risk. I wouldn't advance them a nickel. Not at any interest rate.

When we got back in the car, Dad taught me one of his Navy songs over Mother's disapproval. It was called "Cocaine Bill and Morphine Sue." The chorus went, "Honey have a (sniff), have a (sniff) on me. Honey have a (sniff) on me-e-e."

By nightfall, after stops at several more watering holes, Dad was driving down the middle of the two-lane highway, straddling the lanes. He must have been going over seventy. I curled up on the window ledge above the back seat, drifting in and out of sleep. During my waking moments I took to counting the flattened rabbits along the highway in the glare of the blazing headlights and the red glow of the taillights...

When I entered fourth grade, I knew I was a grown-up. My classroom was on the second floor with the fifth and sixth graders. First, second, and third grades—the baby grades—were on the first floor.

I loved walking up the wooden stairs to my room, each step worn down into dents from years of different feet scuffing across it. I loved the smell of the wax that made the stairs glow. I loved being eight years old, soon to be nine, loved my teacher, loved everything about fourth grade.

Another reason for my happiness was that Mother was expecting a baby. As Dad said, she was going to have "a war baby," one of the thirty million babies born between 1942 and 1950. Mother didn't seem to be unhappy about it, although she told me the baby wasn't planned. The doctor who had delivered me nine years earlier called that pregnancy "a fluke," due to Mother's tipped uterus. It would never happen again, he said. Well, it did. It surprised me that a doctor could be wrong twice about something so important, but I couldn't wait to have some company in the madhouse I called home.

Before long, Mother went to the hospital and had the baby, a boy named after my dad, Charles Corder Breckenridge. More than a week later, Mother came home alone. I could tell my parents were worried, but all they'd say was that the baby had to stay in the hospital for a while. Something about him wasn't right.

Later I found out he was what they called a "Blue Baby." Mother's blood was RH Negative. Her blood type didn't affect me, the first child, but second children of RH Negative mothers always died because their blood wasn't right. It didn't have enough oxygen in it.

The hospital got Mother and Dad's permission to try a new technique, very experimental at the time. A young man at the junior college with the same blood type as my baby brother donated his own blood, and through transfusions the doctors replaced all my brother's bad blood with the college boy's good blood.

Nobody was sure the experiment would work, but it did. After a few weeks, I got a new baby brother. He had soft blonde hair that we combed into a kewpie doll curl on top of his head, blue eyes that stayed blue, and the dearest smile in the world. I loved how he looked and how he smelled. Sweet, like talcum powder and baby oil. I couldn't keep my hands off him.

Every time he made the slightest peep of discontent, I rocked him in Baba's platform rocker. The first time I held him, he put his little hand up to my face. I kissed each one of his tiny fingers, his palm, and the back of his hand. Then, I gave him my finger to hold. I knew he was the most wonderful baby that had ever entered this world.

Soon after he was born, Rosie and I saw a beach movie with a handsome teenage hero named Chad. When I suggested we call our baby Chad, Mother and Dad approved the idea. I couldn't get home after school fast enough to rock and play with him. He was like my own first child.

I worried that his bones might be as bad as mine, but Mother must have eaten better this time, because he seemed strong and sturdy. I also began to worry that the violence might start up again. I wasn't ever going to let this baby go through what I had. To make sure that it didn't, I concocted a plan. If Mother and Dad's fighting started again, I'd run away with Chad. Swallowing my pride, I'd go to Aunt Jo first, and beg her to take us in. If she wouldn't, I'd go to the Dedmans. If they refused, I'd ask Dr. Dedman for other ideas about where we might live. He was a baby doctor, so even if he didn't like me, maybe he'd care about my baby brother.

But the violence didn't start again. In fact, for a while, things got better. One of Dad's deals evidently went through. To celebrate, Mother got out the old, treasured, white Haviland bone china that had originally belonged to Dad's grandmother.

Because it was so old, mother only used it once or twice a year on holidays. If you held a plate up to the window, the light glowed through it. The delicate china looked almost alive. I thought it contained the spirits of both my great-grandmother and my grandmother. I carefully set the white plates on the table and put Mother's sterling silverware on both sides of each plate.

"This china will be yours one day," Mother said, smiling, as she put a beef roast in the oven, with halved potatoes nestled around its pink edges. When the roast was done, I lit the candles, and we ate in their flickering light.

That night, Dad came home with a new television.

"The best set money can buy!" he said.

After dinner, we all watched the election returns on TV for the first time ever. Dad was the only Democrat in his family. The rest were dyed-in-the-wool Republicans who hated government in any form. Dad switched parties because he liked what Franklin D. Roosevelt had done for the country, and especially for poor people.

We cheered when Harry S. Truman barely defeated Thomas Dewey. Cheered again when those racists, Strom Thurmond and George Wallace, were defeated. I asked Dad what the word 'racists' meant. He said they didn't want black children to have good schools.

The next thing Dad bought was a cabin in Payette Lakes, a beautiful area of lakes and woods not far from Boise. Besides the cabin, he bought three horses and all the tack that went with them. I was ecstatic, but I could tell Mother wasn't happy about it. She didn't want to ride or own horses. Dad bought a palomino mare for himself called Santa Fe. She was a well-trained little quarter horse.

He bought a supposedly gentle brown-and-white pinto called Doughhead for Mother. The horse was called Doughhead because he was gelded too late, which made him pigheaded and dumb. Before he was gelded, he'd muscled out like a stallion. He rode like a jackhammer, had a mind of his own, and an iron mouth. When he got the bit in his teeth you couldn't turn or stop him.

After I rode him a couple of times, I said to Dad, "Why in the world did you buy that terrible horse for Mother?"

"Because he's tame, and I wanted her to have a horse that's easy to handle."

"That horse is *not* easy to handle, Dad, and what's more, he's crazy."

"He is not."

"Yes he is. I just hope he doesn't go wild and hurt Mother."

"Don't be silly. He's fine. Just a bit stupid."

For me, Dad bought a little roan with a black mane and tail, and a white blaze on his face—a roan just like Grandmother Breckenridge rode. His name was Lucky Strike. He was formerly owned by a girl named Beverly Strike.

Lucky was part quarter horse and part thoroughbred. Small, fast, and sure on his feet, he was trained as a polo pony. He could turn on a thin dime. Plus he had a single-foot—somewhere between a walk and a trot—that was like sitting in a rocking chair. There wasn't a better horse in the world.

Once, we hired a babysitter for Chad, and rode the horses to our cabin for a weekend getaway. It was a four-hour ride. Mother was tense the whole trip but I was so happy I whistled, while Lucky rocked along, putting one ear back to listen whenever I talked to him. He was the smartest horse I've ever ridden.

When we got to the cabin, we unsaddled the horses, haltered them, and tethered them outside on some grass. I curried them down and the three of them looked beautiful standing there as the sun began to set, flaming red.

Nestled among the pine trees, the cabin overlooked a spring-fed lake. The water was clear and cold, and I learned to suck in a deep breath, put my face down, and float for a few seconds without sinking. At night, I slept in a loft that ran around the top of the cabin, one of three upstairs bedrooms. Mother and Dad slept downstairs. After the fire in our huge stone fireplace had gone out, I went to bed and listened for the mournful cries of mountain lions. Their cries sounded like women wailing. Such an eerie sound, I squirmed to the bottom of my cabin bed and rocked myself to sleep.

One weekend, we brought a young black couple up to the cabin with us, Leo and Christine. Leo was the car washer at Dad's car lot. Once, when Leo was new on the job, he'd done a wonderful job washing and waxing an unusually filthy car, and Dad, delighted, had said without thinking: "Leo, that car looks great! It shines like a nigger's heel!"

As Leo's smile faded, Dad realized what he'd said. Chagrined, he apologized to Leo several times. Later he told that story over and over again, always ending with how bad it made him feel to have done anything to hurt a fine man like Leo. Dad said Leo could have been a doctor or lawyer if he hadn't been born black.

Leo's wife, Christine, was so light-skinned, she had freckles. Her hair was kinky and vaguely reddish. Supposedly, Christine was going to babysit Chad while we were there for the weekend. But Chad had plenty of babysitters, so I knew Dad was just trying to give the young couple a weekend away from town, and perhaps exonerate himself from having put his foot in his mouth.

Once we got there, Dad suggested that Leo and Christine take a walk around the lake, but they hesitated. When Dad urged them, thinking they might like some time alone together, Leo said somebody might think they were up to no good.

"Not many blacks around here, Mr. Breckenridge, Sir," Leo said.

Dad, who never walked if he could drive, said, "Well, let's all take a walk together. How about that?"

I went with them, while Mother stayed home with Chad, who was napping. As we walked, I told Christine I didn't often get to be with another freckled redhead. She smiled shyly, then laughed, and her laugh sounded like a bell.

"Bringing them to the cabin might have been a mistake," Dad said later, "I don't think they had a very good time... Isn't that a hell of a thing, when this is supposed to be a free country?!"

"I don't know if it was a mistake, Dad. They sat on the porch, breathed in the fresh air, and loved it as much as we did. "

"I hope you're right. They're such good people."

In fifth grade, Rosie was lucky enough to get the good teacher, Mrs. Wilson. I got stuck with Miss Herm, who we called Herm the Worm. Bent over like a pretzel, Herm the Worm was so fat, her ankles spilled over the tops of her black, lace-up shoes. When she came to your desk and leaned over you, a sour smell surrounded her like a swarm of flies hovering around a garbage dump.

Miss Herm was a terrible teacher who always carried a killer paddle. Walking around the room, she used it without warning, hitting kids on the head, back, shoulder, or arm. Sometimes she got started and whacked a kid four or five times. It was eerie to hear that piercing "Whack, whack, whack" shatter the silence.

She picked on kids who had the fewest defenses—the poor kids who wore shabby clothes, always too big or too small, and came to school hungry. One of them was a big boy named Alfred Keegan. He'd been held back twice. Another was Joan Klotz, a shy, skinny girl. Joan had two outfits for school, and they were always dirty. Her front teeth were dark and rotten looking, so she held her hand over her mouth when she smiled or talked.

My survival strategy was to sit in the front row and act like I was paying close attention to Miss Herm's droning lectures. I didn't say one word in class during that entire year. I was not only afraid of Herm the Worm, I was afraid of what I might do if she hit me. I knew that humiliating kids whose lives were already hard was wrong, and I wasn't sure I could stop myself from telling her off, jerking the paddle away from her and throwing it out an open window. That wouldn't help my grades, and I'd have the rest of the year to try and get through alive.

One day after school I was riding my bike in the graveyard, even though I was forbidden to go there. The graveyard was for the families of dead people, and you should have a little respect. Also, the roads were dirt and gravel, and your bike wheels could easily skid out from under you.

The only other kids besides me who rode their bikes in that graveyard were the bad boys. Like circus acrobats, they raced one another and did spinouts on their scuffed-up, dusty bikes. I always got off my bike, sat on the green lawn, and watched them. Then I clapped—an enthusiastic audience of one. They smiled shyly. Occasionally, one boy would laugh and bow in my direction.

On the cemetery road, you could go as fast as your legs and your bike allowed. When I came speeding around a corner that day, my wheels skidded out from under me and I went down. It felt like a slow-motion dream. I'd recently lost the rubber grip off my left handlebar, and the end of it—just round raw metal—cut through my T-shirt. It slashed across my chest from under my left arm almost to my nipple. Then, my head hit the road.

When I came to, the blood from the gash in my chest was seeping across the front of my ripped T-shirt. My bike was still between my legs, but we were both flat on the gravel road. I had a terrible headache. Keeping my head still, I rested, dazed, wondering what I was going to do next. I was too injured to stand up or ride my bike home.

My spirits sank as I wondered if a car would ever drive through the graveyard and find me. It wasn't even close to Memorial Day. And what if a car came after dark? The driver would run me over.

I must have dozed off. Hearing someone call my name, I opened my eyes. One of the bad boys was squatting down beside me. He was probably fourteen or fifteen.

"Jill," he asked, "what happened?"

"I took the corner too fast."

"I got to get you home. You're bleeding."

I looked down at the front of my shirt, stained red.

"I got to get you home," he said again, like he was talking to himself, "that's a bad cut."

"I know," I said, glancing down, then away, from my bloody shirt.

"I'll put you on my crossbar," he said. "Can you help?"

"I'll try."

He carefully took the bike from between my legs and laid it on the lawn off the road. Then he wrapped part of my ripped shirt around my left arm and had me hold onto the end of it.

"That's like a splint," he said, "in case you broke it."

He slowly helped me up.

"Put your good arm around my waist."

I did what he said. He eased me onto the crossbar in front of his bicycle seat, and sat me so I could put my right arm around him as he pedaled me home.

"How're you doing?"

"Fine," I lied.

"Hold onto my shirt."

The trip seemed to take hours.

'It won't be long," he kept saying. "Hold on."

When he finally got me home, Mother took one look at me and screamed.

"She'll be all right, Ma'am," he said. "I don't think she broke that arm, but I made her a splint, just in case."

Mother thanked him. She asked if she could give him something for bringing me home, but he said no. She wondered if she could at least get him a new shirt since my blood had stained the front of his.

"No thank you, Ma'am," he said. "My ma can get it out."

Then he left. Another bad boy had saved my life. Maybe it was the same one who pulled me out of the canal. I'll never know. But if he should ever read this, he'll realize I haven't forgotten him.

Mother took me to the hospital and they cleaned up the cut. It didn't even need stitches.

"You're lucky," the young doctor said. "You probably got a slight concussion, but you can sleep that off. You'll have a headache for a while. As for the cut, it's a bleeder but it's not that deep. If it had been just a little lower and longer, you couldn't have nursed your babies."

Mother lowered her eyes, embarrassed. She'd never had any intention of nursing her babies. But I was pleased. Even though it didn't mean much to me then, I knew I hadn't been damaged for life.

By sixth grade, I'd nearly recovered from The Third World War. My swearing nightmares never returned. The giraffe disappeared, as did the bus. I escaped the kidnappers' trash can and untied the ropes around my ankles. But I don't know where I escaped to because the dreams just stopped. Sometimes, I could even fall asleep without rocking myself at the bottom of my bed.

I rode Lucky on any weekend Mother could drive me to the stable. Chet, my former riding instructor, told me that because of his training as a polo pony, Lucky would be a great barrel racer—probably good enough to compete. In the field next to the stable, I started working him in figure-eights around sticks stuck in the ground.

At school, I had the best classes and the best teachers ever. I'd almost caught up with the rest of my class. My only shaky place was math, but I'd resigned myself to that fact. My favorite teacher was Mr. Dorn, who taught art.

He was young and handsome, with short black hair and horn-rimmed glasses. Every girl in sixth grade had a crush on him. Mr. Dorn was a kind and wonderful teacher. The projects we worked on took a long time. I made a big mosaic of a rabbit out of stones and glass. It was four feet high and three feet wide. Mr. Dorn said it was very ambitious, and that I had staying power.

Mother worked full time now and didn't get home till close to dinner, so I spent most afternoons at school working on art projects. I gathered lots of white stones for the rabbit, and colored glass bottles for the background.

After collecting many green and brown bottles, I put them in an old pillowcase and carefully broke them with a hammer, so the pieces didn't get too small. Then I filled in the background of the picture with brown glass dirt and green glass blades of grass. It took me a long time. When I finished, Mr. Dorn gave me an A on the project. Mother said it was the most beautiful picture she'd ever seen. She had it framed and hung it in the living room.

Every night, I practiced the accordion and became good at it. I even played solos with my left hand using only the black base buttons. Those buttons are hard to play because you can't see them. You have to play them by feel. Luckily, the C button has a little dip in it. That's how your fingers know where it is, and they can find the other keys in relation to it.

Even though I kept improving, I never liked playing for an audience, especially at Mother and Dad's parties. People asked me to play, though, so I couldn't get out of it. One night, I played for a while, then took my accordion off and went to the kitchen for some cheese and crackers.

While I was reaching across the counter, I felt a hand on my bottom. When I turned around, there was Bob Campbell leering at me. I slit my eyes, glared my meanest glare, and said, "Do you remember what Aunt Jo said to you?"

Looking shocked, he stepped back and nodded dumbly.

"Well, I'm as mean as she is," I said, fixing his eyes in my glare. Then, I turned around and walked out of the kitchen. For the rest of the evening, he kept his hands to himself. I circulated through rooms filled with cigarette smoke, laughter, and the familiar clink of ice against glass, reluctantly playing whatever was requested, a sulky little Cinderella waiting for the right time to make my escape.

As the middle of the year approached, Mr. Dorn said, "You're a natural leader, Jill, and everyone likes you. Why don't you run for a student office?"

"Which one?" I asked, surprised, since holding an office had never occurred to me.

"You'll have to choose, but you'd be a good seventh grade Girls' Representative."

"I couldn't run for that. It's a really important office, and Merilee Davis is running."

"So?"

"Well, she's really popular and..."

I couldn't say what was really on my mind. Even though we were both in sixth grade—I was eleven and Merilee was twelve—she was a

totally developed young woman. I was a little girl. Like Rosie, Merilee had gotten her period. She had breasts and was shaped like an
hourglass. I was flat as a silver dollar, and skinny.

Another thing I couldn't say was that her parents were very involved in school activities. While my parents had never even been to
a PTA meeting, her parents had both been officers in the organiza-
tion. I knew they'd help Merilee put on her campaign. When she'd run
for—and won—other offices, her posters looked really professional.

"Well, you're popular too," Mr. Dorn said, "and that position
would be great fun for you in seventh grade. You'd represent all the
girls in your class. I think you'd be very good at it."

"I don't know," I said. "I'll think about it."

"Think hard," Mr. Dorn said, "because you don't have long to
declare. If you run, I'll help you in any way I can."

I thought about it for a day, and then decided to run. I didn't tell
Mother or Dad. If I lost, it would be too embarrassing.

I stayed after school, and with Mr. Dorn's help, made lots of
posters. We came up with a great slogan, and I painted it many times
on yellow poster paper:

"WANT SOMEONE WITH LOTS OF PEP?
VOTE FOR JILL FOR GIRLS' REP!"

I hung posters around the school and hoped for the best. Surprisingly, a lot of sixth grade girls said they were going to vote for me.

Even though I didn't think I had a chance, I won the election. Mr. Dorn congratulated me, proudly shaking my hand. It
was too wonderful to believe. I would start seventh grade in a
new school building with a Student Council job I knew I could
do well. I'd have the power to accomplish things that would benefit my classmates. It would be a great beginning to junior high.
I told Mother and Dad about winning, but acted as if it was
nothing much.

Some of the parents came to the auditorium presentation
honoring the newly elected council members, but Dad was out of
town and Mother had to finish up a closing on a house. I was relieved they weren't there, because Mother might think I was getting stuck-up and call me "Miss Priss, Girls' Representative." I

wanted to protect my delight. Winning something so important was almost like being an adult.

One day in November, I came home from school to find Mother standing in the driveway surrounded by scattered newspapers and an explosion of cardboard packing boxes. Next to her were stacks of great-grandmother's bone china. She'd been drinking, and she was furious. Her combs had fallen from her hair, which was now drapped around the top of her head like a lunatic's crooked crown.

One by one, she took up the bone china plates, but instead of wrapping them in sheets of newspaper, she threw them with all her might into the cardboard box.

Keeping my voice steady, I said, "What's wrong, Mother?"

She replied: "We're going to (smash) move (smash) to that little (smash) nothing town of (smash) Shoshone (smash) Idaho!"

After she finished throwing the treasured Haviland china into the cardboard box—every plate, saucer, cup, and serving piece—Mother sat down on the driveway, put her face in her hands, and wept.

5

Uprooted to the Nowhere Hotel

Dad had bought a hotel in Shoshone, Idaho. It was a tiny town with a railroad track running through the middle of it, a track that forgot long ago what a train looked like or how a train sounded as it toot-tooted its approach. Shoshone boasted one movie theater, one restaurant, a tiny grocery store, an even smaller hardware store, and the McFall Hotel, which we now owned.

The only postcard in the lobby displayed a tinted picture of the hotel with a tangerine-colored forties' car and a tour bus parked in front. Above this photograph was the line, "McFall Hotel, Shoshone, Idaho—Gateway to Sun Valley and Arco Atomic Project." The cards were Dad's work of fiction. No tour bus and few cars ever stopped anywhere near the hotel.

At that time, we were pretty dumb about the aftereffects of radiation from A-Bombs. Still, it seems implausible that advertising a nearby uranium mine for atomic bombs would have tempted anyone to stay at our hotel.

For this debacle, I left behind almost everything I knew and loved except my baby brother. I left all my sixth-grade friends, especially my best friend, Rosie, behind, and my future position in junior high school as Girls' Representative. I left behind my neighborhood on Crescent Rim Drive and the leafty-green town of Boise, where I was born and had lived for most of my eleven years. Gone, too, was my Aunt Jo, and our wonderful lake cabin. We even had Puppy put to sleep because he was sick and the vet said he couldn't be fixed. If I'd been a coyote, I would have howled.

Yet somehow, Dad had been able to keep the three horses. He pastured them five miles outside of town where they had lots of room

MCFALL HOTEL, SHOSHONE, IDAHO—GATEWAY TO SUN VALLEY AND ARCO ATOMIC PROJECT

to graze on green grass. They were much happier in their new home than I was.

Not even a drunk explorer would have called Shoshone *les bois.* It was a barren Hades of lava rock and sagebrush, barely held in place against the relentless wind by gravity's pull. Dusty tumbleweeds, blown around like vagabonds, were caught and held in the occasional hand of a barbed-wire fence. The landscape looked like the final scene of a Western B-movie after the cast and crew had walked off the set.

Dad told me the McFall Hotel was on the historic register, someone's far-fetched dream transformed into architecture. I guess it was supposed to look Swiss, with wood scrollwork trim on the outside of the building. But the trim had weathered and the paint had faded and peeled. Even in sixth grade, I knew it wasn't the kind of place where anyone who had a choice would stay.

The lobby, lined with slot machines, smelled musty, but the players didn't seem to mind. The same group of old men, found in every Western bar and hotel lobby, faithfully pulled down the slot handles and predictably got oranges and lemons in exchange for their nickels and dimes. These men and machines were from the same B-movie set, rolled in whenever the script called for a depressing backdrop.

The bar, to the left of the lobby, was dark and smoky, and it, too, was lined with slot machines. I would occassionally hear the jingle of small change as some unfortunate soul hit a winner, thus reviving his vain hope for a real jackpot. The bar also had a jukebox, but few ever bothered to pick out a tune.

If the bar was empty, which was often the case, and the silence weighed heavy on the bartender, Butch, he would feed the machine himself. It was the closest thing to a heartbeat in the whole place. Butch favored the cowboy songs about Old Paint and all the little doggies, or the Nashville songs of lost love, betrayal, and murder. While he polished the bar to a patent leather shine, he played those songs as loud as Dad allowed.

Butch always wore a cowboy hat, jeans, and a cowboy shirt, just like I did. He was handsome, in a square-jawed, gritty kind of way. His girlfriend, Evelyn, worked the bar's cash register. She wore silver jewelry and turquoise-colored blouses and skirts, her elastic, silver-buckled cinch-belt hitched up tight around her tiny waist. Dad thought Evelyn was dipping into the till, but he could never catch her at it.

The restaurant was to the right of the lobby. We ate our meals in there, but seldom ate together because Dad and Mother worked different shifts. She didn't cook a meal the entire time we were there. Every day, I ordered eggs, bacon, and toast for breakfast, just like Mother used to fix for me in Boise.

In back of the hotel, on the other side of the alley, was our so-called yard. It was enclosed by a fence. Long ago, someone must have planted a garden. You could still see traces of it. But, over many years, the grass had turned yellow and most of the trees had succumbed to the extreme weather. The once-upon-a-time bushes and plants had dried into stick skeletons. It was a dead garden. The fence around this dusty shadow of one-time beauty seemed like someone's cynical joke.

But Chad, who was now two, thought the yard was perfect. Finding a beetle on a dry leaf was a thrilling adventure to him. Mother hired a local woman named Owela, who read to him, took him for walks, and treated him like her own child. Chad called her Owe, and he adored her.

I entered sixth grade midyear in Shoshone, confronting an impenetrable wall of students who had known each other since they were babies. The kids knew who I was—in a small town, word gets around quickly—but they acted like I was invisible.

Compared to Boise, the schoolwork was easy. Without even working, I got an A in every class. When I occasionally had homework, I sat at the counter in the restaurant and finished it while I ate dinner.

Dad and Mother tried to shape up the hotel, hiring people to clean the rental rooms and polish the worn wooden furniture in the lobby. Attempting to get rid of the musty smell that permeated the entire hotel, they pried and wrenched the windows open, but the dank odor lingered. Within a week, a dust storm blew through town before they could get the windows closed, and everything acquired a fresh layer of dust.

A river flowed through town not far from the hotel, but it didn't help our garden. Only birds did well there. In early spring, they built nests and multiplied. Baby birds, mainly robins, were always falling from their nests. Because Mother didn't cook, the warming oven in the kitchen became my incubator. It always housed three or four tiny orphans.

I spent much of my free time on the riverbank digging up angleworms for their wide-open mouths. But no matter how many worms I fed them, they never got enough, and soon died. In the beginning, I dug graves for them around the edge of the yard with a tablespoon. After erecting crosses made from two sticks tied together with string, I would read a Bible verse from one of the many Gideon Bibles in the rental rooms. At first I tried to find a good passage, but it took too long, so I began to select passages at random, closing my eyes and dropping my finger onto a page.

This method met with mixed success. Some departing babies got lines like: "This observance will be a reminder, like something tied on your hand or your forehead." Exodus 13:9. Other chicks got a better send-off: "I cry aloud to God; I cry aloud and he hears me." Psalm 77:1.

I finally determined to choose my verses exclusively from Psalms, though the method wasn't foolproof. Sometimes God was furious. I refused to read memorial lines like: "Smoke poured out of his nostrils, a consuming flame, and burning coals from his mouth." Psalm 18.8.

After several weeks in the funeral business, my energy flagged, and I was relieved when my incubator was empty.

Since the daily paper was always on the restaurant counter, I started reading the news every morning. This provided me with some company and made the time pass more quickly while I waited for my bacon and eggs to come up. I glanced at the paper again during dinner, my favorite meal. For the entire time we lived there, I had a hamburger, a chocolate milkshake, and French fries every night.

Once a month, three or four men came in the back door of the restaurant to see Dad. They were dark-haired, short, and skinny, wearing sleazy black suits and hats with brims. To me these visitors looked like sinister little paper dolls, cut from the same pattern as the men Dad had met at the Sonoma Inn on our trip to Winnemucca. They stood out because all the locals in Shoshone wore cowboy clothes.

Dad ate with them in the back of the restaurant. They didn't pay for their meals, and Dad never introduced them to me. Since they stared cold-eyed at me, I stared cold-eyed back at them. Because I read the newspaper, I knew what they were—crooks, plain and simple. Men like that shot innocent people and cut them up or stuffed them into barrels and sank them under water. I wasn't about to lower my eyes to them.

Like a child in Pompeii who decided not to run, I stood, defiant, and watched the approaching catastrophe—its reds and blacks, its hissing, steaming mass, its raw horror and beauty—as it advanced on me. After all, I was trapped here. Whatever was going on in Shoshone was way bigger than I was, so why not stand my ground and watch the disaster roar toward me.

No one from town ever ate in our restaurant. I guess they didn't like the food. Dad eventually had a long talk with the cook. He was convinced the guy was buying cheap beef and low quality produce

The bar at the McFall Hotel. photo by Chad C. Breckenridge

and spending the savings on booze, though he could never prove it. Strapped with a crooked cook and a light-fingered cashier, Butch, the bartender, was the only one he trusted. Unfortunately, the cashier was Butch's girlfriend.

"I know what Butch sees in her," Dad said. "She's a good-looking woman. But I hope he doesn't leave his wallet on the bedside table."

Our apartment at the back of the hotel came furnished, and it won the hotel's prize for musty. We'd stored our furniture in Boise, leaving Baba's platform rocker behind. Our apartment offered up a sad substitute that creaked when it rocked. You always knew when Owe was reading to Chad because you could hear the rocker complaining all the way to the lobby.

After we'd been there a week or two, I asked Dad, "Why in the world did you buy this place? It's a dump!"

"Because it's close to Sun Valley, Honey," he said. "Before long, Sun Valley will be too expensive for people to stay there. Then, this place will boom."

When I asked Mother how far Sun Valley was from Shoshone, she said it was about a two-and-a-half hour drive—if you drove fast. I thought, "So people are going to drive five hours a day to ski?" I didn't think so.

At first, I was too miserable to develop a social strategy at school, but after two weeks of eating alone, I decided it was time to make some friends. I noticed that the farm girls in my grade stuck together and so did the town girls, but in both groups, the unpopular girls were friendlier. Eventually, a few of them invited me to join them during lunch. From here I continued to watch the other girls closely.

The most popular town girl in my class was Alice Fromm. She was a big-boned girl, tall for her age, with carrot-red hair. I had a class with Alice and talked to her every chance I got. She lived in town like I did, but she didn't ride horseback or do any of the outdoor things I loved. Alice would never be a Rosie to me, but I wanted to be her friend. When I asked her over to the hotel for dinner, she said she was busy.

Every night, I finished my dinner quickly because I'd discovered a colony of wild cats in the back alley. The cats lived in crumbling shacks behind our crumbling hotel. I hid and watched them from behind barrels of rancid kitchen grease stored in the alley. Grease coated and crusted everything back there, even the inside of my nose and throat, as I crouched behind the barrels, spying.

Lean and wild, some of the cats were all black or all white. The rest were every combination of black and white dots, plaids, stripes, and circles you could imagine. Every time I came close, they scattered like minnows from a dropped rock.

My favorite was a half-grown black kitten, as wild as I was. I had to catch that kitten before it grew up so I could tame it. Once I'd caught it, I would stroke its fur and look into its yellow-moon eyes, gradually winning it over with kindness. Then, it would be my guide, sharing its secrets with me, sharing its freedom from walls and human alphabets. I wanted the night to be part of my world too. The black kitten and I would travel together by moonlight, avoiding all human animals.

Every night I baited a box trap and propped it up by a stick on one end. The stick was attached by a string to a jelly lid full of dog food. Every morning, I found the trap sprung, cat paw prints circling the empty jelly lid.

I would have asked Leon, the janitor, for ideas, but he didn't speak to anyone. Hunched over, greasy hair falling across his forehead, he kept his eyes fixed on the ground, except when he threw rocks at the cats. Maybe their nightly yowling bothered him, since the door to the dark McFall basement where he lived opened onto the alley. Leon ignored me, but he occasionally cast a sly sidelong glance my way. Dad said he was an alcoholic and spent all his money on booze. His paper bags of trash held only empty liquor bottles.

Determined to catch my black kitten, I went to the hardware store to buy a more professional trap. The only ones the store carried either killed or maimed animals. When I asked the owner, Mr. Sturm, if a fishing net was strong enough to hold a trapped cat, he looked at me through thick glasses and said, "Fish nets is meant for fish. They won't do somethin' they ain't meant to."

After several weeks of finding my trap sprung, its bait eaten by the cats, I faced facts. I'd have no guide. Whenever I heard the cats yowling to the moon, it reminded me that I couldn't enter the unknown with them. I'd have to travel alone.

I took the two opened cans of dog food I had used for bait and left them at the top of Leon's basement stairs. A few days later, I saw the empty cans in a paper trash bag along with his empty liquor bottles.

One Sunday, Dad drove me out to where the horses were pastured. He said they were getting wild, and we needed to work the kinks out of them. We caught Lucky and Santa Fe, then haltered and tied them up. But Doughhead was crafty. Whenever we got close, he'd whirl and bolt away. After we'd traipsed back and forth across the pasture several times, we trapped him in a corner against a barbed wire fence and got a halter on him.

"Why don't you start with him," Dad said. "Ride him bareback for awhile, and then we'll ride the other two together."

"You have to be kidding, Dad," I said. "No one could ride that horse with a rope and halter. He's got a hard mouth, and he's crazy."

"That's ridiculous," Dad said. "Hop on. You're a good rider."

Skeptical, I climbed on while Dad threw the rope over his neck and tied it to a ring in the halter to make a rein. He slapped

Doughhead on the rump. The horse snorted and reared, then took off at a dead run. I gripped my knees tightly and held on. I pulled back on the halter rope with all my strength and did everything I could to rein him in, but he just ran faster.

There were lots of gullies in the pasture and it was a bumpy ride. I was scared but I knew if he kept on like this I could ride him until he ran out of gas. Then, without warning, he swerved and ran toward the barbed wire fence. I'd heard of vicious loco horses pulling this trick, and I knew what he was up to.

He would race straight toward the fence. Right before he hit it, he'd swerve and throw me, flying at the speed he was running, into the barbed wire. Riders had been killed that way. Before he got close to that fence, I had to jump and land as far as I could from his flying hooves.

I took a deep breath and jumped off to the right. As I did, he perversely swerved right and I slid under him. Covering my head with both arms, I curled up. His front hooves missed my head by a fraction of an inch. One of his back hooves caught the inside of my right leg and scraped off the skin between my knee and shin. Lying there for a moment, I realized I was still alive, just shaken. But I was so mad at Dad that I couldn't see straight.

When Dad told the story later, he said that he ran toward me, sure I was badly injured, if not dead. Since I'd fallen behind a rise, he couldn't see me. Suddenly, my head reared up out of the grass looking for him. When I saw him, I shouted, "Damn you, Daddy! Damn you!" At that point in the story, he threw his head back and laughed. I laughed too, but vowed to listen to my own judgment the next time.

One day, an old friend of Mother and Dad's showed up for a visit. Her name was Martha Braun, but everyone called her Ol' Mart. She told one story after another. Like a tall, regal actress, she had a booming voice, a commanding presence, and short, dyed red hair. Mart knew all the songs from *Oklahoma* and she'd sing them anytime you asked. My favorites were, "I Cain't Say No," and, as Mart said, the song lovers sing the next day, "Oh, What A Beautiful Mornin'."

Mother and Dad said Ol' Mart came from a wealthy, proper family. Her parents didn't believe in women working. They wouldn't consider sending her to college because they thought she'd be seduced by the stage. Her mother was determined that regardless of Mart's singing and acting ability, she would never go into show business like some common tramp or trollop.

Ol' Mart

Mart begged, but her mother wouldn't even allow her to attend secretarial school so she could support herself. When Mart was eighteen, her parents married her off to Collin Braun, who was thirty. She and Collin never had any children. "Thank the good Lord!" Ol' Mart would say.

"If you can believe it," she said, "that man, who never said no to a drink, started buying top-of-the line race horses. Not just one, but three, four, five of them! If that wasn't enough, he started betting on them. His drinking, those horses, and that gambling just wiped us out! Then he ups and dies on me without any insurance. Not a dime! Not a copper penny!"

She pointed her second finger at me, and shook it up and down as she said, "Honey, promise me you'll never marry a gambling man!" I solemnly promised. But when I thought about the men Mother and her friends had married, it didn't look hopeful. I vowed to do better.

"Don't get me wrong, Jilly," Ol' Mart said, "I was simply crazy about that man. What a sense of humor! And he could tell a story like no man alive!"

Although Mart got a big inheritance from her family, Collin went through it fast. She paused a moment, remembering.

"Jilly, I just thank God for my jew-els. That's all I have left."

Because she loved showing them off, I asked to see her jewels again.

"Just a minute—I have them pinned right inside my boo-zum."

She reached down inside the front of her dress and brought out a whole bag of diamonds, emeralds, pearls, rubies and who-knows-what-all-else. They were all set in yellow or white gold and fashioned into rings, brooches, bracelets, and necklaces.

"This is the sum total of my possessions," she said, "these jew-els and Ol' Liz."

Ol' Liz was her black Cadillac, which she treated like a baby. She parked it off the street in a safe place where no one could scratch or steal it.

Mother and Dad said she was welcome to stay as long as she wanted. I'm sure they didn't charge her, because she had no money. Ol' Mart lived with us for the entire time we were in Shoshone, doing what she could to help in the hotel.

I didn't have a single close friend that first summer, so I went to the pasture almost every day to ride. If I wanted to ride bareback, I wrapped the bridle around my handlebars and rode my bike to the stable. If I wanted to use my English saddle, I threw my bridle over my shoulder. Carrying my English saddle and saddle blanket, I walked to the highway and hitched a ride.

Because the horses weren't ridden enough, they were wild. It took a while to catch Lucky, but I bribed him with sugar cubes or an apple. Sometimes I rode him into town and gave Chad a ride in front of me on the saddle. Patting Lucky's mane, he laughed. I didn't keep Chad in the saddle long, because Lucky was spirited. If he shied or reared, I'd be hard pressed to quiet him down and hold onto a baby at the same time. Although Chad loved Owela, he always cried when I handed him back to her after a ride.

Riding Lucky, I traced the mysterious curves of the river out of town, studying the beaver houses or watching an otter family playing water tag. In time I began to travel farther from the hotel. Sometimes I practiced trotting Lucky without a saddle, my body glued to his back like an Indian brave. Controlling my breathing so I'd be less easily detected, I surveyed the scene for enemies. They were all around. Diamondback rattle-snakes curled, sunning, on lava rocks. Some-times, Lucky sidestepped or snorted, then stopped. I knew he smelled a snake and was giving it a wide berth.

We climbed lava-rock hills. At the top of one, I came across a fortress made of lava. Riding around it, I found an entrance and rode Lucky in-side. Sand covered a level floor surrounded by rock walls. I tied Lucky to a small bush and dug a hole for my treasure—two rattlesnake skins, one with its rattles still attached; several bits of agate; and three broken arrowheads—which I then

Chad and me riding a friend's collie.

covered with a slab of rock. Cracks in the walls allowed me to look out on all sides to spot any foes riding my way.

Even in broad daylight, I often heard coyotes howling to one an-other. When I howled back with my practiced "ow, ow, ow, owww-www," they answered me as if I were one of them.

When school started that fall, Alice refused two more of my invita-tions, but I didn't give up. She finally said yes. The first time she came to the hotel for dinner, we ate at the counter in the restaurant. I told her to order anything she wanted.

"I suppose I should order meat, potatoes, and a vegetable like we have at home."

"If you want to, but I'm having a hamburger."

"For dinner?" She smiled furtively, as if eating a hamburger for dinner was the naughtiest thing she'd ever heard of.

"Sure, I have one every night."

"You do?" she said, her eyebrows arching. "What else do you have?"

"Oh, I have French fries and a chocolate milkshake."

"Every night?"

"Yes."

Giggling, she said, "Well, I guess I'll have that too."

While we were eating our forbidden dinner, we chattered about school. Then I took her back to meet Ol' Mart, who told the entire story of her tragic marriage, and showed her the je-wels in her boo-zum. After that introduction, my friendship with Alice was sealed.

That fall, while Mother and Ol' Mart took over at the hotel, Dad and I had some adventures together. I think he was trying to make up for everything I'd left behind in Boise. He made me feel there was no one on earth he'd rather be with.

One late afternoon, we rode our horses out to an enormous cra-ter; it might have been a couple of miles across. Dad said it was an extinct volcano. An animal trail circled around and around inside the crater, going all the way to the bottom.

"Look over there," Dad said, pointing.

So far away they looked like tiny toys, we saw a mountain lion tracking two deer. Apparently, they couldn't see or smell the tawny cougar inching along behind them. Dad said one of those deer was going to make the cougar a tasty meal. That reminded me of his story about when he was a boy herding sheep and lightning struck. I asked him to tell it. He laughed, and jumped right in.

He began by pointing out the beautiful sunset in electric pink and red on the horizon. He said, as a boy, he loved the spectacular Western sunsets. But, like all herders, he worried about unpredictable Western weather. In spring, torrential showers turned gullies into raging rivers within five minutes. During dry summers, when lightning struck any-thing flammable, it touched off blazing wildfires that toasted herders and their flocks before they could gather their thoughts.

One night, in the middle of a fierce electrical storm, Dad left the dry warmth of his sheep wagon. It was parked on a ridge, and he was afraid lightning would strike it there. He spent the night with his sheepdog Jennie halfway down the slope. Although he threw a blanket and tarp over the two of them, it was so wet and windy, they got soaked.

The sheep were at the bottom of the ridge huddled around a small tree. When Dad heard a deafening crack, he lifted his blanket to see a lightning bolt. After striking a boulder at the top of the ridge, it ricocheted down the hill like a fiery snake until it hit the little tree.

When Jennie woke Dad at first light, he found the tree reduced to a black stick. Thirty-five electrocuted sheep were scattered around it. Except for several meals he cooked up right away, there was no way to save all that meat. It took him two days to skin the dead sheep for their wool. Turkey vultures gathered for the feast, and they drew other predators. During the day, Jennie barked and Dad shot his rifle at coyotes and wolves to scare them away, but at night, every wild animal with a taste for carrion gathered around to chew on those carcasses. The sound of cougars yowling and snarling over the raw meat made Dad's skin crawl.

After several months of training Lucky, I took Dad with me to show him how well the little horse worked the figure-eights around poles I'd set up in the pasture. As Lucky and I waited behind the starting line, he pranced, eager to race. When we were ready, I signaled Dad and he shouted, "Ready, set, go!" We took off at a gallop, as Dad timed us with his watch.

Lucky loved an audience. He raced with everything he had, not once touching a pole with his body or nicking one with his hooves. When we'd done two rounds of figure-eights and streaked across the finish line, Dad shouted, "You two are fabulous!" He looked down at his watch. "And fast too. A quarter horse couldn't have cut tighter turns than you did!"

"Thanks, Dad," I said, proudly, holding back an eager horse that wanted to have another go at it. Lucky was a born competitor.

"There are lots of little rodeos around here," Dad said. "We'll get you two into some of them. You'll give the locals a run for their money!"

Dad bought a single horse trailer, and on many weekends during the fall and early winter, he drove Lucky and me to rodeos where we competed in races. Although I'd trained Lucky well and knew he was fast, I didn't know how we'd do against other kids and horses more experienced than we were. Dad said I'd probably be competing against boys, some of them older and bigger than I was. He told me not to worry about winning, but just give it my best.

Dad had evidently put his foot down with Mother. Too nervous to watch, she didn't come with us, but she never tried to stop me. Mother didn't know it, but figure-eight courses and barrel racing are tricky—and dangerous—because the horse has to change its front leg lead as it goes around every pole or barrel. If Lucky made one false move going that fast, he'd go down with me on his back.

At the first rodeo, Dad entered us in the barrel race. One at a time, five horses and their riders went up to the starting line. Barrels were spaced out in a row. After the starting gun fired, a judge timed each racer with his stopwatch. At a run, we wove our way through the barrels, then whirled and raced back the same way. The horse that completed the course fastest, just skimming the barrels without knocking them over, won.

The four boys competing that day were bigger and older than I was. They rode quarter horses, larger and flashier than Lucky. He was a roan. The four quarter horse competitors could have beaten Lucky in a quarter-of-a-mile straight race, but I was confident they'd have trouble matching his speed and agility around those barrels.

Lucky pranced up to the starting line. He couldn't wait to race; it was in his blood. Once the starting gun fired, I hardly needed to rein him around the barrels. When it was all over, the announcer called out, "The winner of the blue ribbon and a thirty-dollar prize for the barrel race is Jill Breckenridge, who just turned twelve years old. She hails from Shoshone, Idaho."

When we got back to the McFall, Dad told everyone within shouting distance I'd won, and they all shook my hand. Even Mother acted pleased, but she looked scared. Good news always frightened her, since her motto was, "Expect the worst; then you'll never be surprised." Butch, the bartender, smiled broadly as he slapped me on the back. Evelyn winked and slipped me five dollars, probably pilfered from Dad's cash register.

After that first victory, we traveled to rodeos almost every weekend. In between them, I worked Lucky around the poles. He just got faster.

Alice came over to the hotel for dinner often now. One night she told me that her father had recently killed a rattlesnake on their front steps with a hoe. The next day, another rattler appeared in exactly the same spot—evidently the mate of the first one. Mr. Fromm killed it too.

As we ate our hamburgers, I asked Alice why no one from town ever ate at our restaurant.

"Because they eat at The Grill across the street," she said.

"I know. Why is that?" I asked.

She looked embarrassed, but said, "Someone from here owns it, and I guess they like the food better too. They say the cook at the McFall is rude to them."

Soon after, Dad caught the cook doing something that helped explain why people shied away from our restaurant. A man ordered a dinner steak, rare, and got it well done. The customer was polite, but sent the steak back to get it done the way he'd ordered it. Dad walked into the kitchen at just the right time, and saw the whole incident. A waitress brought the steak back to the cook, explained the problem, and left. The cook, who didn't see Dad, spit on the steak. When the waitress came back, he handed her the plate, saying, "See how he likes that."

Before the waitress delivered the steak, Dad stopped her, fired the cook, and prepared another steak himself, but it took so long, the customer left in a huff. Dad had a hard time finding another cook. Although everyone pinch-hitted, no one could handle the job. The new cook Dad hired wasn't much better than the one he'd fired, but Dad hoped that at least the new one wouldn't spit on the food.

The sleazy men came to the hotel more often now. I'm not sure if they were the same or different ones because they all looked alike, wearing dark suits and hats pulled down to just above their eyes. One night, while I was eating dinner, Dad argued with them. The visitors' voices dropped to an ominous drone. As Dad's voice rose, his face turned red. I imagined Pompeii's hot lava, hissing and spitting, flowing our way.

In Shoshone, as in Boise, Mother made me practice the accordion. She was too busy working to supervise me, so I kicked the music stand all over my room. I was relieved that I didn't have to play at parties or in The Accordion Band—relieved, too, that my parents were drinking less.

Ol' Mart was a good influence. She never had more than one drink before dinner. If anyone offered her another, she'd say, "No thanks, darlin'. I've lived through that nightmare with Collin. Once is enough!"

A school talent show was announced, and I was asked to play. Even though I didn't want to, I didn't know how to say no. Besides, I told myself, it would be a snap. I'd played those same songs hundreds of times.

I wore my accordion costume to the event—a black taffeta skirt and white satin blouse with full sleeves. When we arrived at school, I was surprised to see that the auditorium was packed. I wasn't prepared for the difference between a small party of adults, most of whom I didn't like, and an auditorium filled with my classmates and their parents. My heart started jumping around all over my body, beating in my chest, my throat, and my ears. I couldn't make it go back to where it belonged.

Because Dad and Ol' Mart had to work at the hotel, only Mother was there for my stage debut. Several acts preceded mine. First was a tap-dancing girl with wavy blonde hair and scarlet lipstick; then a boy in a yellow shirt appeared on stage and juggled oranges. (He dropped three of the six.) Next, a girl sang "Comin' Through the Rye" in a phony Irish kind of way.

When it was my turn, I took a deep breath, went out on stage, and announced, "My first number will be 'Beer Barrel Polka.'" I played it flawlessly, and everyone clapped. As I walked offstage, they kept clapping. Although I'd planned an encore, like a pro, I let them clap a while longer.

Blushing at the applause, I walked back on stage and said, "For my next number, I'll play 'Tea For Two.'" I put my right hand on the white keys, and my left hand on the black base buttons, then paused. My hands were in place, but my mind was blank. I took a deep breath and stood there a moment, hoping the song would come back to me.

"Tea For Two" was an easy song. I knew it well. But it had flown the coop. I called it back, begged it in every desperate way I could imagine, but it had traveled far away beyond rhyme or reason.

After what seemed like an hour, I bowed my head.

"Thank you very much," I said, and walked off the stage.

Everyone clapped politely. After the talent show was over, I waited backstage for a long time before I came out. The auditorium was empty except for Mother, sitting in the last row next to the exit door. When I walked up to her, carrying my accordion in its box, she didn't speak to me. She didn't speak all the way home or the next day either. Mother thought I'd done it on purpose.

That was the end of my accordion career.

Soon after, Dad took me to another rodeo where there were two events I could enter. They both paid money. In the first one, eight boys and I casually rode down to the other end of the arena, took off one of our cowboy boots and left it there in a pile with the other boots. Then, we rode back and lined up on our horses at the starting line.

When the gun went off, we raced to the pile of single boots, jumped off our horses, pawed through the boots until we found our own, put it on, and raced back. Some of the horses were dancing around, but Lucky waited calmly while I pulled on my boot, climbed back on, and raced toward the finish line. We were competing against an older boy, at least a head taller than I was, who rode a big rangy horse. We flat-out ran our horses, and Lucky gave it his best, but the boy and his horse beat us by a nose.

The boy must have lived nearby because a lot of people cheered for him. By the next race, a timed barrel race, a few fans cheered for me too. Nine of us unsaddled our horses and left our saddles and saddle blankets at one end of the arena. Mine was the only English saddle. Bareback, we rode to the opposite end of the ring while the barrels were set up. One at a time, we raced to the barrels, wove through them, raced to the saddles, hopped off, saddled our horses, mounted them, raced back, wove through the barrels again, and galloped across the finish line.

This time, I was first to race. Lucky's ears were eagerly cocked forward, but he was calm and businesslike. He whipped around those barrels so easily, he hardly worked up a sweat. Then, he stood stock-still while I saddled him. We raced back to the barrels. Lucky wove through them again, and we raced across the finish line.

After several other boys raced badly, it was the older boy's turn again. His horse was jumpy, but he raced to the barrels and wove through them, not sticking as close to them as Lucky had. Then, he raced to the other end of the arena where the saddles were waiting. The gelding was skittish but the boy finally managed to get him saddled. Then he mounted and galloped back.

As he approached the barrels, his horse was going too fast, and he took the first barrel wide. When his horse came to the second one, he skimmed it too close and knocked it over with his shoulder. That disqualified them, leaving me the winner.

The crowd cheered and cheered for me—the underdog. Lucky, every bit as proud as I was, arched his neck and pranced when we rode toward the judge to get our ribbon and the fifty-dollar purse.

A cowboy asked if I wanted to sell my horse, and I said, "Not a chance!" That made Dad laugh.

We both whistled as we loaded Lucky into the trailer. Driving back to the hotel, we sang "Cocaine Bill and Morphine Sue" twice.

Dad introduced me to a boy named Sam, whom he'd hired to do some work around the hotel. Sam was dark-haired and handsome. A junior in high school, he was four years older than I was, and much more sophisticated. When he asked me out, I was nervous, but not knowing what else to do, I said yes. My parents were pleased when they heard about it, but, as a seventh grader, I had no idea how to act on a date.

I told them I was scared and didn't want to go, but Dad said, "Sam's a good boy. You'll be fine." Still, I worried. He was so much older. I'd never even kissed a boy, and had no interest in it at all. Alice was no help because she'd never been on a date either. Besides, she thought Sam was cute.

"Well," I said to myself, "you'll soon find out what a date's like. Maybe we'll just talk. That would be okay."

Mother, anxious to get me out of cowboy clothes, bought me a purple dress that snapped in front. It had a mandarin collar, and was belted tight at the waist with a full skirt. Because the top snap was low, and too close to my button-sized breasts, I safety-pinned the neck of my dress closed a couple of inches below my collarbone.

Sam picked me up in his car and we went to see a Tarzan movie at the only theater in town, which we agreed was terrible. Sam then took me to the ourskirts of town and we parked. We talked for a while, I told him about a terrifying movie I'd seen with Rosie called *The Thing*. When I told him I'd missed most of it, because I was crouched on the theater floor, too scared to watch, he laughed.

Then, he kissed me. It was sort of sweet. "This isn't too bad," I thought. But when he stuck his tongue inside my mouth, I nearly gagged. I'd heard about French kissing. It sounded yukky, and it was even yukkier than I imagined. I pulled away.

Sam tried to get his hand inside the front of my safety-pinned-shut dress, but luckily, the pin held. Even I didn't touch myself there, and I wasn't about to let him. When he flopped over on top of me and started humping my leg, like I'd seen stray dogs do in the dusty streets, I pushed him off.

"I want to go home," I said.

"Are you sure?" Sam asked, looking surprised.

"Yes, take me home."

When I got back to the hotel, the skirt of my purple dress was wrinkled in front. The dress I'd thought was so grown-up now seemed hateful. Maybe if I'd worn something else, the embarrassing scene in the car would never have happened.

I was mad at my parents too. Dad, of all people, must know how older boys act. And if he was so dumb, why didn't Mother speak up? I should never have trusted their judgment—I could have kicked myself all the way to Boise and back.

When my parents asked if I had a good time, I said yes. I didn't care to talk about it.

One night, as I ate my customary dinner, I saw Dad in the back of the restaurant surrounded by four dark-suited men. Two of them stood behind the table with their arms folded. They watched while Dad argued with the men sitting on either side of him. Dad's voice was louder than their low, steady drone. One of the sitting men, who wore a dark blue hat with a red band, pointed his finger at Dad like a warning. It got very quiet, and I almost heard the gurgle of hot lava surging around my feet. Then, the four men left by the back door.

Soon after their visit, without any explanation, I was told we were moving back to Boise. We'd been gone exactly a year. I dreaded the move back. It wasn't that I loved Shoshone, but I'd have to enter seventh grade in Boise midyear.

Rosie and I had exchanged a few letters at first. When she stopped writing. I knew that she and my other friends had gone on without me.

6

Miss Priss Supports Her Family

Musty smelling and dusty, we crawled back to Boise with barely the clothes on our backs. We couldn't move into Baba's old house on Crescent Rim Drive because my parents had sold it. Even though I'd fallen out of love with that house during the warfare, I still loved the neighborhood and living across the street from Rosie.

We moved into The Chalet Apartments, down the hill from Crescent Rim Drive, not far from Capital Boulevard. The Chalets were close to Dad's old used car dealership, which he took over again. There, he bandaged his financial wounds, let the broken bones of his pride set, and planned his next escapade. My parents never explained to me why we left Shoshone or why Dad came back to his old dealership.

At the time, and later, I wondered why Dad ever bought the Mc-Fall Hotel and moved us to Shoshone in the first place. Did he really believe the hotel would be successful? Two residents stayed there during the entire year we owned it, and they only stopped because their cars broke down.

Why did Dad go there? Before our move, trouble had been brewing for some time, with all his unexplained trips, our mysterious drive to the Sonoma Inn in Winnemucca, and his regular meetings with the shady men. I think whatever trouble was brewing came to a head when he got beaten up.

Were the shady, dark-suited men in Nevada and Idaho gangsters? The Mafia was very active in the West during the early fifties. Many hotels and bars in both states where gambling flourished were under Mafia control. Their illegal profits had to be money-laundered in some way. What better way than to set up shell companies in losing

138 / MISS PRISS AND THE CON MAN

hotels and funnel illegal profits through them? The McFall was making almost no money, so it would have been a perfect candidate for that kind of scheme.

Our year in Shoshone could be explained in one of two ways. The first scenario is that somehow Dad got hooked up with the Mob, and he served a one-year sentence in Shoshone for a sin against organized crime. It's hard to know what the sin was because he never gambled, so he didn't fall into debt that way. But he must have owed them. Although Dad sold both Baba's house and our cabin, he had nothing to show for it. Maybe he paid all that money to the Mob, but it took him another year to work the debt off completely.

The second scenario is that he really did fall for the myth of the "McFall Hotel, Gateway to Sun Valley and the Arco Project." It's hard to believe Dad was that gullible, but, as The King of Wishful Thinking, it's possible. Maybe he sold our properties to buy the hotel. Since so many Western hotels were Mafia owned, he might have discovered later he'd inadvertently hooked up with organized crime.

Although either one of these scenarios is possible, the first one seems more likely to me. I think he was beaten up to let him know who was boss. His payback to the Mob was money laundering their illegal gains for exactly one year in Shoshone. Maybe he was arguing with the gangsters before we left Shoshone because they refused to give him any pay for time served. He was forced to return to Boise with his pockets empty.

Back in Boise, I was too busy adjusting to my new situation to think much about why we'd returned. When Mother and Dad told me we were going to live in The Chalet Apartments, it sounded like a classy place. I looked up the word "chalet" in the dictionary, and began to imagine that our new home would be a wooden Alpine structure with sloping roofs and overhanging eaves. A Heidi kind of thing. It sounded romantic.

The Chalet Apartments *were* built from wood—that much was accurate. But otherwise the place was a complex of small, cheap apartments set close together, building after building after building. The second definition offered by the dictionary—"the hut of an Alpine herder"—turned out to be is closer to the truth.

I was too embarrassed to have friends over to The Chalet. Not only were the buildings tacky, but so were the people who lived in them. Most were Army Air Corps couples, the husbands stationed at the nearby Mountain Home Air Base. They were poor, and they didn't keep their kids or their apartments clean.

The grounds of The Chalet weren't kept up either. With so little care or water, the lawns were dry and yellow. A few bushes struggled valiantly to stay alive, but they were losing the battle.

The only good thing about living there was that we got Baba's furniture out of storage, and I had my platform rocker back. Baba's beautiful marble-top table sat in the front entryway. The white marble was smooth and cool to the touch.

Chad was the happiest member of the family in The Chalet. He rode his new red trike on the endless sidewalks around the buildings, which was all he needed to be happy. When I wasn't following him around, I rocked him in the platform rocker and read books to him, which comforted me too.

My biggest sorrow when we left Shoshone was leaving the horses behind. It was devastating to lose Lucky at the peak of our winning streak. I never knew what happened to him. He wasn't young. I had fantasies of riding him for a few more years, then putting him out to pasture for a well deserved retirement. Dad said he'd found the horses a good home. Since I couldn't trust him to tell me the truth, I never asked for specifics. Maybe he sent them to the glue factory.

Entering a new Boise school halfway through seventh grade was as hard as I feared. All my friends had new friends, and they'd formed their junior high groups. The kids were polite, and seemed glad to see me, but I was an outsider. Worst of all, I had to endure the name thing again.

It's not a good idea to give a child one name and call her something else, especially if the given name is a weird one, like Josephine. Since my last name began with B, I was always seated, alphabetically, in the first row of the room. I liked sitting in front. It helped me look interested, even in boring classes.

The hardest part in every new class was that first day. The teacher got everyone seated, then started calling roll, beginning with "Judy

Anderson? Tom Babcock?" and so on. It was never long enough before my turn came.

"Josephine Breckenridge?"

Like a clown who's tripped over her big-toed shoes, I raised my hand to a roomful of laughter.

"Jill—I'm called Jill."

"Jill?" she asked, writing my name down in her roll book.

"Yes, Jill," I said.

The clown takes off her mashed hat and bows.

My mother, my aunt, and I were all Josephines, but my mother and aunt were usually called Jo. I had read that Josephine was the Emperor Napoleon's wife, and when anyone asked about my name, I used to say that Josephine was beautiful and Napoleon was wild about her. Later I discovered that the Empress of France was scandalously unfaithful, so I stopped comparing myself to her. As Ol' Mart's mother would have said, she was a tramp and a trollop.

No analysis or rationalization helped me survive that first day of a new class. The process never got easier, and the laughter never lessened.

School, itself, was no problem however. None of my classes were hard, and I knew many people from before I moved away. I could greet people in the hall, at least, which made me feel less lonely.

I never asked who served out my term as Girls' Representative. I assumed it was Merilee Davis, the girl I beat. I didn't want to know. Leaving Boise had ended my political career. I never ran for office again, though it was discouraging to lose what I'd worked so hard to win. I didn't trust my parents to stay put anymore. Our transience had killed any comforting assumption of permanence that I once had.

Mother got a job working at the real estate office again, and during the summer I babysat Chad. Mother paid me, and I liked earning the money. Being with Chad was the only thing that made me happy during that lonely summer. I loved his twinkly blue eyes and impish smile. He was very bright. Not a loudmouth like me. He observed and studied things, mulling them over in his mind. Before he weighed in on anything, he'd thought it through.

When he got into trouble, he said to Mother, "Don't tell Jilly." Mother promised she wouldn't, but she usually did. I was the mother of three children. My parents were the difficult ones.

Incorrigible: i-n-c-o-r-r-i-g-i-b-l-e…incapable of being corrected, incurable. My little brother is an angel, but my parents are incorrigible.

During the day, I often babysat for the Air Force families who lived in The Chalet. I took Chad along with me. When the other kids went down for their naps, I put Chad on the couch for his nap too. If I babysat at night, he stayed home with Mother. Dad was always at the car dealership or traveling around on some deal or another, so he wasn't around much.

Once I got to know The Chalet residents better, I found they weren't so bad. The women just had too many children and too little help caring for them. Most of the apartments were cluttered with toys and clothes, the sinks overflowing with dirty dishes, but the young mothers seemed to be doing the best they could.

When I babysat at night, I bathed the kids. If there were books, I read stories to them. If not, I told them a story from one of the children's books I read to Chad at home. After I put the kids to bed and tucked them in, I did the dishes in the sink and picked up the apartment. When I babysat during the day, I did the dishes while the kids were napping.

The parents were very appreciative, especially the women. Reaching deep into their slim pocketbooks, they always paid me a little more than the going rate for babysitters, fifty cents an hour.

Twice during the summer, I visited Rosie. After walking my bike up the long hill past the Depot to Crescent Rim Drive, I rode my bike to her house. It was good to see Mrs. Dedman again, and she seemed glad to see me. Rosie and I still enjoyed one another, but she had new friends, a new horse, and a new life.

I went to the stable one day to watch her ride. She wore English riding clothes—even a black beanie hat. She'd jumped for a while, but decided she liked gaited horses better. Her bay thoroughbred was large and spirited. Using two reins instead of one, Rosie took her horse through its paces for me. He was a powerful animal, and she rode him beautifully. She'd won many blue ribbons in horse shows. I was proud of her. When I got back to The Chalet after those two visits, I felt sad. I missed Lucky, missed a lot of things I couldn't even name. So I seldom went to Rosie's house.

That summer, while Rosie was taking riding lessons, training her horse, and winning blue ribbons, I was babysitting. I earned several hundred dollars. For the first time, I bought all my own school clothes. In the past, whenever I asked Mother for money, she looked so nervous; I knew this was what she wanted. From then on, I always worked and took care of my own clothing and expenses.

Two older boys at The Chalet began to bully Chad. They were probably seven—more than twice his age. One day, I was sitting on the steps of our building with Chad, and he pointed them out to me. When I started after them, they ran. I easily caught up with them, grabbed one by his arm and the other by his shirt collar, then jerked them to a stop.

"I hear you've been bullying my little brother."

They both shook their heads and said, almost in unison, "No we haven't."

"Yes you have, and I want it to stop. If you ever bother him again, I'll beat you up. Do you understand?"

Their eyes opened wide as baseballs as they shook their heads up and down in a yes motion. That was the last time Chad had any trouble with them.

After school started again, Nancy Davidson was in several of my eighth-grade classes. I knew and liked her in grade school, but we'd never been close. She invited me to her house one day after school. It was farther back on the rim than ours had been—it was a beautiful house with lovely furniture. Her family, like all the Davidsons, had lots of money.

Although her mom and dad weren't divorced, they weren't like other married couples. Mother told me that her dad lived a double life. Since he was having a long-term affair with another woman in town, he was up all night with her, and slept all day. When I was at Nancy's house, I never saw her father.

Mrs. Davidson had barely survived a stroke. One eye and one

side of her face drooped down. She wasn't able to look you in the eye or talk to you. The first time I met her, it was early in the afternoon, but I smelled liquor on her breath. Maybe she felt so bad about looking strange, she drank all day. Mother said that Nancy's dad was a heavy drinker too.

Because Nancy and I had fewer common interests, she couldn't compete with Rosie as a friend, and her mother was certainly not Mrs. Dedman, but our crazy family lives gave us much in common—even more than Nancy knew. She was related to Rodney Davidson, who had touched off my family's World War III, but I never mentioned his name to her.

It was obvious that Nancy's parents had money: neither of them worked. Her house was perfectly furnished and decorated—beautiful but cold. The Davidsons owned many things, but their house was filled with unnamed sorrows that sat in every chair, and regrets that stretched out on every sofa. That house was a lesson to me about how money can wear a beautiful mask to hide something that's not pretty.

Although I was still grieving about losing Rosie and Lucky, I seldom talked to Mother about anything private. She just used it against me. One day, she asked a direct question.

"Why are you so unhappy?"

There were too many reasons to count, but I was caught off guard, and said the first thing that came to mind.

"Because I'm so ugly."

"You are not," Mother said. "You have beautiful hair." She ran her hand across the top of my head, stroking my hair.

Pulling away, I said, "Who cares about hair if you don't have any eyes?"

"What do you mean?"

"I hate these pale eyebrows and eyelashes! I look eyeless."

The next Saturday, Mother took me to a beauty shop called Permanent Beauty, where she got her haircuts and permanents.

"You have natural wave," Flossie, the beautician said, running her fingers through my long hair, "and nice features. We'll just show off those good traits." She cut my hair to a medium length that waved and curled softly around my face. Then she shaped bangs across my forehead. Finally, she gave me a Brow and Lash Tint. She put cream around my eyes and eyebrows so the dye wouldn't get on my skin. After telling me to close my eyes and keep them closed or it would sting, she dyed my eyebrows and eyelashes a dark brown.

"You have nice thick eyebrows and long lashes," Flossie said after she finished. "They took the dye well. If you come back every month or so, we'll just touch them up."

When I opened my eyes and looked in the mirror, I actually had eyes—and above them, eyebrows! At the drugstore, Mother bought me brown mascara and a brown eyebrow pencil.

"To fill in the gaps," she said.

One subject Mother knew everything about was make-up. After we got home, she showed me how to put on just a little bit, so it didn't look like I was wearing any. I threw my arms around her and thanked her without reservation.

On Monday morning, I picked out just the right outfit and got dressed. I couldn't wait to get to school, although I was worried about it too. What if my friends didn't like the way I looked, or, even worse, what if they laughed? When I got to school, the boys didn't say anything, although some of them stared. My girlfriends thought I looked great. They gathered around and begged me to tell them all about my transformation.

This was another lesson about surface appearance and beauty. I liked the way I looked now better than the way I looked before. As a result, I liked myself better too. Even though what's inside is all that should matter, in the real world, it doesn't always work out that way.

One of Nancy's good friends was Florence Mendiola, so I got to know her too. Florence was Basque and a Mormon. Her religion required her to wear a white cotton T-shirt under her clothes even in gym class, even in bed at night under her pajamas. It had something to do with a woman's modesty. None of us understood the custom, but Florence had a beautiful smile and a nice personality. She did well in school, and she was very popular. But we were glad we didn't have to wear white cotton T-shirts all the time.

Growing up in Boise, I never heard any prejudiced remarks about black or Chinese people, and none about Catholics or Jews, but I heard a lot of negative remarks about Mormons. My parents never talked about Mormons that way, but I often heard the term "Jack Mormon."

One night, when the dinner dishes were done and the last laugh from *I Love Lucy* had faded, I asked Mother and Dad what those words meant. I said my friend, Florence, was Mormon, and she was really nice.

"Well, first off," Dad said, "on weekends, Boise is full of Jack Mormons from Salt Lake City. That term means Mormons who don't follow the rules of their religion. People say that at home, they act proper, but here in Boise they smoke, drink, and chase after women."

"Why do they do that?"

"Every religion has lots of different kinds of people, Jilly. Many of them don't abide by what they hear in church on Sunday. Most of us fall pretty short."

Dad thought for a minute, and then added, "The history of the Mormons in the West is a bloody and complex one, Honey. In the beginning, they were welcomed to Utah and other states. But, when their numbers grew, warfare broke out. Not only white against Indian, and Indian against white, but also white settlers against white Mormon settlers. "

Dad told me a story he'd heard many times from my grandmother. She was usually fair-minded, but she was dead-set against Mormons because her best friend was one of the emigrant children who survived The Mountain Meadows Massacre.

In late August of 1857, Brigham Young's adopted son, Major John Lee, hatched a murderous plan with the help of some other young Mormon men. He first sent Indian allies to attack the Francher Party's wagon train. This party consisted of 140 emigrant men, women, and children from Arkansas and Missouri who had set up camp for the night in Mountain Meadows, before proceeding on their way farther west.

Once the Indian attack was under way, Lee carried out the rest of his plan. He promised to help the emigrants escape if they followed his precise instructions. The party must first send out wagons carrying all their children, seven years old and younger. Wagons carrying the women and older children must come next. Finally, the men must walk out, each one accompanied by a Mormon defender to guarantee safe passage.

At a prearranged signal, Lee's Mormon escorts and Indian allies slaughtered one hundred and twenty men, women and older children. To silence any eyewitnesses, all wounded emigrants were killed in cold blood. Of the entire Francher Party, the only members spared were the seventeen children, from two months to seven years old, who were sent out in the first wagon.

My grandmother's friend was among those surviving children. One of the older girls, she remembered everything that happened. After the massacre, she was taken into a Mormon family. Her new Mormon mother wore her murdered mother's clothes.

Dad said the Mormon men responsible for the massacre were captured and executed, but many Westerners still felt resentful. They thought the Morman Church never took responsibility for covering up the massacre.

Mother and Dad still drank, but less than usual, it seemed to me. Maybe it was because I was babysitting so much, I wasn't around to see it. They never had parties or invited anyone over. They must have been as ashamed of The Chalet as I was. Dad's business failures made us feel like outlaws. But it was a relief not to play the accordion, and a relief not to be with Susan or the Campbells. If my folks did go to the Campbell's house, I was either babysitting or I stayed at home with Chad.

We still visited the Budges occasionally. My old friend, Bruce, had a little brother now, named Bill. He was Chad's age. The four of us ate our Chinese food at the Budge's kitchen table. Bruce was still sweet to me, but he didn't like Bill as much as I liked Chad. He seemed jealous of him.

Bruce's mother, Mary, had gone downhill fast. Her skin was pale gray, and she looked older. She was always drunk now, staggering and slurring her words. Her arms were covered with sores from when she passed out holding a lighted cigarette and burned herself.

Mother and Dad told me that Bruce had gotten into some serious trouble the past year. He stole a car, and on another occasion drove the get-away car when his friends robbed a sporting goods store. The police caught him both times and put him in jail. But his uncle was an important judge. He got Bruce released.

I told Bruce that I hoped he'd learned his lesson. He flashed a big grin at me and said, "Now Jill, don't worry your pretty head about it." Bruce was rumored to be a ladies' man. I was afraid that he and Dad were two of a kind.

Though I was doing a lot of babysitting, it became clear that my family needed money, so I started looking in the want ads for a better job. But all the jobs listed were for grown-ups. Finally, one Sunday, I spotted a position that might suit me: Chicken Plucker. I called and told them about my babysitting experience, and they said they'd be glad to have me on board. I'd just have to come in for an interview and fill out some forms. When Mother came home from work, I couldn't wait to tell her. When I did, she looked stricken.

"Work in a chicken-processing plant? Over my dead body!"

"I thought you'd be pleased."

"Well, I'm not pleased, and you're not working as a chicken plucker!"

"Why?"

"Because it's a terrible job!"

"Mother..."

She put her hand up to shush me.

"No more. You're not going to pluck chickens, and that's that!"

Thus ended my chicken-plucking career.

As word about my babysitting skills spread around Mountain Home Air Base, people started to call me day and night. That summer, I often worked at the Air Force nursery too, and I took Chad along. The families there seemed to be even harder off than the military families at The Chalet, but they always treated me well. As the end of summer approached, I'd saved over five hundred dollars. It seemed like a million dollars to me.

Just when I was looking forward to ninth grade in Boise, Mother and Dad made an announcement. We were moving again—this time to Pasadena in Southern California.

Dad was going to be part of a first-time-ever international hotel deal in Los Angeles. He said it was an idea whose time had come. Since it would be warm in California all year long, Chad and I could be outside without ever worrying about the weather. My parents had already made arrangements to store our furniture, and they'd rented a furnished house in a nice neighborhood.

7

California Freeways and Facades

Loading up his family again, Dad headed west. He fit into the second migratory flock of men who traveled across the Oregon Trail in search of a better life. The first flock was made up of well-off people like Baba's family. The second flock was made up mostly of single men following the siren call of gold or other riches. If they didn't strike it big in one town, they moved on to the next.

The few women who accompanied this second group were determined survivors. They'd already lost their men to dreams and ambitions, so these practical women chose between two dismal alternatives. They could stay behind with their fatherless children and starve, or tag along and ride the dream in the slim hope they might improve their sorry state.

The Pacific Ocean stopped Dad's westward roll—for the time being, at least. The furnished house he'd rented for us was on Brigden Road, a tree-lined street in Pasadena, California. A creamy stucco house, it was what we later called a rambler. It boasted no basement or second floor, only a meandering first floor that covered all the bases. With two bedrooms and a den, it was roomy. With light green shag carpeting, it was comfortable. With pale leather living room couches and chairs, it beckoned you to take a break.

It had a nice kitchen, dining room, and even a grill on a patio off the living room, where Dad barbecued steak or chicken. Large living room windows welcomed in an abundance of green outdoor foliage. On either side of the front steps was a small kumquat tree—native trees of China, Dad said—that always held tart oval mini-oranges. The lawn in the fenced-in back yard was healthy, and roses and gardenias bloomed profusely most of the year.

It was the nicest place we'd ever lived in, and I wondered who was paying the bill. It couldn't have come cheap.

One thing I didn't like about Southern California was the smog. It came mostly from car exhaust, and got trapped in our valley by the mountains. Smog looked like low-hanging smoke. It made your eyes sting and water. Dabbing them with a Kleenex just made them hurt and water more.

Chad had lots of room to play, but there seemed to be no children nearby.

Mother got a job as a claims processor and adjustor at a property and health insurance company in downtown Pasadena, while I baby-sat Chad. Her take-home pay was $350 a month before taxes, a good salary for a woman in the early fifties.

Although our rented house was beautiful, the neighborhood baffled me because we seldom saw any neighbors. To the left of us, on the other side of a solid patio fence, you could hear people splashing in their swimming pool and talking, but in the seven years we lived there, I never saw any of them.

On the other side of us lived an older woman that Mother somehow got to know—an invalid with Parkinson's disease. The woman was too shy to join us for holiday dinners, but Mother always took her a plate of food.

Until school started, Chad and I lived alone in a small paradise of warbling birds and fragrant flowers. It was like we'd moved to a tropical version of Mars—beautiful, but foreign and very lonely.

Dad traveled a lot, and when he was home he was usually working on his International Hotel deal. It was going to be in Los Angeles, which we began calling L.A., like everyone else. He and Mr. Stewart, the head of the deal, were in total agreement on the plan. It would include a diverse group of restaurants and a hotel. The restaurant complex would include several restaurants serving American, French, Italian, Mexican, and Chinese food.

Dad said the plan was way ahead of its time. In the future, we were going to live closer and closer together. We needed to know different kinds of people and appreciate different kinds of food and customs. His hotel would offer rooms decorated in the styles of the countries inspiring the restaurant food.

When I met Mr. Stewart, my heart did a double back-flip. He was as handsome as Dad, but younger and blonde. Very respectful, he never acted creepy with me like Bob Campbell had. He was my first big love.

Mr. Stewart told me about his large stable and his herd of palomino horses. I could imagine how elegant he'd look riding them. Evidently, his wife was older than he was, but she loved horses too. Mother invited them over for dinner several times, but they were always busy.

I soon realized where all the Southern California people were. They were driving their cars on the freeways. There seemed to be hundreds of freeways, looping over and around one another, then lassoing all the nearby sprawling communities and tying them together whether they wanted to be joined or not.

"Actually," Dad said proudly, "the first freeway in the nation was built here. The Arroyo Seco Parkway between Pasadena and L.A. It's six miles long."

In disbelief at his enthusiasm, I said, "Once they got started, I guess they just couldn't stop."

"This is the future, Jill," he said, not laughing at my joke.

Evidently, in Dad's dream of the future, smog from car exhaust would hang like a poisoned shawl over the entire area. It seemed more like a nightmare to me.

Traffic wasn't bad most of the time, but people honked if they thought you weren't going fast enough. Then they got as close to your bumper as possible without actually knocking you off the freeway. Driving on those freeways made me nervous, but it terrified Mother. Whenever she drove, it took us twice as long to get anywhere. She'd keep the speedometer at forty, her knuckles white on the wheel. People behind us would honk and shout insults as they roared past.

In anxious desperation, Mother sometimes swerved over and drove on the shoulder. I found the possibility of crashing into a deserted car scarier than contending with other cars on the freeway. This brought out the Miss Priss in me, and touched off The Freeway Wars.

"Mother, get back on the freeway! What you're doing is illegal!"

"No! I can't! I simply won't!" she snapped, hunching over the wheel.

"Well, you have to, or they'll arrest us!"

"So be it. No amount of money will get me back on that deathtrap!"

Our voices rose until we were shouting at each other, but no pleading or bullying on my part convinced her to re-enter the race. But after driving on the apron for a while, Mother invariably returned to the freeway fray.

When we got home, she'd say, "What an orrrdeeeeal!" Looking up that word, in honor of Mrs. Dedman's spelling lessons, I found that ordeal means a primitive kind of trial where accused people were made to go through poison, fire, or water. The few who miraculously survived were considered innocent. "Driving on the freeway with Mother is an ordeal."

In a calmer moment, I asked Mother why she was so scared in the car, and she told me the story. It was a Saturday night in summer, and she and a close friend had arranged a double date. When the two boys arrived, in a black convertible with the top down, they were very drunk. Against their better judgment, Mother and her friend climbed in. They headed up into the mountains outside Boise. Mother's date was driving much too fast. On a curving mountain road, in spite of Mother's pleading, he increased his speed and lost control of the car. It rolled over and off the road.

Mother's date had his arm around her shoulder. He pushed her down on the floor in the front seat and threw himself on top of her. They stayed inside the car as it rolled over several times, but the couple in the back seat was thrown out. The boy barely survived his injuries, but Mother's friend fell under the car and was crushed. She died instantly.

Driving with Dad was a totally different experience. He drove safely and surely. Several times a year he went to the IRS office in L.A., and he always asked me to ride along and keep him company. Even though he was jolly on the trip over, as the interview approached his mood darkened.

He'd come up shy on his taxes again and been ordered to make it right. I waited in the car while he handed over his money—either in cash or a money order. Dad was a Democrat, loved America, and thought it was the greatest country in the world. But like many Westerners, he didn't believe in giving a nickel of his hard-earned money to support the government.

The Freeway Wars Mother and I engaged in were part of a larger shift in our relationship. At thirteen, I'd lurched into adolescence at the same time that Mother was stumbling into menopause. Both conditions fueled the tension between us, and we argued often.

When Dad was gone Mother's drinking increased, and a disturbing pattern developed in our already strained relationship. In the first phase, she was sticky sweet—lots of hugging and kissing in a Betty Boop sort of way. After three or four days had passed, she began to ruminate, then she glowered... thinking... thinking...

Then came the pathetic phase. "Poor me, I don't do anything but work; I never have any fun; nobody appreciates me; I'm just about to the end of my rope; and I've had it up to here!" These emotions fueled a series of Jekyll and Hyde transformations. Leaving Betty Boop behind, she got pathetic, then drunk and mean. Let the battle begin!

I was always willing and able to accommodate her, lobbing hand grenades like, "I hate you!" or "I hate your guts!" If Mother wasn't already armed with a cooking spoon or spatula, she quickly found one before chasing me around the house.

Mother tried to kiss and make up after every skirmish, but I would have none of it. I knew that in a week or so—predictable as sunrise and sunset—liquor's putrid flower would blossom again. Although I needed and wanted Mother's love, I didn't trust or respect her. It was all so complex and conflicting, I stayed as far away from her as possible.

The truth was, we were both miserable. All Mother did was work—she got that right. The one-time flapper who loved nothing more than to don a pretty dress and become the life of the party, never went out. She never had what she called fun. And I was desperately lonely, having been dumped into a neighborhood devoid of humanity, surrounded by ominous coils of freeways, and suffocated by smog.

That summer between eighth and ninth grade, I didn't have a single friend, had lost my horse and the excitement of rodeo competition, and grown disillusioned with adults. I was very lonely, but I wanted to be alone.

If you were a cowboy, you never had to lose everything. No matter where you rode, you kept the same moon and stars, the same coyotes and crickets singing you to sleep at night. Your horse didn't care where you went as long as you were together. He simply nuzzled your shoulder.

Miss Priss, wearing her cowboy boots, cowboy hat, jeans, and embroidered cowboy shirt, mounts Lucky, and rides far, far away.

Since Chad and I had no friends, Mother took us to the pet store to buy some company. We bought Yertle the Turtle, who lived in a green plastic dish sitting on a shelf above the kitchen sink. Every time you turned on the water in the sink, he crawled up and poked his green head, on its red-striped neck, out of his shell, begging for food. Yertle the Turtle ate packaged turtle food, but he preferred tiny bits of raw hamburger or newly swatted flies.

One day we bought a bright green parakeet I named Pete. The storeowner swore he was young, and said if we spent a little time teaching him, he would talk. I finger-trained him, and he loved to come out of his cage, sit on my shoulder, and travel around the house with me, nibbling gently on my ear or shirt collar.

Mother bought Fifi, a gray, miniature poodle puppy. Fifi was Crazy Dog #1. (Every dog we owned after moving to Southern California, went nuts shortly after entering our house.) Even when she was no longer a puppy, Fifi continued to run around in frenzied circles. Mother spoiled her rotten, but I could have kicked that hysterical little powder puff out the front door and into the street.

Occasionally, Mother and I went to the movies. We saw the first 3-D movie, *Bwana Devil*, wearing the dark glasses they gave us as we entered the theater. Lions with their jaws open wide flew right at you. It was unsettling.

But the theater itself was more frightening still. The *Los Angeles Times* occasionally featured front-page stories about shoot-outs between drug dealers and the police. Whenever the lights were on, Mother and I looked around furtively, trying to spot any dealers so we could get out of there before the shooting started.

When school finally began, I was both scared and elated. I knew enough not to wear cowboy clothes on the first day. I wore my best outfit—a chartreuse blouse, fitted at the waist, with a pointed collar and a full chartreuse skirt that faded into gray.

As I walked the school that first day, I noticed groups of girls walking both ahead of and behind me. Where had they been all summer? In time, I found out that all the girls in my neighborhood had gone to Webster Elementary—they'd been friends forever. I was the only one walking alone. I noticed right away that none of them dressed the way I did. They wore conservative straight skirts and blouses. Although they stared at me, they didn't laugh. Still, I felt like a firecracker going off in church.

Right away, my favorite class was biology. The teacher, Mrs. Mundt, was the best teacher I'd had since my Boise art teacher. When she talked about different species of plants and animals, her round face glowed with delight. Her room was full of snakes, birds, hamsters, tropical fish, and white mice. The first week, she seemed delighted when I asked if I could help her take care of the animals. I'd found a home away from home.

When Mother got back from work at five-thirty or six, she asked how school had gone. I said fine. She never asked any further questions, and I didn't volunteer any information.

Our family time was watching television. Every night, we carried our dinners into the living room on metal TV trays with legs. We laughed together during the television programs, especially during Dad's favorite, *The Jackie Gleason Show*, on Saturday nights. We loved it when Gleason was Ralph in The Honeymooners, holding his fist up and threatening Alice with a "Pow! Right in the kisser!" Unlike real life, where real fists are put to work, Ralph was simply a sputtering windbag. Alice always stared him down, hands planted firmly on her hips.

Sunday nights, we watched *Meet the Press*. That's how I knew Dwight D. Eisenhower swamped the Democrat, Adlai Stevenson, who Dad was rooting for.

Mother signed me up for ice skating lessons at the Pasadena Arena and I took a lesson once a week, then practiced my spins and jumps for an hour afterwards. I quit when I started making friends; they were more important to me than skating by myself.

One of my first friends was Pat Sheldon. She was cute and smart. On weekends, we played tennis at the school tennis courts, spending most of our time chasing balls. Our mothers liked each other too— they had drinking and Canasta in common. Once a week they got together at Pat's house, played cards, and got pie-eyed. When Mother came back from Sheldon's, I always wondered how she'd driven the car home without crashing it.

By mid-November of ninth grade, I knew a lot of people at school and felt more comfortable there. The running joke in gym class was that since I was the only girl in the class who hadn't gotten her period, I was probably a boy. Even though Mother had told me to expect it any day, when I woke one morning to find blood spotting my bottom sheet, I called her, terrified.

As she ran into my bedroom, I said, "Mother, I don't know what's wrong with me. I must be hurt!" She laughed, which I didn't appreciate. Then she gave me a sanitary belt and a Kotex, showing me how to hook the ends of the Kotex through two little tabs on the belt. I had to wear the pad between my legs. That was the only time I almost yearned to be a boy. The urge passed when I remembered how much equipment they had to carry around between their legs all the time.

Then the cramps began. When I complained about the pain, Mother said, "I hope you're not going to be like some of those sappy girls at Westlake who were always complaining about their cramps and staying in bed for the day." She said *their cramps* sarcastically, screwing up her face. Then, she added, "I never had the cramps in my life!"

That was the end of my cramps career.

I hadn't planned on talking about my period at school. Once it came, I felt shy about it. But after playing basketball in gym class, we had to take showers. "Oh no," I thought. "What should I do about the Kotex?" I didn't have the slightest idea.

"Do you wear this dumb pad into the shower or not?" I finally asked one of the girls. She laughed, and announced to the entire gym class, "Hey, everyone! Jill's a girl after all! She got her period!" In various stages of dress and undress, the other girls came running toward me. They did a victory dance around me on the wet cement floor as the showerheads blasted steaming torrents into the shower stalls around us.

Two or three afternoons a week, while I helped Mrs. Mundt clean out the animal cages, we had long talks. She was like a second mother to any girl who needed one, and there were plenty of girls in need. One girl in our class, Maria Sanchez, whose family had recently emigrated from Mexico, was often in the room talking to Mrs. Mundt. They spoke in whispers, but before long everyone knew Maria was pregnant. Mrs. Mundt was helping her. Maria soon left school, which made us sad. She was sweet and very bright.

Mrs. Mundt always had lots of white mice, since the adult mice had nothing else to do but run around on their exercise wheels, breed, and have babies. She gave me a mouse couple and a cage for them. I added them to our menagerie at home.

Not long after, I became friends with Cyndy Beeson and Lorrie Guerriero, who both lived in my neighborhood. One of Lorrie's best friends was Marty Bucklen, a cute blonde with a ponytail, but Marty lived across town, so I didn't get to know her right away.

Cyndy was a straight arrow. Her father was an engineer and her mother was a housewife. Although her mother was quiet and wimpy, she did one rebellious thing. She smoked in the bathroom while Mr. Beeson was at work.

Lorrie's parents had moved to Pasadena from Youngstown, Ohio, to escape the Mafia. Lorrie said every Italian man her parents knew—

even the honest ones—got roped into working for the Mob. Her family traveled as far away from organized crime as possible. Lorrie's mother, Sue, worked as a secretary in L.A., and her father, Leonard, was a rug cleaner.

After school, we often went with Lorrie to her tiny house while she stirred her mom's delicious spaghetti sauce, made not with just hamburger but with real chunks of beef. We waited while Lorrie did her chores, but we always ended up at my house. Chad was in school, and I had to be there when he got home. Everyone liked my house best anyway. They loved my parents—thought they were more fun and with-it than their own. Because we had the den all to ourselves, it became our hideaway.

The other reason we went to my house was that we'd all started to smoke. I didn't like smoking at first, but I kept at it until the coughing and choking abated. Dad was smoking Marlboros in his cigarette holder at the time, and Mother was smoking L & Ms. I stole a few cigarettes from her and smoked on the way home from school until I got the hang of it. Lorrie and Cyndy couldn't risk getting caught by their parents so they didn't smoke on the street. They came to my house and we smoked in the den. We attempted to air out the room by leaving the double doors to the patio open.

One day, Mother walked in. She sniffed and laughed, waving the smoke away with her hand.

"My goodness," she said, laughing. "I thought there was a forest fire in here." From then on, we didn't hide our smoking.

Although Chad loved Lorrie, Dad didn't. He was pleasant to her, but she was the only one of my friends he had reservations about. She was both naughty and beautiful, with shoulder-length black hair and long, slender hands. At parties, when she wanted to dance, if no one would dance with her, she danced alone. Dad must have recognized a kindred spirit.

Lorrie thought Dad was perfect. She never realized he didn't feel the same way about her. Because her mother was fussy about her house, Lorrie wasn't allowed to have pets, so she loved our animals too. She often spent time in the kitchen talking to Yertle, the turtle, and Pete, the bird.

Pete said "Hello!" to her every time she came into the kitchen, and "Hello!" every time she left, which delighted her. I didn't tell her he said "Hello!" to anyone who came in and out of the kitchen. Because I hadn't spent much time teaching him to talk, that was the only word in Pete's vocabulary. Not that he wasn't smart. He learned a new word after you'd said it to him just a few times.

Day after day, Lorrie left us alone in the den and spent time talking to Pete. She never reported back on her progress. When she returned to the den, she joined us in seriously practicing our deep inhales. Then we worked on the advanced sophistication of letting smoke drift out of our mouths while we inhaled it back in through our noses.

After Mary Budge's doctor husband divorced her and married his nurse, Mary moved to Pasadena with her youngest son, Bill. Bruce, who was my age, had been sent to a military school until he straightened out and quit driving getaway cars for robberies.

Mary rented an apartment close by, and Chad loved having Bill to play with again. It was a big responsibility for Mother, though, since Mary had become a hopeless alcoholic. Dr. Budge sent her away several times to "take the cure," but it never took. She always started drinking again as soon as she came home.

Mother helped Mary get a job as a nurse, her career before she married Dr. Budge. But she had trouble holding a job because, once she started drinking, she couldn't stop. Bill often called Mother to come over and help him, and I went over too. Mary was usually passed out in bed, cigarettes smoldering in ashtrays on the dresser, on the bedside table, and on the bed itself. Cigarette-burn sores festered on her arms. We often cleaned up the place and fixed some food for the two of them. Mother always nursed Mary back to health and helped her get another job.

"Luckily," Mother said, "there's a real need for nurses, or nobody'd hire her. Not with her work record."

We were concerned about Mary and Bill, but we could only do so much. Our own situation was anything but secure. Dad had gotten a hint—how or what, he never said—that something wasn't right about the International Hotel deal. It had to do with Mr. Stewart.

"Don't you like him anymore?" I asked, worried I'd never get to ride Mr. Stewart's palomino horses, which I'd been angling for.

"No, it's not that," Dad said. "Something just isn't right."

Dad hadn't backed out of the deal yet, but he said it wasn't looking good.

My parents finally found a couple they liked. Dad met the husband in a Chinese restaurant in L.A. I didn't know it at the time, but Dad was already trying to raise money for his next deal, and Clayt and Rae Carlton were two of his first investors. Dad said they were "characters." In Idaho parlance, that might mean "eccentric." To my parents, it usually meant "crazy as squirrels, and drank too much." Because of these two qualities, they were known as good scouts and lots of fun. We were invited over to have dinner with them.

They lived in a one-room apartment in L.A. Even the bed was in the only room, which was papered with large, open-wide red roses. We sat on the bed, or on chairs arranged on either side of it, while Chad played with his little cars and trucks on the floor. Rae prepared all the food in the bathroom, on a shelf beside the bathroom sink. She cooked on two hot plates next to the TV and did the dishes in the bathtub, already brimming with stacked dishes and pots and pans from previous meals.

The four adults had several drinks as I fidgeted over my third 7-Up. Considering her limited space and equipment, Rae put together a good meal of fried chicken, rice, and a tossed salad. I don't know where she stored the salad, because I never saw a refrigerator. Maybe they kept it in the clothes closet beneath Clayt's shirts.

Mother and Dad's friends in Boise were bad enough, but the Carltons were a giant step downhill. I didn't have much of an appetite for dinner because I couldn't erase the picture from my mind of Rae cutting up the chicken, then flushing its fatty skin down the toilet. I wondered where she washed the lettuce.

Rae must have read the disapproval on my face. The next time the Carltons came to our house for dinner, she brought Chad and me each a present. I was surprised and pleased. It was clear that Rae preferred Chad; she didn't like me any more than I liked her. Now I wondered if I'd been wrong about her. After the adults downed a few drinks, Chad opened his present. He loved his little silver truck.

I couldn't imagine what my present was, a slender package about a foot long. Excited, I tore the paper off until my hands held a garishly painted Hawaiian girl, naked to the waist. She wore a green plaster grass skirt, and, above that, a plaster necklace of flowers that didn't begin to cover her two huge breasts with pointed scarlet nipples.

Humiliated, I glared at Rae and Mother as I walked, with as much dignity as I could muster, out of the living room. Both women laughed. Mother called after me, "What's the matter, Miss Priss? Can't take a joke?"

My classes at school were going well, but I'd begun to notice a disturbing problem with retaining what I learned. Given enough time and drilling, I'd trained myself to memorize whole pages of data. This worked well for me in the short run. I was getting a straight A in every class.

In the classes I cared about, like biology, I retained the material pretty well. But in the required classes I didn't like—French and beginning algebra—I retained the material just long enough to get through the test. After I got my necessary A, the letters, numbers, words, sentences, paragraphs, and equations, flew up up and away like flocks of blackbirds.

The problem got worse as the semester proceeded. By mid-term, I'd waved good-bye to the French vocabulary words and verb declensions. I'd also said bye-bye to the early theorems and equations covered in beginning algebra. Are they called theorems and equations? I can't remember because they're gone, gone, gone.

I knew I had to keep a nearly straight A average so I could go to college. That was my survival plan. How college would help me escape my parents' life, I had not the slightest clue. But I knew I had to keep my grade average up.

Competing with my urgent need to remember school data was the fact that I'd survived the war years of my early childhood by willfully learning to forget all about it. I'd become both an overachieving learner and an overachieving unlearner. The learning came after a lot of effort and time memorizing; the unlearning happened automatically.

This erasing didn't matter much in my French class because our mild-mannered teacher didn't care if we cheated. During every test, most of the class, me included, left our books open on the floor by our chairs, and copied directly from them. The teacher, reading at his desk, never looked up until he collected the papers. That was the way I kept my A in French.

I had no such luck in beginning algebra, where I was forced to review relentlessly before every test. After an incredible amount of work, I scraped through with a low B.

One morning Dad was in the kitchen making coffee when Mother and I heard him laughing. We ran into the kitchen and found him leaning against the counter in stiches. As he was measuring out the coffee grounds, without any warning, Pete, the bird, had clearly said, "Charlie, Charlie Breckenridge, hello you old son-of-a-bitch!" Pete repeated the sentence one more time for our benefit. From that moment on, Lorrie could do no wrong.

The parakeet didn't learn any new words, but he continued to come up with creative combinations of the few words he did know. Some mornings, he repeated the whole sentence, "Charlie, Charlie Breckenridge, hello you old son-of-a-bitch!" Other times, he simplified it to, "Hello Charlie," or "Hello, you old son-of-a-bitch!" Occasionally he distilled the sentence down to its main point, "Son-of-a-bitch! Son-of-a-bitch!"

Soon after starting tenth grade, Cyndy, Lorrie, and I discovered The Peeper in our neighborhood. Cyndy, the first one to fall beneath his unwelcome gaze, was so modest that even showering in gym class mortified her. She had straight blonde hair, cut short and primly shaping her face, so she looked like the little Dutch girl on the Dutch Cleanser can.

Cyndy never talked about anything personal, but one day while the three of us walked to school, she told us what had happened the night before. Her bathroom had one window, so high and private it didn't have a curtain over it. Cyndy was changing her Kotex when she felt somebody's eyes on her. She looked up. Framed by the window, she saw the face of a man about her father's age watching her.

She screamed for her dad, who ran outside. He found a wooden box The Peeper had dragged under the window to stand on. The police said there wasn't much they could do. He probably lived in the neighborhood. We girls shuddered with horror.

My own dad was seldom home during the fall, but he returned in time for the Christmas holidays, out-of-sorts and cranky. I knew the hotel deal must be falling through. On Christmas Eve, he drank his usual pitcher of martinis before dinner, which didn't help his sour mood. He sat in his chair, glowering. As Chad put out his note and cookies for Santa, Dad didn't even fake good cheer.

I read *The Night Before Christmas* to Chad and put him to bed. After he was asleep, Mother, Dad, and I began setting up the gifts Chad had requested from Santa—a new trike, a circus tent with acrobats, and a starter electric train set. None of them came assembled.

Dad worked assembling the trike while I set up the circus tent. My job was easy—just a few colored cardboard pieces with tabs that hooked together. Then, I hung clowns from the rungs of their wooden circus ladders by their hooked hands or feet. Mother unwrapped what seemed like hundreds of train pieces and placed them, one by one, on the carpet. Dad fit the trike handlebars together and started attaching them to the front wheel.

After a few minutes, he slammed the handlebars down on the green shag rug and said, "This damned thing doesn't make any sense at all! They must have left some parts out!"

Trying to be helpful, Mother said, "Are there any directions we could look at?"

At this suggestion, Dad stood up and threw the trike's front tire down on the rug.

"There's no rhyme nor reason to this damned thing! If you're so smart, put it together yourself!"

He stalked off to the bedroom. We could hear him slamming drawers in and out. After banging the medicine cabinet door shut several times, he finally went to bed.

Mother and I looked at each other helplessly. One of the few things we were in total agreement about was our adoration of Chad. Unprepared for the task as we were, we rolled up our Rosie the Riveter sleeves and plunged in. We didn't know how to put the trike together either, but we knew we had to do it for Chad. As I studied the directions, it became clear what was called for were tools Dad didn't have—a screwdriver and a pair of pliers. I used a dull kitchen knife as a screwdriver and serrated scissors as makeshift pliers, while Mother struggled to get the train track together.

Once the trike was assembled, I helped Mother with the train. At first, I read the directions while she carried them out, but her hands shook so much, she had trouble with the little pieces, so we switched roles. On our knees, we crouched over the unassembled train set. Like mystics awaiting a brilliant flash of illumination from above, we mumbled the electric train words to one another, "Switcher, transformer, rerailer," and haltingly assembled the train set. It took most of the night, but we got the job done.

When Chad got up, he was astonished that the cookies he left out had all been eaten. And he was awestruck watching the train spinning around its curved track. (We'd even figured out how to make it toot and puff smoke.) He put two of the little clowns on a passing flatcar, christening his new toy.

On Christmas morning, Dad rose, rested and cheerful. We opened our presents. Then, Mother and I relaxed while he fixed breakfast. After Dad left the room, I said to Mother that if Santa Claus were as temperamental as Dad, the children would never get any presents. We both laughed.

In the kitchen, we heard Dad singing, "Chestnuts Roasting On An Open Fire," as he cooked our Christmas breakfast—spicy sausages and gravy, golden biscuits with butter and syrup, and brains with scrambled eggs and capers. Grateful for any gift given, we sat down together and ate.

My brother Chad with Fritzy.

By the next summer, it became clear that Dad's deal had fallen through. I couldn't get anything out of my parents except that he'd smelled a rat and pulled out. Mother was also sad because Fifi, Crazy Dog #1, had whirled herself into the street for the umpteenth time and been run over by a passing car. To assuage her grief, Mother went right out and bought a dachshund puppy, Fritzie, who was soon in training to be Crazy Dog #2. Fritzie chewed up everything he could get his tiny pointed teeth into.

The best thing about that summer was another visit from Ol' Mart, the thwarted actress who had lived with us in Shoshone. She came for the weekend and stayed two years. I slept in the den because I needed to study late. Mart slept in the extra bed in the back bedroom with Chad. When she was around, everything lightened up. My friends always wanted to be with her. We sat at her feet while she told us stories and showed us her jew-els over and over again.

Mart's biggest worry was that the bill collectors would repossess Ol' Liz, her black Cadillac. Afraid to park the car in our driveway where it could be easily seen, she hid it in different locations around the neighborhood and moved it several times a day.

During tenth grade, I saw less of Pat, because she was busy being student body president—the first girl ever to hold that office. She also spent a lot of time with her boyfriend, Dave, who she'd gone with since seventh grade. She didn't have much time to hang out with me, but I had other friends now, and I still enjoyed the time Pat and I spent together.

Although I was happy at school and with my friends, I was still uncomfortable about my looks. In those days, the ideal girl was a wholesome tanned blonde with long straight hair curling under in a pageboy. I was too tall, thin, pale, freckled, curly-haired, and long-legged to measure up. I was also redheaded, gangly, and awkward, words that are emphatic enough without a 'too.'

Mother decided I should take modeling lessons to build up my confidence and learn to walk gracefully. She signed me up with The William Adrian Modeling Agency in Pasadena, and the following Wednesday night, she shakily drove me through town to a run-down warehouse district with dark, deserted-looking buildings, waiting in the locked car in front of the dilapidated building until my two-hour class was over.

Nervous as a cat on her way to a dog show, I carried a paper bag holding the bathing suit and high-heeled shoes I'd been instructed to bring up a long flight of wooden stairs. At the top of these stairs was the home of The William Adrian Modeling Agency. It consisted of one messy office. But Mr. Adrian had wrangled permission to use the wooden landing between the top of the stairs and the office as his classroom.

Mr. Adrian was a short, stocky man, probably in his late fifties. Nearly bald, he'd combed several strings of greasy black hair across the top of his head. A stroke had left one of his eyes unscathed, but the other eye gazed up toward the sky in a permanent search for fame and fortune. His mouth, on the gazing-up side of his face, drooped down at the corner so even when he laughed, you were never sure he meant it. He'd managed to merge the mask of comedy and the mask of tragedy into one face.

His assistant, Gloria, ran the modeling classes. Her round face was framed by brown hair she wore in a pageboy. Because of her heavy make-up, it was hard to tell how old she was—probably somewhere between eighteen and thirty. Probably on the younger side. Probably more than his assistant. Long before women were allowed in the military, Gloria had the demeanor and bark of an Army Sergeant.

The other four girls there looked as scared as I was. Two of them were overweight, though they both wore tight-fitting clothing. Another girl was barely four feet tall and skinny, with short, blond hair that stuck straight out from her head. Only one of us looked like she had some potential—Marjorie, a dark-haired girl with fingernails chewed down to the quick. That wouldn't help her get nail ads, but her hair was beautiful and she had a good figure. I was the skinny, awkward, embarrassed one.

Gloria ordered us to put on our bathing suits and high heels. The five of us changed in the broom closet, a long dark room lit by a single bare bulb and lined with brooms, mops, and dustpans. It smelled of the waxy sawdust used to clean wood floors. Gloria said we might as well get used to inferior changing rooms. That's the way it would be when we did fashion shows and TV programs later.

"I changed once on the floor behind the front seat of a car," she said, as we girls glanced at each other, bug-eyed. That's not what we'd imagined when we signed up.

We made an attempt at modesty within the confines of the closet, turning our backs toward one another, staggering around, groping toward the wall to maintain our balance, and draping our clothes over the damp mop heads and dusty rags hanging on the hooks along the wall. After wriggling into our bathing suits, we slipped on our black high heels, concurring in whispers that we'd been told to wear black high heels—only black. Every girl's heels were at least three inches high.

The classes Gloria taught were Walking, Talking, Turning, Stairs and Sitting, and Make-up. In that order. The first thing she had us do was walk around and around in a circle on the landing, our high heels firing machine-gun staccatos into the wood floor, our fingers modestly pulling the bathing suits down over our behinds, as Gloria barked out orders.

"Marjorie, stand up straight! You look like a Chinese peasant! Rene, suck in your gut! Jill, wipe that apologetic look off your face! Come on now girls, you're having fun, not marching to the slaughter house!"

I didn't say anything, but I begged to differ. My feet hurt, and I didn't appreciate being stared at by William and his brother, Calvin, who had joined him for the cattle drive. The two men sized us up like they were appraising us for rib roasts and porterhouse steaks. They didn't look overjoyed with today's herd.

Part of the appraisal was measuring. Gloria showed us how to accomplish this task with a measuring tape. I pulled the tape firmly around my back and across my nipples for the bust—34 inches. Then, around the smallest part of my middle, just beneath my ribcage, for the waist—22 inches. Finally, around the fleshiest part of my hips—34 inches.

Each one of us reported our measurements, top down, as William seriously recorded them in his little notebook. He began with me at 34/22/34. The two heavier girls were 38/36/44 and 36/30/37. The short blonde girl was 30/19/32. Marjorie, the dark-haired girl who bit her fingernails, was 35/26/36. Mr. Adrian seemed to like her numbers best.

I didn't learn till later that Marilyn Monroe's dimensions were 37/23/37, the perfect dimensions for a sex goddess. None of us could compete with those numbers except Gloria. With her large breasts, she was sexy, but her figure was considered too heavy for bathing suit or ramp modeling. The thinner girls got that work.

After class was over, the five of us hobbled back to the broom closet and changed back into our regular clothes. My feet hurt. We groaned in relief when we took off our high heels and put on our bobby sox and white bucks. Daunted, I gingerly descended the stairs to Mother's car. When she asked how the class went, I said, "Fine."

"What do you mean, fine?" she asked, irritably. "What did you do?"

"Oh, we walked around and stuff."

"You mean they taught you how to walk?"

"I guess so."

"Well, that sounds good."

For the next five weeks, we had a class every Wednesday night. Mother spent a lot of time in the Caddie waiting patiently out front. Mr. Adrian allowed no mothers upstairs, nor were they allowed anywhere near where we modeled or adorned TV show sets. He bullied and bossed our mothers around. Perhaps they were cowed by his insulting manner, afraid of his derision, or just desperately hoped he could accomplish with their daughters what they couldn't. Not one mother stood up to him, fearing that Mr. Adrian might drop her daughter from his classes and put an end to the girl's modeling career before it began.

In each night of the five remaining classes, we spent the first hour walking in our bathing suits and high heels before moving on to the next installment. The second class, Talking, was mainly about listening. Evidently that was what we were supposed to do when we were with "the opposite sex," as Gloria called men.

In the Turning class we learned how to stop, put our hands on our hips, take one step back with our left foot, then pull our right foot back to meet it and make a "T." At that point we would step forward again with that right foot and execute a turn, then turn one more time to end up going in the same direction as before. At fashion shows where we walked on a ramp or between tables, the several turns allowed us to make a complete turn-around and display all sides of our outfits. It felt graceful and dramatic, almost like dancing.

The class called Stairs and Sitting could have been reduced to a single sentence: "Keep your knees together, and your skirt pulled down over them."

The last class, Make-up, was the most fun of all. Gloria brought a huge sectioned tray outfitted with every color of face make-up imaginable, along with rouge, eye shadow, mascara, eyeliner, and eyebrow pencils. Mr. Adrian said that I should wear green eye shadow because it looked best with my long red hair, which I had begun to set in soft rollers at night and then comb into a pageboy.

Gloria's tray looked like the equipment of a serious artist. That's what make-up meant to me. It allowed you to repair, as much as nature would allow, what had gone amiss the first time around. You simply applied some paint and a few strategic lines.

Until then, I'd worn only a light amount of mascara and eyebrow pencil. But when I descended the stairs to Mother's car after that last class, I had been transformed by liquid face make-up, eyeliner, and green eye shadow. Mother's expression, close to horror, gave me the impression she did not much approve of my new look, but I thought I looked glamorous, sexy, and at least twenty years old. What tenth grade girl could ask for more?

A few weeks later, I began dating Steve Farrell, also a tenth-grader, who played boogie-woogie piano for the school dances. His hands on the keyboard moved almost too fast to follow. When listening to his music, if you couldn't dance, you tapped your foot.

He drove a new red-and-black Chevy with tail fins. Hanging from his rearview mirror were black angora dice with white spots his former girlfriend had knit for him. When I climbed into his car, I was free! For the first time, I had wheels—even though they weren't actually my wheels.

By that time I fully understood the hierarchy of beauty. First, there was the most beautiful to least beautiful, which meant most perfect to least perfect. Then, there was live or photographic work. Live work paid less. Since my relationship with the camera was hostile, I qualified only for live work—and for smaller paychecks. These jobs were often during the day, which was tricky because of school and Mother's job. It would have been worse if I'd been photogenic. One of my friends, Patti Fosdick, a beautiful blonde who looked like Grace Kelly, did Breck Shampoo ads. She missed a lot of school but she made a lot of money.

One afternoon, Mother drove me into L.A. to appear briefly on a TV show for the first time. She was reluctant to take time off work, because she couldn't risk losing her job. Dad was traveling around again trying to set up another deal, and he'd become very unreliable about sending any money home. But William Adrian's last words to her on the phone had been: "If you don't get Jill there in time for this job, she'll never work for me again!"

Mother faked a dentist appointment to get me out of school. As we passed the Hollywood sign, high up on its Hollywood hill, I thought it looked mighty good up there. Mother was driving on the apron of the freeway again. Going about forty, she crouched over the wheel like a racecar driver, but she was so terrified of freeways I'd stopped fighting with her about it.

As we passed the sign Mother told me a story. During the war, it became too expensive to replace the four thousand light bulbs in the original 1923 sign, so it was replaced with a new one that had tall, fifty-foot letters. A young starlet, Peg Entwhistle, was depressed because she couldn't get an acting role, even though she'd already made two films. Using a construction ladder, she climbed to the top of the "H" and jumped to her death. That same day a letter arrived at her apartment offering her a role in a play about a suicide.

My first TV show role was disappointing. I was part of a fake nightclub audience around a fake set. The show featured mediocre musical acts for which we were the adoring audience. Sitting around our little cocktail tables drinking Cokes, we feigned delight and clapped after every song as if we'd really liked it. I made twenty-five dollars that day, after Mr. Adrian took out a sizable cut.

What I loved best about being on those shows was the make-up. You were supposed to arrive without any on, or very little. The crew made you up before the show, using beautiful eye shadow and lots of face make-up. Under the set's lights, with heavy face make-up on, my freckles were invisible. I was in non-redhead heaven, feeling close to perfection.

A girl, soon to be a woman, never sees herself clearly. She only sees the flaws in what she got, or grieves over what she didn't get. Most of her good qualities are hidden from her. I thought my parents were the dreamers, but I was one too. A dreamer masks the truth to see something the way she wants it to be. Make-up gave me the more perfect face I desired, and divorced me from the face I had—the face that looked frightened and damaged and sad. If people saw me the way I wanted to see myself, maybe they'd believe the dream. Then, maybe I could believe it too.

During the day, I started wearing TV set make-up. No eye shadow except at night, but I wore heavy face make-up all the time now. When I walked to Lorri or Cyndy's houses, men driving by in cars stopped, leered, and asked if I wanted a ride. Insulted and outraged by their audacity, I said, "Get lost, or I'll call the police!" and they roared away.

Once, a man driving by was gawking, his head turned away from the road toward me. He went through a stop sign and almost hit another car. Years later, I realized the cruising men probably thought I was a young prostitute trolling in a quiet, residential neighborhood. They couldn't believe their good fortune.

These reactions from men gave me a certain kind of power, but it wasn't what I wanted. Although I couldn't have articulated it, I wanted something as simple as having people like me. If they liked me, maybe I could like myself—or maybe I could like this Hollywood version of myself.

In a high school picture taken of me at the time, I look sultry. It was hard work to achieve that look, since my lower lip didn't naturally stick out that way. After much practicing, I became adept at sliding my tongue through my slightly parted teeth and putting the tip of my tongue under my lower lip to hold it out in a practiced pout.

Although the expression looked sexy, I couldn't talk with my mouth in that fortified position. "What time is it?" would have come out as, "Bat pime iph ith?"

Once, after a date with Steve, we parked and made-out. Leaving the radio on, we kissed for a while, then French kissed for a while, then petted for a while. I didn't allow Steve's hand under my clothes at first. When the petting got too hot and heavy, I got scared, faked concern, and looked at my watch.

"Oh, Steve," I'd say, "I have to get home or my folks will kill me!" A fiction, because I never had hours. Dad was gone most of the time, and Mother staggered off to bed by nine. Steve grumbled, but he took me home, my pancake make-up smeared across the collar and shoulders of his shirt.

Mother was dead-set against my new make-up. This seemed odd, since she wore even more than I did, covering up the damage from her x-ray treatments. She must have feared that the modeling class she financed had spawned, not a future movie star, but a future call girl.

After countless fights, she resorted to another tactic. She stopped saying anything directly about my make-up, and took up pantomime. Before I left for school in the morning, she scrutinized me, then made a kind-of wiping-off motion with her hand against her cheek, as in, "Can't you take some of that off?" The minute she made that wiping-off motion, I'd explode like an H-bomb. One time, in exasperation, she said, "It looks like a mask, Jill. A mask!"

Stunned and hurt, I said, "You should talk, wrinkles!"

Armed with a metal cooking spoon, she chased me around the house, but I hastily swept up my books and ran out the front door to school.

Our nicest family times were centered on the TV. Dad bought a color set soon after they appeared on the market, though only a few of the channels broadcast in color. With Dad gone so much and Mother always worried about money, Ol' Mart continued to bring some lighthearted sparkle to our evenings. She laughed louder and harder over the *I Love Lucy* show than any of us. On commercial breaks, she ran out to move Ol' Liz so the bill collectors wouldn't nab her.

We loved *The Loretta Young Show* too. We all thought Loretta was beautiful, and a wonderful actress. One night, as usual, Ol' Mart had taken out the "uppers" of her false teeth because they hurt, and put them on the side table to give her gums a rest. Suddenly, she started screaming. Fritzie, Crazy Dog #2, had not only chewed up Ol' Mart's false teeth, he'd swallowed them before Mart could do a thing about it.

One night, Mother, Ol' Mart, Chad, and I were watching a jungle movie together. The explorers were plowing their way through the dense underbrush when a commercial came on. The commercial was about Pard Dog Food with Chlorophyll, which Mother fed to Fritzie, even though it didn't cure his bad breath. The sound of rustling underbrush continued, and we realized there wasn't any underbrush in the dog food commercial's landscape.

All of us, even Chad, turned around at the same time to see The Peeper staring at us through the living room window. Yelling at the top of our lungs, we ran out the front door after him, but he bolted from the bushes. As we got close to him, he melted away. Mother thought he must live close by, he knew his way around the neighborhood so well. With Dad seldom home, he seemed to have chosen our house to haunt.

Several months after Dad pulled out of the International Hotel deal, he was served with a subpoena to testify in the trial of Mr. Bailey Stewart. It turned out the police had been hunting Mr. Stewart for years.

This was the only bad deal Dad ever got out of in time.

The International Hotel was a great idea, though very idealistic during the 1950s, when few people cared a jot about foreigners or foreign food. A few decades later, entrepreneurs in Florida, California, and Las Vegas were building virtual foreign lands complete with virtual landscapes and virtual foods.

The reason Mr. Stewart was arrested, however, had nothing to do with the International Hotel deal. Mr. Stewart's latest wealthy older wife had died under mysterious circumstances. Evidently, she wasn't the only one. His first two older wealthy wives, who'd owned stables as well, had simply disappeared. After years of searching, investigators had finally found one of the first two wives buried under the wooden floor of her stable. Mr. Stewart, my first great love, was a Bluebeard.

8

Boat Shows and Rose Parades

At the beginning of eleventh grade, I was fifteen. Chad, in second grade, was six—my age when the worst violence raged in our household. Without ever discussing it, Mother, Ol' Mart, and I united in making sure his early childhood was less traumatic than mine had been. I read to Chad before he went to bed at night; Mother fixed her usual bacon and eggs for breakfast, christening each new day with smoky grease; and Ol' Mart made us all laugh.

We three women went through the daily walk and talk of our lives as if we didn't see the end in sight. In spite of the volcanic cracks that appeared when warfare erupted between Mother and me, we pulled together for Chad's sake, holding onto the fringe of normal life as it drifted away from us.

I got a job working at Fields, a small but popular clothing store in downtown Pasadena. Fields was the fashion center for every teenage girl hooked on clothes. I quickly spent my paychecks buying cashmere sweaters at about thirty dollars apiece. I eventually accumulated thirty-two of them, an extravaganza that cost me more than a thousand dollars. This amount didn't include the matching straight skirts and socks we girls wore with our white buck shoes. Although it was difficult to ignore the wreckage behind me and the catastrophe lurking ahead, I walked resolutely forward, eyes closed and wallet open.

There was a certain logic to my incessant purchases. I was investing in surface appearances, putting my faith in the "now" rather than a doubtful future. The concept of saving was as foreign to me as driving on the left side of the road. From what I could see, luck and good fortune were clearly here today and gone tomorrow. If you didn't spend your money while you had it, you were just a damned fool.

Mother never bought anything for herself because she knew from past experience she'd need what little money she earned for essentials like food and rent. She was frugal, but miserably unhappy. Dad, on the other hand, had a closet full of beautiful clothes, and his wardrobe pleased him greatly. When Mother got into one of her poor-me moods (precursor to a bender) she'd say, "I haven't had a new dress in years." I'd think, "Then buy one and quit whining about it!"

You don't love the victim in the house; you love the one with power.

Although I had growing doubts about that power, my tacit deal with Dad was Don't Ask, Don't Tell. Our boat was already rocking, and I wasn't about to capsize it. Besides, I never connected my father's instability, frequent disappearances, and womanizing with Mother's misery. I held him responsible only for loving me, which he did abundantly when he was home. Because Mother and I were both female, I fought for my life. There was no danger of me becoming Dad, but I could become Mother—wrinkled and pathetic, bitter and drunk.

Later, it became clear that during these years, Dad was racing back and forth across the world, living the high life on other people's capital. He alternately raised and spent huge sums of money—a process of self-destruction accelerated by pills and anesthetized by gin and expensive women. We saw him for only brief intervals when he returned to rest and recover. Mother, Ol' Mart, and I, like any crew of doomed shipmates cursed with a crazy captain and tossed by hurricane winds, sailed ahead and pretended the sea was calm and the sun was shining.

But at the same time, I found it all very confusing. So many of my presumptions had been tipped upside down. The childhood promise of a happy, secure family life had withered; the assumption that what you saw accurately portrayed what you got had been proven naive. In Shoshone, the crooks at least *looked* armed and dangerous. Here in Pasadena, Mr. Stewart looked like a model citizen, though he turned out to be a serial killer. My trust in a world you could examine and accurately judge was crumbling. The world I'd come to know was a slapdash affair constructed of cardboard and papered with dollar bills, the faces on the bills masked and morphing.

Whenever Dad was out of town, Mother drove his aqua Cadillac to work. I learned to drive her olive green '37 Buick, and enjoyed ferrying Lorrie and Cyndy along with me back and forth to our new school, Pasadena High School. It was part of a huge campus. Our junior and senior high school grades were housed with the two-year Pasadena City College, and our graduating class was over twelve hundred students.

We girls loved being on the same campus with college students. Loved arriving at school in Mother's Buick, with its louvered hood and green visor shading the front window.

As always, school was my haven, the place I could be my best self. Not that the city high school was perfect. We'd inherited the dregs of the teaching corps. Our teachers were primarily old men, forced to teach until retirement; a few widows, whose dead husbands hadn't provided for them; and a few history teachers, hired to coach football.

But the teaching staff wasn't what I cared most about. My friends were my main priority, and I had a new *old* friend at school. Bruce Budge had come to Pasadena from his military academy to live with his mother, Mary. He went to P.H.S. too. Even more handsome than I remembered, he was as wonderful to me as ever.

In my junior year of high school, 1954, the Supreme Court ordered all schools to be integrated since "Separate But Equal" was only separate but not equal. The law didn't really affect us at P.H.S. or P.C.C. Although the races weren't openly mixing and interdating yet, our school and our school dances were already integrated. We learned to dance by watching the black kids strut their stuff.

After "Sh-Boom" became a hit, rock 'n' roll music was the overwhelming craze at school. We loved its heavy beat and thinly veiled sexual references. We danced fast to "Sh-Boom" and to "Shake, Rattle and Roll." For slow numbers, we chose "Goodnight, Sweetheart, Goodnight" or "Sincerely." We hated Elvis Presley and his poor imitation of our black friends. The beat of rock 'n' roll fueled our

178 / Miss Priss and the Con Man

adolescent madness, and made our skin itch with desire. Our adolescent bodies had no choice but to obey the beat.

I'd grown into my body as it developed curves, and I no longer hated it. At night, pulling the drapes across the porch doors, I danced to rock 'n' roll on the den radio. In front of the large mirror, which hung above the couch that became my bed at night, I swayed, naked, to the beat. I was in love with the music and with how my body moved, as if charged with music's fluid electricity.

Inspired by the culture of black music and the lingo of the Beats, our list of slang expressions grew and changed almost daily. A person in the know was "cool" or "way out," and the opposite of cool was a "square" or "nerd." One of the biggest fights I ever had with Mother was when I said, "Oh, Mother, don't *sweat* it." She was furious. I hadn't meant to insult her. "Don't sweat it" was an expression we kids said to one another all the time. What we meant was, "Don't worry about it."

Ol' Mart almost always remained neutral in our family dramas. In the two years she lived with us, she got involved just once. I was studying in the den as Mother made dinner. I heard Mart yelling as she ran from the living room to the kitchen.

"Chaddie, Ol' Mart just has to tell... Ol' Mart just has to tell your mama about this!"

She'd caught Chad playing with matches behind the couch on the green shag rug. He promised never to do it again.

Dad traveled, mostly out of the country, on his new deal, which was to bring farmers from Hong Kong, where there was money but no land, to Caracas, where there was land but no money. In Hong Kong, several retired generals were trying to help refugee farmers, escapees from The Cultural Revolution, make a new start. Dad was traveling between the two countries, signing up both farmers and investors.

He'd found land for the farmers to settle on not far from Caracas. Now, he was trying to fit all the pieces of the puzzle together. It soon became clear that some of the puzzle pieces had been cut badly or had disappeared from the box altogether.

Dad was gone for more extended periods of time. His long distance phone bills, delivered into Mother's shaking hands, had mushroomed to between three and five thousand dollars a month. Dad seldom sent enough money to pay those bills, or any of the other bills that were steadily accumulating. Months went by when we didn't even hear from him. On her meager salary, Mother tried to chip away at our debt, but she kept falling farther behind.

Bill collectors called incessantly. Most of the calls came in the afternoon before Mother returned from work. I'd begun doing the cleaning for her after school, splitting the job up over a week. Our phone reliably rang between the dusting and vacuuming, between the vacuuming and scrubbing, and between the scrubbing and scouring. Sometimes it rang three or four times in a row, each caller different, as if all the bill collectors in Bad Credit Land were standing in a long line waiting their turn to harass us.

At first, when they asked for Mother, I said she wasn't home. They asked who I was. When I said I was her daughter, they demanded, in hard-edged voices, that I write down their ultimatums for Mother. It was so punishing to go through their repeated scolding, I made a deal with the truth. I turned my back on it—not forever, just for now—and assumed the role of maid. An indifferent maid who said the Mrs. wasn't home; an ignorant maid who didn't know when the Mrs. would be back. I got my routine down pat.

Ol' Mart, adorable as ever, couldn't offer any help. She was running away from her own unpaid bills, so she never answered the phone. But the relentless bill collectors calling Mother unsettled Mart. She was terrified they were going to repossess Ol' Liz.

Though Ol' Mart was searching frantically for a job herself, her efforts were fruitless because she had no marketable skills, no experience, and no work record. Since her family employed maids, cooks, and gardeners, she didn't even know how to clean or baby-sit. Every morning, she started poring over the Want Ads at the kitchen table next to the phone. When I got home from school, she was often in that same position, the receiver resting, exhausted, on its side as she crossed out another ad in the wrinkled, coffee-stained newspaper.

As the stack of unpaid bills grew, it was all Mother could do to work and stay on top of the bills that were essential. She had neither time nor energy to keep up with the cooking and washing, and resigned from both of those jobs. Arriving home from work exhausted, she cared only about pouring a drink the minute she walked in the front door.

She began serving us the new Swanson Frozen TV Dinners. Ol' Mart and Chad didn't complain, but I did. These so called dinners tasted like someone had wadded up colored pictures of food, stuffed the crushed paper into the geometric compartments of aluminum trays, and dumped too-salty gravy on top.

On those rare occasions when Mother cooked what might nominally pass for a real dinner, it was invariably hamburger, boiled potatoes, and a head-lettuce salad.

The weekly wash was another problem. Mother would put it in the washer, and pour liquid bleach from the bottle directly on top of the clothes before the tank had filled with water. After two of my favorite blouses were ruined this way, I began doing my own wash. We all began doing our own wash, except Chad. Mother went easy on his clothes.

As everything around us deteriorated, Fritzie, Crazy Dog #2, went from chewing up Ol' Mart's false teeth to chewing up the bedding. He reveled in destroying our blankets. If the beds were made, he didn't disturb them, but if they were unmade for even a minute, the sneak climbed up on them, did his damage and jumped down before we could catch him. All of us had an ever-increasing number of chewed holes in our once lovely blankets.

Mother had no social life outside the house except her Canasta games with Mrs. Sheldon, until she managed to track down Lucille, her best friend from Westlake. They had even more in common than when they were students because Lucille had made a bad marriage too. Her alcoholic husband seldom found or kept a job. He had the work record of a Kleenex. At least he went to AA and wasn't drinking anymore. Lucille, like Mother, worked—the one in ten women who did, as Mother once said, sadly quoting from an article in *Ladies Home Journal.*

In a monologue for my benefit, Mother often compared Lucille's husband to the husband of one of her Boise friends. Supposedly, the Boise woman had many boyfriends who would have married her in a minute, but she chose the steady one. Maybe she didn't love him as much as the other ones at first, but he was such a good man, such a good provider, that she learned to love him over time. I got the message—choose money and stability over love. But no argument demonizing love has ever won over a melodramatic teenage girl.

At my urging, and Lucille's, Mother occasionally went to Alcoholics Anonymous meetings. From the start, she repeatedly broke the two most important rules. Under the No-Talk Rule, all participants were supposed to remain anonymous. After every meeting, Mother not only blabbed everybody's stories to anyone who would listen, she also named names. People introduce themselves in AA meetings using only their first name, as in "Hello. My name is Joesphine, and I'm an alcoholic." But Mother often repeated the last name, as well, since many of the speakers in the groups she chose to attend were Hollywood stars or other celebrities.

As Mother regaled us with the group members' binges, exploits, lust, and debauchery, I figured out why she went. These recovering people were an extension of the list of "characters" she already knew and loved. They were just like her and the Boise friends she'd grown up with.

The second rule she broke was the Abstinence Rule. After her evening meeting, Mother stopped at the grocery store, bought bread or milk, and to reward herself for attending the AA meeting, she picked up a bottle of vodka too.

Sometimes Steve's music was the only thing that cheered me up. When Pat became Homecoming Queen, he played at the school party after the game. Pat looked beautiful in her white formal, and everybody loved Steve's boogie-woogie music. I sat next to the piano in a sultry pose wearing my aqua dress. It was a scoop-necked sheath, tight-fitting except for the flounce that flared out above my knees and went to mid-calf.

My modeling career continued to provide me with spending money. Mother drove me to L.A. at her torturously slow speed. On several occasions we were further delayed by accidents, and I had to put on my make-up in the car. Once, I even had to change into my bathing suit as we were driving. I scrunched down on the floor, as far as the glove compartment would allow, and slipped off my clothes. A trucker, high up in his cab, passed us, grinned broadly and honked twice. After squirming into my bathing suit, I pulled my shorts up over it. Gloria would have been proud of me. I'd become a real model.

I was tired after spending the night in typically fitful sleep, having graduated from soft hair rollers to the wire-and-brush variety. Never mind that I had naturally curly hair—only a straight pageboy was popular. When you tried to sleep on wire rollers, it felt like hundreds of pins were piercing your skull. Sophisticated torture, it wore you down slowly, but by the next morning your hair would be coerced into a perfect pageboy.

On several weekends, I modeled at Car and Boat Shows—the jobs I hated most. But you didn't say no to William Adrian. At least these shows paid more than sitting around a TV studio set. The boat show was held in an auditorium that looked blocks long. In the middle of the auditorium, amid all the boats and boating equipment, a large portable swimming pool had been filled with water. An undulating ramp circled the pool. We four girls, elevated high above the men ogling us, walked around the pool, one at a time, in our bathing suits and high heels. Gloria, the only one of us not in a bathing suit, kept up a running banter.

"How about adorning your boat with one of these girls, huh boys? Here's Terri. She'd certainly add a touch of class to any ocean scene, wouldn't she?"

Cheers and whistles.

"Or, Jill, with that beautiful hair. How many men here love redheads?"

More cheers and whistles.

I seldom looked down because I was afraid of losing my balance. When I snuck a quick look, the hungry expressions on the men's faces frightened me. In the background, loud organ music provided a parody of worship—change your life, come to God, buy a boat, then buy a girl to accessorize it.

As we walked around the pool, men's eyes undressed us one at a time. This was not a sport I enjoyed, but I rode myself around the curves of that ramp, not winning any ribbons but resigned to ride the only horse I had until it finished the course.

When I wasn't working or at school, I spent as much time with Chad as possible. I was reading *Huckleberry Finn* to him at night. He never wanted to close the book and go to sleep. Although he had neighborhood friends now, Bill was still his best friend.

Since Lorrie was an only child, she loved spending time with Chad and Bill. The boys always wanted to get an Orange Julius, so Lorrie and I took them on double dates. They tucked their shirts in and slicked their hair back with water. I drove the green Buick with Bill sitting next to me. Chad and Lorrie sat in the back seat, Chad in perfect rapture.

The boys were at the age when they were still beautiful. The down on their cheeks lightly covered creamy skin that would later erupt into pimples when adolescence squared their faces' contours. As the boys sipped their Orange Julius drinks slowly, they glanced up at us with large, adoring eyes.

At school, I was struggling through one of the worst classes I'd ever taken, advanced algebra. Since I could remember nothing about last year's beginning algebra, and since I'd nearly flunked that class anyway, it was hopeless.

Gone were all the equations starring X and Y. Long gone the sadistic story problems, where trains went 500 bales of hour carrying 50 miles per hay, adding up logically to how many miles can be baled per hay. Day after day I puttered along, but I was running on empty.

It was my good fortune to sit next to Cyndy, who let me copy her answers. Otherwise, I would have flunked every test. I was ashamed of myself, but could think of no other way to make it through the course. But I missed exactly the same problems she missed and got exactly the

184 / Miss Priss and the Con Man

same scores. Three weeks into the class, the teacher caught on. He announced that, because the class was so large, it would be divided. Cyndy was moved into another room along with half the class.

I failed the next test, as did Sammy Iglesias. He sat to my right and had spent the first three weeks copying *my* answers. We were both dashed. Without fulfilling the math requirement, we couldn't go on to college. We'd be doomed to inherit the lives of our parents.

Lorrie, Marty, Cyndy, and I started many fads that year. We often talked on the phone at night and decided what we'd wear the next day. One day it might be cashmere sweaters and straight skirts; the next we'd all wear belted dresses with full skirts supported by several crinolines, starched stiff with sugar water. Once we all wore striped tops, which were just coming in, and by the next week, the halls were filled with girls in striped tops.

Emerson wrote that we become what we worship. We four girls belonged to the tribe of Superficials—girls who chose the camouflage of outside appearance, who hunted popularity for our sustenance, and fed on clothes and boys for our daily bread. Some of us discovered later that we really belonged to another tribe.

My first California friend, Pat, knew people in every clique, and some who were in no cliques at all. They were the Substantials, that minority who love good books, movies, plays, and poetry. Pat's friends later became scientists, social workers, artists, and musicians. That tribe finds its reality in ideas, finds its core in principle, its truth in literature, its heart and soul in beauty. After I was married, I would walk the path from one identity to another, but I didn't know that yet.

We ate lunch at Bob's Big Boy across the street from school, so I got to eat hamburgers every day again. Bruce, my friend from Boise, ate there too, although he hung around with a different bunch of kids than I did. Bruce was not only tall and good-looking, he was very muscular. He said military school was like prison. After class, there was nothing to do but work out and develop your muscles.

Another group of boys, a year older than we were, ate at Bob's too. One of those boys was Tom Carlson, who I'd gone on a double date with before I started going with Steve. The four of us went to a movie, out for a burger, and then home. Tom walked me to the front door. We didn't kiss goodnight. It wasn't a bad date, but we never went out again.

As I walked into Bob's one day, Bruce pulled me aside and said that Tom was saying he'd slept with me. Shocked, I told Bruce I only went out with Tom once, and he never even kissed me. Bruce said, "I didn't think so—he won't be talking like that for long."

Tom, a slender boy of medium height, was sitting with his friends at the table next to mine that day. Bruce was across the room at a table with his friends. When I was halfway through my Bob's Big Boy Special hamburger, Bruce walked across the room to Tom's table, leaned over, and said something to him. Tom turned around as Bruce grabbed his shirt collar and jerked him up to eye level.

"I've heard what you've been saying about Jill," Bruce said loudly. "It isn't true, is it?"

Tom mumbled something.

"I can't hear you?" Bruce said loudly.

"No," Tom said a little louder, "it isn't true."

"Say that again," Bruce said even louder. "I couldn't hear you."

"No, it isn't true," Tom said, nearly as loud.

Bruce dropped him back into his chair and said, "If I hear you've even mentioned Jill's name again, I'll smash your face flat." Then, he walked back to his table.

I was going steady with Steve, and most Saturday nights, when he wasn't playing for some school party or event, we went out to hear jazz. Since Miles Davis had kicked off the first Newport Jazz Festival in Rhode Island, jazz was blooming on both coasts. Steve said our West Coast Jazz was every bit as fine as anything the East Coast could brag about.

Steve and I often listened to jazz records at his house. His parents, Louise and George Farrell, liked me as much as I liked them. George owned a successful liquor store in a wealthy part of town, and Louise was a housewife. Their English-style brick house looked like Rosie's house, across the street from Baba's. Steve's house even had the same sunken living room and wood paneling as Rosie's.

Louise and George had wonderful parties, and they invited my folks. The four of them became friends. The Farrells didn't drink as much as my parents, but they loved good liquor. They invited not only their own friends but lots of Steve's friends to their parties. We kids drank Coke and 7-Up, had grown-up conversations, and enjoyed being treated like adults.

When we parked to make out, Steve and I were now engaged in serious necking and petting. Steve wanted to go all the way, but I had no intention of ruining my life. Girl after girl from our high school "had to get married." The thought of dropping out of school in eleventh grade to get married and have a baby made me shudder.

One night, when we were parked not far from my house, we were heavy into necking. I was rumpled but fully dressed when I caught sight of The Peeper. His eyes, in a pale face framed by the car window, were fixed on me. Steve jumped out and chased him but The Peeper eluded him and disappeared into the darkness.

Dad continued traveling around the world and the bills kept piling up, until the phone was disconnected for "Non pay," as the phone company called it. Night after night, Mother sat at the kitchen table with a drink in one hand and a cigarette in the other. Sometimes I sat with her to keep her company.

"What an *orrrdeeeeal!*" she'd say. Then shaking her head and sighing, she'd add, "Well, it could be worse—we could all be dead."

I couldn't argue with that logic.

Mother was doing her best, so I never complained about the phone. I didn't tell anyone at school about it either. During the several times it happened, when my friends wanted to call me, I'd say, "Let me call you. We're waiting for Dad to check in from overseas, and I can't tie up the line."

On such evenings, I would eat a hamburger at The Headliner, and then call from the pay phone in the nearby drugstore. If my friends were suspicious, they never let on to me.

Lorrie and Marty wanted to be cheerleaders their senior year. Tryouts were held in the spring of junior year. Cyndy was too shy to try out, and I hesitated. Since my interrupted victory of winning Girls' Representative in sixth grade, I'd had no interest in school activities. Who knew when Dad might bundle us up and haul us off to another location?

But cheerleading was something I knew I could do well. It was the first high school activity I'd cared about. And I cared passionately. The three of us went to a few cheerleading classes taught by the seniors, then practiced at home. Since I was both limber and coordinated, the steps were easy for me. But I took nothing for granted and practiced almost every day.

Living so close to Hollywood, the possibility of fame and fortune was always in the back of our teenage minds. We pictured ourselves on a gigantic screen, at the same time watching and being watched. One of our jokes was, "You look great! This is the day a talent scout's going to discover you!"

Many pretty girls went on to junior college at P.C.C. hoping to become queen of The Tournament of Roses. The queen and her princesses were always chosen from junior college girls. Many of the girls on other floats, however, were from The William Adrian Modeling Agency. That's how I got to be one of the two princesses on the San Francisco float my junior year of high school.

I was the redheaded princess wearing an aqua net formal. The queen was a beautiful black-haired girl in a white formal. The brunette princess, in a pink formal, was William's girlfriend, Gloria, her ample bosom bulging over the top of her dress.

We girls arrived at the corner of Orange Grove and Colorado Boulevard at 7 a.m. on New Year's day. Our driver, Larry, had participated in the parade for years. He told us it had taken twenty to forty flowers to cover one square foot of our float. For the past few weeks, thousands of volunteers had decorated the floats with more than eighteen million flowers.

This was the 64th Tournament of Roses Parade. It was a cold Pasadena morning when we arrived at the corner of Orange Grove and Colorado Boulevard. Mother, jittery as a hummingbird, got me there early. Slogans were the theme that year, and ours was, "For God and

Country." The smell of roses and carnations surrounded our float like a perfumed halo. It was so cold, I draped two coats over my shoulders and wrapped sweaters around my hands and feet.

Close to 8:00 a.m., the floats, marching units, and equestrian teams crawled into action as the brass bands rattled and the metal shod horses' hooves clopped. I threw my coats and sweaters down to Mother as we pulled out. The Parade followed Colorado Boulevard for five miles to Sierra Madre Boulevard, where it turned north. A few minutes after the Parade began, when we'd donned our permanent smiles and metronome waves, the temperature dropped dramatically.

Still smiling, we girls shivered, glancing at one another. It began to mist, a fine mist at first. More glances back and forth. The temperature dropped again. We began clenching and unclenching our toes inside our high-heeled shoes, trying to keep the blood circulating. Then it began to sleet—a relentless, freezing sleet.

After fifteen minutes, sleet covered our cold shoulders, our numb feet, and our curled-under hair. Through clenched teeth, we hissed half-intelligible sentences to one another, "Cold, God, freezing!" or "My toes...freeze, fall off!" or "Get me out...nightmare!"

But no one got us out. We were all For God and Country, but that didn't make us any warmer. For two-and-a-half more hours, we rode—waving, smiling, teeth chattering, lips turning blue. Only our driver stayed warm from the engine heat.

By the time the float crawled to the end of its torturous journey and parked in the float display area at Victory Park, our feet were so numb, we couldn't walk. Our lips were so stiff, we could barely form words. Male volunteers wrapped us in blankets, then got on either side of us and carried us off the float and into our parents' warm cars.

After recovering from the parade, I began the second semester of my junior year. My classes were both bad and good. I'd managed to squeak through advanced algebra with a low C. Now, I was struggling through geometry, my last math requirement. For some reason, geometric shapes made more sense to me than algebraic equations. With hard work and lots of reviewing, I knew I could pass the course.

My favorite class that semester—and during my two years of high school—was English composition. I was fortunate enough to have one of the few young teachers in the school, Mr. Gilchrist. He was the first good teacher I'd had since Mrs. Mundt in ninth grade biology.

Mr. Gilchrist, nearly bursting with his love for writing, read us excerpts of excellent writing, gave us handouts of excellent writing, and showed us how to achieve excellent writing class after wonderful class. I'd never experienced such human passion for words and their uses.

One of our assignments was to write an opinion paper on any topic we cared deeply about. I'd never had an excuse to express my ideas on paper before. I wrote a piece, about two pages long, on the dangers of our fast pace of living. Using freeways as an illustration, I said that speed allowed us to loop over and around one another until we were all tied up in knots.

I wrote about Dad flying at incredible speeds around the world, speeds that prevented him from seeing his own yellow rose buds unfurl, layer by layer, from their dark centers into light. I said that traveling at high speeds doesn't bring real happiness. Speed isn't where we find new ideas, paint a picture, or take a photograph that will give us pleasure for years to come. We have to slow down to find that kind of happiness.

But slow has to be the right kind of slow. It can't be the slow of Mother's driving on the freeway apron at forty miles an hour—a slow braked by fear instead of fueled by purpose. That kind of fear slows us down, but it blinds us too. Slow has to be a decision that involves real choice.

I was anxious to see what Mr. Gilchrist would think of my essay. A couple of days after I'd turned it in, at the end of class, he passed back our papers—all of them but mine. Then he asked me to wait a minute. After the room emptied, he looked at me intently.

"Jill," he said, "this is a remarkable paper. I know you wrote it, yourself, because you've used examples from your own life."

Taken off guard, I barely whispered, "Yes, I did. Thank you."

"Really, Jill, this is one of the best papers I've ever received. I hope you're going on to college."

"Yes, I am."

"I hope you'll take writing classes, because you have natural talent. And, Jill, I'd like to read your paper to the class tomorrow. I want you to hear it read aloud, and the other students can learn from it. Is that all right?"

"I guess so," I said.

After leaving the room, I worried about him reading my paper in class. It might be embarrassing.

The next day, since I sat in the front row, I didn't have to see how the other kids were reacting to my paper. I sat hunched over, jaw clenched, studying my hands in my lap. When he finished reading, everyone clapped. Then, Mr. Gilchrist talked about why he thought my paper worked. I barely heard what he said.

After class, several of the kids came up and said they'd never thought about speed before, but they felt exactly the same way. I showed the paper to Steve and my other close friends, but not to Mother and Dad. I was afraid Mother might laugh. Also, she and Dad might take my examples of slow and fast personally.

Later in the semester, I came home to find Ol' Mart elated. She'd found a job as a house mother for a Montana college sorority. The sorority provided room and board, plus a good paycheck and benefits.

For the first time in her life, Ol' Mart was going to be able to support herself using the skills we always knew she had.

When my girlfriends came over to say good-bye, we all knelt around her in an adoring circle. On demand, she told her tragic story again and got out her jew-els. We slipped on her emerald and diamond rings, holding our spread-out fingers in front of us, studying their effect on our hands; wore her sapphire bracelet, turning it toward the light to release its sparkle; and draped her carved jade necklace and ropes of real pearls around our necks, happily bearing the weight of exorbitant beauty.

Ol' Mart was *so proud*. We were proud of her too. But I hated to see her leave. With Dad gone so much and the money he sent ever-dwindling, she was the only spark of light and laughter in the house besides Chad. Now, one of those sparks would be extinguished.

Soon after Ol' Mart left, the tryouts for cheerleader were held. I'd practiced in front of the den mirror for months. I knew I was good. Seven other girls tried out besides Lorrie, Marty, and me. Since the tryouts were alphabetical, I was second. My performance was flawless. After analytically watching the other girls, I concluded that nobody had matched my performance. I knew I'd be picked for the squad.

Two days later, the list of cheerleaders was put up in the hall. "Breckenridge, Breckenridge," I whispered to myself, scanning. Lorrie and Marty's names were on it, but mine wasn't. I read the list over three times, thinking I must have missed my name. But the list was alphabetical—my name should have been at the top. After the truth sank in, I cut my last two classes, the first time I'd ever cut a class, and went home. Until I left the school building, I could barely keep from crying, but on the way home, I got mad.

"So this is the way it is?" I thought. "I'm going to have to work and work for everything I get, and more often than not, I won't even get that."

I lit an L & M, took a deep breath, and exhaled.

"Okay," I said out loud, "If that's the way it's going to be..."

Even though Mother knew I was trying out for cheerleader in the spring, she never asked me about it, and I never said anything.

Two days later, at the end of homeroom, I got a pass asking me to report to Mrs. Jones, the Dean of Girl Students. I'd never met her, but I recognized her from the tryouts. She'd been sitting with the other judges, all teachers.

"Please, sit down, Jill," she said, kindly. I sat in the chair across from her desk.

"Let me get to the point right away," she said. "I'm sure you know that you were the best cheerleader of all the girls that tried out..." She paused.

"Then why didn't I...?"

"The reason you didn't make the squad, Jill, had nothing to do with your ability. You must have practiced hard to become that accomplished."

She paused again, and then continued. "You know our cheerleaders are...have always been, the all-American-girl type..."

When I saw where the conversation was going, my body stiffened.

"Yes?" I said, warily.

She reached for the right words. "Jill, you're a pretty girl and your teachers, especially Mr. Gilchrist, say you're a nice girl...very talented...

"They've been talking about me behind my back," I thought, and felt my face redden.

"Yes, a very pretty girl," she continued, "it's the make-up you wear...it makes you look...I don't know...hard...harder than you are..."

I knew three things for sure: First, Mrs. Jones was trying to do me a favor. Second, it was too late. Nothing she said, nothing I could do was going to get me on the squad. And third, no one, *no one,* was going to take away my mask and shield. They were *mine and mine alone.* How dare this woman I didn't even know bring up something so personal. I stood up.

"Is that all you want to say?"

"Well, yes," she said. "I just thought you might consider..."

"May I go now?"

"Yes... I just wanted to..."

"Thank-you," I said, and walked out of her office. Walked out of the school and drove home, cutting the rest of my classes for the second time in my life.

As I tried to recover from my disappointment and embarrassment over not making the squad, things got steadily worse at home. The stack of unpaid bills kept growing. One evening after dinner, I found Mother in the bedroom sitting on the edge of her single bed, an opened letter in her hand. I sat down next to her and saw the envelope. It was postmarked "Acapulco," and addressed to Dad. I could smell the envelope too. It reeked of perfume. One of Dad's other women had written him at home.

"Do you want to read it?" Mother asked, handing it my way.

"No," I said, politely. "No thank-you."

Once again, Mother said, as if to herself, "He's always had women. I've never minded it, really, if he just wouldn't spend so much money on them..."

After we sat frozen in silence for a while, I left to do my homework. I didn't want to know the details of my parents' personal life. I knew too much already. My deal was to work hard on my schoolwork, and to take care of my own expenses. That's the best I could do. The rest was up to them.

After recieving that letter from Acapulco, Mother seemed to give up. She started taking Chad into her bedroom to sleep in Dad's bed at night. As soon as she'd tucked him in, she would shut the bedroom door and lock it from the inside with a hook and latch she'd installed. Every night, whether I was doing homework or reading a schoolbook in the den, I would hear her latch click and know that Mother was once again locking out the world, including me. A pack of wolves could have leapt through the window and devoured me. In her alcoholic stupor, she wouldn't have heard a thing.

I was scared at night too. The house was big, with many windows, and The Peeper's ghostly face often appeared at one of them. But I never spoke to Mother about my own nightly agony. She'd made a deal with any outside threat—she offered me up as a sacrifice. Every night, I lay in bed, frozen with fear, repeating the childhood prayer she'd taught me until I finally fell asleep.

I was mad at Mother, and I'd begun to have reservations about Steve as well. I loved his music and his talent. Perhaps I loved him, too, but I didn't know for sure. The constant battling about my virginity was tiring, but there was something else. I found out, after one of our many virginity fights, that he'd been hanging around Cyndy's house. It was a double betrayal. I was furious at both of them. Contrite, they said it would never happen again. But I felt uneasy.

Steve's parents rented a house close to Hermosa Beach for the weekend and they invited us to meet them there. As we headed toward the Lighthouse, Steve took the Santa Monica Freeway, speeding past Venice, Marina del Rey, and El Segundo. We couldn't wait to hear Howard Rumsey's Lighthouse All-Stars and the featured trumpet player, Chet Baker.

That night at the Lighthouse existed out of time—clear, with a full moon and enough stars to decorate a million Christmas trees. The club overlooked an ocean turned magic by moonlight and a beach reaching into eternity. Chet's first song was "My Funny Valentine," the song that reminded me of Steve. The audience went wild.

Between sets, we retrieved our blanket (tucked under a bush by the club), left our shoes there, and walked along the beach holding hands, breathing in the scent of ocean water and seaweed. As we lay on the blanket under that endless night sky, making out and petting, the ocean kept whispering, "More, more..."

Steve said the same thing in different words. I was fully dressed except for my striped cotton T-shirt, which was wadded up around my neck, and my bra, which was tossed across the sand. We were moving, moving together, until an earthquake grabbed and shook me. Without meaning to, I moaned, then grabbed and held onto Steve's back so I wouldn't fall into the ocean and drown.

I realized whatever had happened to me was well worth waiting for. But I wouldn't go further, no matter how many times Steve begged, "Please, Please..."

"No," I said, "no."

Steve put his head on my bare shoulder. The next set began in the club, and the sound of Chet's trumpet swirled sensuously around our charged bodies.

"If I had my way," Steve said, "I'd get you pregnant, and we'd *have* to get married."

His statement horrified me and strengthened my resolve. For maybe the hundredth time, only this time my voice was tired and cold, I said, "Steve, I'm not going to go all the way with you—or with anyone. Not until I'm married."

He stood up, sulking, turned his back on me, and stared across the ocean, tucking in his shirt. When we walked back to the club, we weren't holding hands.

During the second set, Chet played a song we both loved, "I Fall In Love Too Easily." Its next line continued, "I fall in love too fast. I fall in love too terribly hard for love to ever last."

Dad was home that summer more than usual. Whenever he was there, we got into a routine pretty fast. He did the shopping and cooking, spent hours hosing down the patio and front driveway, and took care of the yard. I did the inside cleaning. Mother worked all day, then came home, exhausted, and drank all evening. Dad finished off his usual pitcher of martinis every night as well, but he never showed it.

Although his meals were better than Mother's, the menu was always the same. One night, he grilled chicken, the next night, steak. Every night, he baked potatoes and tossed a salad. "What's wrong with these people?" I wondered. "Haven't they ever heard of variety?!" At least Dad alternated between two meals. Mother fixed only one—unless you considered Swanson's Frozen TV Dinners a meal.

Intersperced with these daily activities, Dad was on the phone incessantly, either urging people on or yelling at them. He'd get permission for the farmers to enter Venezuela, and the Hong Kong people wouldn't be ready with their passports. By the time the passports were finally set, there'd be a delay over regulations in Caracas.

He said not having enough capital to live on as he put the deal together was his biggest problem. I thought, "You aren't the only one suffering. You should watch poor Mother struggle with the unpaid bills, or know how I feel lying to bill collectors."

My trust in Dad's ability to put a deal—any deal—together was fading, but he was the only horse we had running in the race. Everything we owned or wanted to own was riding on him, so I tried to keep my doubts from jinxing our luck.

Dad's lawyer, Fred Beech, came to the house several times. Dark, thin, and shifty-eyed, he looked so slimy and crooked, I didn't like being in the same room with him. But Chester Lee, the man Dad hired to be his translator in China, was just the opposite. Mr. Lee was an honest, decent man. Dad had met him at his L.A. restaurant, The Chinese Dragon, and they'd become good friends.

One day, I went to the IRS with Dad as he paid his past dues. All the way to L.A. and back, he talked about the deal. How the land outside Caracas had finally been bought, and how they were negotiating to put together a herd of cattle, tractors for the land, and an irrigation system. Once the deal was in place, we'd give up our house in Pasadena and move to a ranch outside Caracas.

"A foreign language like Spanish is easy, Jilly, when you speak it every day. You'll pick it up fast. We'll have our own horse ranch. You can breed palominos—develop your own line of fabulous horses."

"That sounds great," I said, immediately drawn into his plan.

"One of my partners there," Dad said, "has a darling son. He's about eighteen, dark, handsome and rich. You'll like him."

For the horse ranch alone, I was ready to pack up and move to Caracas. The handsome son was simply a bonus. It sounded like a movie I'd be happy to co-star in.

When you live in Southern California, especially as a teenager, your real life, the life of film, and the lives of film stars merge. You hear and read so much about the stars, you begin to think of them as neighbors—even family.

In September of my senior year in high school, James Dean was killed at an intersection north of Los Angeles. He was driving his 1955 Porsche Spyder much too fast. His close friend, Elizabeth Taylor, who'd given Jimmy a cat named Marcus, was bereft. Jimmy was twenty-four. I was sixteen.

Four days after his death, *Rebel Without a Cause* was released. We kids saw it several times. Like the flocks of marsh birds that dive and swoop in unison, we were hooked. After the movie became popular, even good girls who'd abstained from bad behavior wanted to smoke and act snotty, and tough boys got even tougher, attempting to outdo the things they'd seen on the big screen. Only the most popular athletes and student government boys didn't climb onto a Jimmy Dean motorcycle. We girls agreed they may have been the most popular boys, but they weren't the most sexy.

Pat's boyfriend, Dave, wasn't swayed by the fad, nor was Pat, who was Student Body Vice President. She was also the editor of our school newspaper and wrote a weekly column called "Postscripts."

Marty was dating a nice boy named Jim Pomroy, who came from a wealthy family. On the other hand, Lorrie was going with one of the tough boys, Don Huntress. His blonde hair was slicked back in a ducktail. He was gorgeous, and dangerous. Fortunately, Don wasn't a greaser, one of the scummy boys, but he was tall, tough, and muscular—a born fighter. Although Marty, Cyndy, and I liked Don, we worried about Lorrie. She was wild, and we didn't want her to get in trouble.

What I only partially realized at the time was that many of the "bad boys" in my high school were cut from the same bolt of rough cloth as the boys I had known in Boise when I was a child. Although Westerners subscribed to the myth that there are no classes, it was becoming clear to me that both Boise and Pasadena had rich people, poor people, and those in between. However, in the West, the pedigrees were shorter than in the long-settled East, and people were judged more on what they'd accomplished than on who their great-grandparents were.

My outlaw family dwelt beyond class distinctions, but different levels of outlaw behavior existed even there. On a scale of notorious, we fit in somewhere between the occasional horse thief and Billy the Kid. Even though Dad's reputation would have cut us out of the respectable middle class, we had middle-class aspirations. Like everyone else, we believed that with hard work and talent, we could

198/ Miss Priss and the Con Man

rise at least to fortune, and maybe even to fame. But because of Dad, our position between rich and poor shifted with the wind. One day, we approached rich; the next day we lost everything.

Christmas in California was always a parody. In the same block with the flowering paintbrush trees dropping their red bristles, with round purple agapantha exploding on drinking-straw stems, with fragrant gardenias and roses, there stood jolly old Saint Nick, high up on someone's rooftop, sporting his red plastic suit and accompanied by his reindeer Rudolph.

As Christmas drew near, Dad appeared for the holidays. He was so cranky, I knew the deal was in terrible shape. Nor did he make an effort to shape the place up the way he usually did. The garden hose remained coiled, the grill stood cold. Everything but the phone was neglected.

He didn't even notice that Fritzie, Crazy Dog #2, had transformed all our blankets into swiss cheese. That sneaky mutt hid under the beds or behind the couch and made guerilla blanket attacks both day and night. Every time the little creep saw me, he ran in the opposite direction—wise on his part.

One day, when Dad went outside to pick up the paper, Fritzie ran past him out the door and into the street, where a beat-up old Ford truck going about twenty miles an hour clipped him. We rushed after the dog and found him stretched out motionless in the street. There wasn't a mark on him. He looked like he was taking a little nap, but he was very dead. The Mexican man driving the truck felt terrible, though I reassured him it wasn't his fault. I was tempted to kiss him on the cheek.

But Fritzie's damage was done. Dead or alive, a dog can't pay reparations. We were stuck with our ventilated blankets because we had no money to replace them. Southern California houses get chilly in winter, and I cursed that deceased Crazy Dog #2 every time I got into bed on a cold night.

Mother immediately came home with Lulu, Crazy Dog #3, a gray miniature poodle. We'd already had one bad poodle experience with FiFi, Crazy Dog #1. Would she never learn? This new dog had a sweet disposition, but, as she grew beyond puppydom, it became clear she wasn't devoted to being housebroken—at least, so you could depend on her. One time, she was able to wait; the next time, she didn't make it. Lulu had a moody bladder.

In early spring, when Dad was traveling around the world again, Mother parked his aqua and cream-colored Cadillac in front of The Headliner. After she'd picked up some cigarettes, she walked back to the car. As she slipped behind the steering wheel, a big black man, evidently planning to rob her, steal the Cadillac, or both, opened the passenger door and slid smoothly into the front seat beside her. Without missing a beat, Mother said, "Get out of my car this minute! My husband's a member of the *Mafia*, and he'll have you killed!"

The would-be robber, in one continuous movement, opened the passenger door, slid his large frame out, and ran. What we girls loved best about the story—and we told it over and over again—was, when mother said the word, *Mafia*, she mispronounced it, nasally rhyming the first 'a' with raffle or daffy—*Maafia*. "Get out of my car this minute! My husband's a member of the *Maafia*, and he'll have you killed!"

The story quickly spread around school. I never knew when someone would walk up to me, jab me in the chest with a stiff second finger, and say, "My husband's a member of the *Maafia*, and he'll have you killed!"

We girls had followed the romance of Grace Kelly and Prince Ranier since they met. When they were married a year later, in April of 1956, I was particularly interested because Grace first met Prince Ranier while modelling for Ipana Toothpaste. So far, I'd only met creeps, toadies, and perverts in my modeling career.

After refusing several jobs from William Adrian, he seldom called me, which was fine with me. I'd grown tired of modeling's sordid surroundings and irrational demands. I was also fed up with the nightly misery of wire-and-brush rollers. Although they kept my long hair curling obediently into a pageboy, their spines were merciless.

I decided to have my hair cut short. Steve protested, but I told him my hair *was mine,* after all.

I had my hair cut in a Pixie cut, no more than an inch long anywhere on my head. Without my long red hair, maybe men wouldn't stare at me so much. My girlfriends loved the new look, but I hadn't counted on how severe the style was for the mid-fifties.

As I walked along Brigden Road one day, a man drove by. He slowed down, his eyes fixed on me in utter astonishment. As he passed, his car went forward, but his head kept turning toward me. He gawked until his car bounced over the curb and nearly ran into the corner streetlight.

A week later, as Mother drove home from playing Canasta with Pat's mother, Ruth, she did run into a streetlight on a busy major street. She bent the light pole less than she bent the bumper of Dad's aqua Caddie. Dad loved that car. She knew he'd be furious.

Mother also knew she was too drunk to pass a sobriety test. Terrified, she left the Caddie, still chewing on the light pole, and *walked* home—it was several miles—in her three-inch heels!

I was out with Steve, but heard later that when she arrived home, Chad was sitting in the living room with the police. They were all watching TV, waiting for her.

Luckily, the long walk in the cool night air and her blistered feet sobered her up. She was charged only with Reckless Driving and Leaving the Scene of an Accident. These were still serious charges, and she knew her insurance premiums would go way up. (They did.)

A month later, after school, I'd just finished vacuuming when two suspicious-looking men rang the doorbell. One man wore a black trench coat and the other wore a beige one. Hesitantly, I opened the front door.

"Yes?" I said, holding the door open a crack.

"Is Mrs. Breckenridge home?" Mr. Black Coat asked.

"No, I'm sorry, she's at work."

"When will she be home?" Mr. Beige Coat asked.

"About 5:30 or 6:00."

"Well, maybe you can help us," Mr. Black Coat said.

Mr. Beige Coat added, "We're here about a claim she filed for a stolen accordion."

I connected the dots in an instant. Mother's car insurance went up after she hit the light pole, and she couldn't pay the premium. She couldn't get to work without a car, so she'd turned in a false claim to raise money.

I also knew the accordion was in the garage. Since we'd moved to Pasadena, it had rested, unplayed, in its black accordion box against the garage wall. Luckily the garage door was pulled down, because you saw the black box the minute you entered the garage. In spite of a valiant attempt at self-control, my eyes drifted toward the garage. Two pairs of eyes drifted along with mine.

"When did you notice it was gone?" Mr. Black Coat asked me.

I could have killed Mother! I didn't want to lie, and I had no idea what she'd put on the claim. So I did the only thing I could think of—I remained staunchly vague.

"Gee, I'm not sure. I always drive that green Buick parked out front."

I beckoned to the front, and their eyes followed my hand as I added, "Mother parks in the garage. She noticed it was gone first."

I'd had a lot of practice lying during the last two years, and, when backed into a corner, I'd become good at it. But I shouldn't have mentioned the word *garage*. It might have given them ideas.

"Who plays the instrument?" Mr. Black Coat asked.

"I do," I said, making sure my verb was present tense. If I didn't play the accordion anymore, it would be logical for a woman, who worked in the insurance business and was hard up for money, to file a false claim on it.

"Well, thank you," Mr. Beige Coat said, "We'll be on our way then."

"Thank you," Mr. Black Coat added, "and please tell your mother we'll get back to her on this."

After they left and I'd stopped shaking, I was furious at Mother. I wondered how many other false claims she'd filed. When she came home, I landed on her.

"How could you *do* that to me!" I said. "How could you put me in that position without even warning me?"

Looking sheepish, she said, "I didn't know they'd come here."

"Mother, that's not true," I said, realizing everyone in our house was a liar except Chad and Lulu, Crazy Dog #3. Insurance claims were Mother's business. She knew investigators would come to the house before preparing their report.

She also knew I'd be forced to lie. Knew I had Dad's gift of gab, and I'd be better at it than she was. She probably figured it was best for her *not* to be home when the investigators came.

"Why did you do it? Putting me in that position—it was a terrible thing to do."

Mother looked hard at me, her eyes narrowing.

"You want a phone, don't you?"

In the kitchen, Mother mixed herself a real drink, not a sneak drink, and we sat at the table together. She sighed several times, and said, "What an *orrrdeeeeal!* Well, it could be worse…" and I chimed in with her as we both said, "We could all be dead."

Afraid to leave my non-stolen accordion at home for the inspectors to find, Mother loaded it into the trunk of the aqua Cadillac. She drove around with that old black and white accordion in her trunk for years.

Soon the bill collectors, who were already calling at all hours of the day and night, began coming right to the house. After dinner one night, I looked outside between a crack in the dining room curtains and saw a black car parked in front.

"Mother," I whispered, "do you know who's out there?"

She hunched over, guerrilla-style, scurried over to me, and peeked through the crack in the curtains.

"No," she whispered, "I don't recognize the car."

By that time the two men were walking up the driveway toward the house. Mother took a second look and said, "Those are the bill collectors who were here a week ago. I told them not to come back, that I was paying off the bills as fast as I could."

Running to the kitchen for a wooden spoon, she said, "I've had about enough of them!" Before I could stop her, she flew out the front door like a flaming comet toward the bill collectors. Astonished by this turn of events, the men hightailed it back to their car with Mother in hot pursuit. She whapped the spoon vigorously across the windows of the car as they pulled away.

Although they never came back, shortly after that incident, the phone was disconnected again for "Non-pay," and I went through another two-week spell of lying to friends about why they couldn't call me, and going to the drug store every night to make calls. One day, our phone service was miraculously restored. I looked around the house to see if anything else was missing, anything that Mother might have reported stolen and stuffed into her trunk.

Steve and I drove down to Hermosa Beach again, this time to hear pianist Dave Brubeck and his dreamy alto sax player Paul Desmond. Their music was smooth as glass. Brubeck's "Look For The Silver Lining" and "Take Five" mesmerized us. We walked along the pier because it was too cold to lie on the beach. Waves whispered their keening "Good-bye, good-bye."

After that, because I was working so much, Steve went to Hermosa Beach by himself or with his family. He jammed several times with Cal Tjader's group after the club closed at night. Cal thought Steve was very talented. After advising him to take up the vibes too, Cal gave him one of his own sets. At that moment, Steve decided he wanted to be a musician. I knew it was the right thing for him to do.

I also knew it wasn't right for me. Knew, as well, that Steve wasn't the one for me. I'd grown tired of his pressure about sex, was fed up with his pouts and sulks. He'd already strayed once into Cyndy's backyard. Besides that, I saw what a musician's life was like. The musician was always gone, his wife left behind to sweep up the mess. It looked too much like home. Talented as Steve was, I knew I'd never want to be his wife.

We went to Hermosa Beach one last time to hear Chet Baker. The first song he played was "Tenderly." Although it was a love song, it made me cry. The last number in the set was "I Get Along Without You Very Well." By the end of the song, I knew I had to break up with Steve.

With graduation from high school approaching, I decided to continue my studies at the University of Colorado in Boulder. Aunt Jo had originally told me about the college and how beautiful it was. My cousin Nancy (Uncle Jim's daughter) went there. Aunt Jo was as determined as I was to get me into college.

"Charlie," she said to Dad on the phone, with me on the other extension, "that girl has a good mind. You send her to college!"

"Of course I will," he said, irritation in his voice.

"I mean it, Charlie," she said.

I could imagine her set jaw and her thinned lips making a determined straight line.

"And you send her all the way through too!" she added.

Aunt Jo also hoped I'd pledge a sorority. She'd been a Delta Gamma at the University of Idaho. Her sorority sisters were still her best friends. She went to all the initiations of new pledges, and cried at every one. I knew she hoped I'd pledge D.G. at a Western college.

I didn't need any convincing, since I wanted to live in the real West again. The University of Colorado's reputation as a party school, and its lackluster academic standing didn't bother me. At the time, I had no academic aspirations. Boulder was beautiful; it was close to the mountains and far from home. That was enough for me.

During the summer, I delightedly prepared for college. My only reservation was how much I'd miss Chad. I hated leaving him alone without me to soften the effects of our parents.

Halfway through the summer, I did two important things. First, I stopped wearing make-up almost entirely, putting on just a little mascara and eyebrow pencil to fill in the gaps. I was sorry to leave make-up behind. It was my beautiful best friend that no one liked but me.

But I wanted to start college with a clean slate and a fresh face. If I decided to pledge a sorority, I didn't want to suffer another rejection because of my make-up. At C.U., after the first year in freshman dorms, students lived in the Greek sorority and fraternity houses. That's where all the action was.

The second thing I did was to break up with Steve. He wasn't happy about it, but he didn't seem surprised. I wasn't thrilled when he said he'd been accepted at The University of Colorado too.

Almost all my close friends were going on to college. Only Don, the bad boy, decided to get a job right after graduation. Pat was going to St. Olaf in Northfield, Minnesota, along with her boyfriend, Dave. Lorrie was going to U.C.L.A. Marty and Bruce were going to Berkeley, and Cyndy was going to Stanford. Ten of us from P.H.S. were going to C.U., including Marty's old boyfriend, Jim Pomroy. Jim's folks had a wonderful sit-down dinner for us to celebrate our graduation and future college careers.

My freshman roommate in Ferrand Hall would be Patti Fosdick, my modeling friend who looked like Grace Kelly and did Breck Shampoo ads. Her parents planned on driving us to Colorado. I was finally escaping from home. Although I felt sorry for Mother, I was relieved to escape her drinking and mood swings. And I was more than ready to leave Dad's martini meanness and failing deals behind. I wanted my own life.

Sitting with my arm around Chad, I said good-bye and told him he'd always be a huge part of my life. We'd talk on the phone often.

The morning I left for college, Dad was in Hong Kong and Chad was spending the night with Bill Budge. Mother, framed by the tart fruit of the cumquat trees, was weeping. As the Fosdick's car pulled away, she waved. I waved back, misty-eyed, but my feelings were for Chad. I couldn't squeeze out a single tear about leaving home.

9

Campus Courtship

The University of Colorado was even more wonderful than I'd imagined. In 1956, Boulder was still a sleepy Western town that happened to have a college on The Hill rising above it. The campus sprawled across a grassy, tree-filled landscape dotted with picturesque stone buildings and graced by a flowing stream.

In the distance, the Flatiron Mountains rose into a clear blue sky—a stark contrast to Southern California, where the foothills were often draped by a malevolent shawl of smog. In Colorado, clear days were the rule rather than the exception, and I gloried in the unspoiled panorama. I'd come home.

Patti and I roomed together, up three flights of stairs to number 403, Ferrand Hall. We each had our own single bed, desk, and chest of drawers; we also, I soon learned, had a different set of habits and assumptions. Since I didn't have a sister, living with Patti was an education.

Although she was always kind and generous, Patti wore the mantle of privilege that surrounds astonishing beauty. She layered on bright red lipstick three or four times a day as she stood in front of her bureau mirror. Then, she blotted her lips with one tissue of Kleenex that she never threw away. Over several weeks, the discarded tissues on her bureau sprouted into a white mountain abloom with hundreds of red lips.

Patti usually went to bed about 9:00, just as I was settling into serious studying. She didn't fit the dumb blonde stereotype, however, maintaining her straight-A average simply by going to lectures. I seldom saw her cracking a book.

In order for me to get my A average, I not only had to crack a book, I had to underline it in different colors, scribble notes in it, break its spine, and its will. Then, praying that the material wouldn't desert me until after the test, I pored over my downed rainbow of colored lines and words until I was so tired the colors blurred and blended. Turning my desk light down to its dimmest voltage, I soldiered on into the night as quietly as I could. But Patti couldn't sleep with the light on, and she suggested I study somewhere else. That meant I had to set up shop in the fourth floor lounge every night. Since the lounge overflowed with noisy girls taking a break from studying, it was hard to concentrate there. This arrangement seemed unfair, but I couldn't ask Patti to find a dark spot somewhere to sleep while I got equal time in our room.

When Aunt Jo called, she wanted to hear about everything I was doing. She always left me with a family story. When my energy or spirits flagged, those stories about my Western ancestors sustained me. Their lives hadn't been easy either.

Aunt Jo said that my grandmother, Anna Corder Breckenridge, rode out in her buckboard every dusty, windy, wet, cold, or blistering day to deliver her eggs. This delivery occurred after she'd done all the chores and other duties demanded by a ranch, a husband, and four children. Grandmother's egg money helped buy winter coats for the children. It got my father out of jail, and it would have sent two of the children, Uncle Jim and Aunt Jo, to college. But The Great Depression gobbled up all her savings.

The youngest in her family, Aunt Jo learned hard lessons from her mother who was burdened by four children she hadn't asked for, and later lost every penny she'd tirelessly saved. Aunt Jo realized you had to take charge of your own life. And, you must have significant savings stored in a safe place. Later, she learned there were situations where no savings were safe.

Aunt Jo also understood her father's burden of being a sheep rancher in a region that worshipped cattle.

Inheriting her mother's vision, Aunt Jo looked ahead to the future with grit and grim humor—a family inheritance. She saved what she could, took out loans for college to supplement her savings, got her education degree, taught country kids in a one-room schoolhouse, and completely paid off the loans before she got married.

Aunt Jo said I was fortunate that my parents were paying my college expenses so I could get a degree without going into debt.

"At least your dad's kept his word this far," she said one day on the phone.

"He'll come through," I said. "He promised."

"I hope you're right," she said, a note of skepticism in her voice.

Besides having my college expenses paid, I also felt fortunate to live in a dorm where the dining room served delicious food. Ferrand Hall was my four-star restaurant. It served a completely different dinner every day. Every day! One day, I feasted on ham, sweet potatoes, and green beans; the next day, on turkey, dressing, mashed potatoes, and peas; the next day, on meat loaf, baked potatoes, and corn; and on and on and on. The menu variations astonished and delighted me.

As I walked down the stairs to the dining room, the smell of freshly baked cinnamon or dinner rolls wafted up the stairwell. What I loved best was that they served a different desert every day—lemon meringue pie, chocolate cake, angel food cake, apple pie with vanilla ice cream, sugar cookies, chocolate pudding, and both butterscotch and chocolate brownies. My favorite desert was the brownies. It didn't take long for the girls who were watching their weight to start giving theirs to me. I gratefully devoured all that came my way.

Academics at C.U. was much less popular than the local watering holes, The Sink and Tulagis. From late morning on, the bars were filled with kids drinking 2.0 % beer. My extended history in Western bars, with their relentless neon signs blinking red and blue, the smell of beer and cigarette smoke, the loud music, the shouts and laughter, made both watering holes unpleasantly familiar to me.

Bars weren't my idea of fun. But they couldn't be avoided, since most college parties took place at one of the two—except for the occasional "kegger" in the woods. Kids often drank so much beer, they threw up until they nearly turned inside out or lapsed into unconscious stupors. Many of these kids had never tasted liquor before, so they didn't know how to drink. For the first time, I was grateful for the hard lessons alcohol had taught me.

Aunt Jo was pleased that I wanted to pledge a sorority. During Pledge Week, hundreds of eighteen- and nineteen-year-old prospective pledges in high heels lurched back and forth between Greek houses across a large campus. My feet complained about wearing three-and-a-half inch heels, and my mouth ached from smiling five-and-a-half inch smiles.

By the last house, we looked like a retinue of staggering circus poodles, grinning from ear to ear, tails wagging wearily under our skirts. Even the dumbest poodle knew enough not to run around in circles wearing uncomfortable shoes.

I wondered how to decide on the house I wanted, but it turned out to be easy. I didn't click with the girls in some houses. The Kappas were stuck-up and snotty. The girls in some other houses were not my type. Although I liked the Pi Phis and Thetas, I liked the Delta Gammas best. Fortunately, they liked me too.

When I told Aunt Jo on the phone that I'd pledged D.G., she cried. She came out for the initiation, the hors d'oeuvres (every event at the D.G. house was preceded by hors d'oeuvres), the dinner, and the initiation ceremony. As Aunt Jo pinned her gold Delta Gamma Anchor, with its tiny seed pearls, on my dress, she cried again.

After dinner, we talked a long time. I asked her to tell me more about her own education and marriage. She said, after working her way through college, she taught in a one-room school for several years. Then, she met and married Uncle Am.

Week by week, she saved whatever she could squirrel away from her meager allowance for food, utilities, and clothing. Over several years, she accumulated $5,000. One day, when she went to the bank to put more savings into her account, she learned a hard lesson: your savings could disappear even without the Depression.

"I'm sorry, Mrs. Adams," the bank clerk said, "but your husband withdrew the money and closed that account."

Livid, Aunt Jo went home and confronted Uncle Am.

"Of course I took the money," he said, smiling broadly. "Don't you know, whatever belongs to the wife belongs to the husband? I had some poker debts I needed to pay off."

Although Aunt Jo fumed, the money was gone. Not long after she confronted Uncle Am, her father-in-law appeared at the door. He'd found out about Aunt Jo's former savings because Am was bragging about it.

"I'm ashamed of my son," the elder Mr. Adams said, "and I'm going to make it up to you. I want to double the amount Am stole, and give you $10,000—on two conditions. First, you never tell my son how much I gave you. And second, you never let him get his hands on it."

Aunt Jo promised. But, although she was good at math, she knew nothing about investing. So she put together an investment club, inviting one of her son's teachers and several of her other friends to join. They all agreed to three basic club rules. They'd educate themselves by reading books on investing; they'd read the *Wall Street Journal* every day; and they'd meet once a month. Gradually, steadily, Aunt Jo's portfolio of stocks grew.

She ended her story by saying that even in a stable marriage, I should be a wise spender and saver. Most important, I should always think about my own future.

Unlike Aunt Jo, I was terrible in math. I didn't have a clue what my other academic interests were, because I had none. So I majored in Home Economics. Evidently many girls at C.U. had no academic interests, because Home Ec was a popular major. Patti and I were both shuffled into that academic wasteland, overflowing with saucer-eyed freshman girls.

I set about fulfilling my freshman year requirements, most of which I don't remember. But I'll never forget my three worst classes. One was Beginning Art, the only class I was allowed to choose for myself. I was considering a major in art, since I'd always been good at it.

For my first project, I did a seed mosaic, using dried corn, split green peas, rice, barley, and lentils. I thought it was quite successful. When the art teacher saw it, he could barely suppress a laugh. I decided he thought my project was too easy, so I offered to do a more ambitious project—a glass mosaic, like I'd done in junior high school. Now the art teacher did laugh.

I was baffled until I looked around and saw what the other students were doing. Although I'd never been in a museum, I knew good art when I saw it—and these students were good. What I'd done was baby art. I wanted to learn how to make good art, too. That's why I'd taken the class. But this teacher evidently assumed you already knew what his class proposed to teach you. It didn't make any sense.

The next day, I dropped the class.

My second bad class was Freshman English, another class I thought I'd do well in. Our instructor, a stocky, savage woman, assigned our first essay on the question, "Why I Believe in God." In 1956, none of us could explain why we got up in the morning, much less answer a metaphysical question about faith. But I gamely set out to write a good essay. When the papers were handed back, we learned that the instructor had flunked the entire class.

Our next assignment was to rewrite the essay until we got passing grades, though our instructor gave us nary a hint as to where we were going astray. Many class members never did produce an acceptable essay, but after several rewrites, I got a C.

Maybe I didn't have the talent my high school writing teacher commended. I'd considered declaring an English major, since art hadn't panned out, but this "Why I Believe in God" debacle didn't bode well for that plan.

My third bad class was chemistry, with its impossible list of elements running from Ac/Actinium to Zr/Zirconium—not to mention the equations that described their complicated interactions. When I walked into class the first day and saw the cryptic letters and numbers of the Periodic Table up on the board, my math phobia flared up like a chemical reaction gone haywire, and lasted the entire semester.

Our teacher, Mrs. Culp, was the only person who taught this particular science. It was required for all Home Ec and Nursing students. She was older than the Rocky Mountains and, lucky for me, as predictable as the four seasons. Culp never asked you to complete an equation on a test if she hadn't already written it out and worked through it on the board.

When she lectured, chalk in hand, it was as if she spoke a foreign language. I could neither understand nor remember a word she said, but like a frenetic robot, I recorded each white-chalk letter and number she wrote. Before every test, I nearly lived in Ferrand's fourth floor lounge. Staying up most of several nights, I memorized my class notes and many full pages of equations.

When I saw the test problem, I never tried to do the math. That was hopeless. I searched my memory, overflowing with letters and numbers, until I located the right equation. For example, maybe it was in the middle of page four in my notes. Since I'd memorized the equations from the top to the bottom of every page, that was the only way I could access the answer to a problem. Beginning at the top of page four, on scratch paper, I wrote down the equations from the top of the page until I got to the prize. I prayed to get test equations close to the top of the page. If I got too many bottom-pagers, I couldn't have finished the test in time.

When the chemistry class finally ended, I got an A—a testimony to the efficacy of terror, dogged determination, and many sleepless nights. I called Mother to tell her the good news, called early in the evening, hoping to catch her before she'd rolled over the hill. But I could tell the minute she picked up the phone that by the next morning, she wouldn't even remember that I'd called.

One thing that helped me get through the chemistry class was the food at the dorm, especially the desserts. One day, I put away fourteen butterscotch brownies—a record. We didn't know about eating disorders in those days, so I didn't binge and purge. And I certainly didn't starve. I enjoyed every one of those desserts, as I slowly began putting on pounds.

At Boulder, I met other students quickly. At the beginning of freshman year, the kids didn't pair off into dating couples. We went to group events and parties. It was more fun and less anxious than traditional dating, where you always wondered if your date hated you, or if you'd worn the wrong thing. Group dating also eliminated the blind date, where you often drew a Martian.

The most uncomfortable thing about C.U. was Steve. He began watching me, often hanging around Ferrand Hall, which wasn't even close to his dorm. He lurked around the edges of group events too. When he caught my eye, he glared at me—a look both angry and threatening.

I missed Chad. Whenever I called him, he whispered that Mother was still drinking. I told him to call more often, so he called after he got home from school or when Mother was at Mrs. Sheldon's playing Canasta. When I heard his sweet voice, I had to fight back tears. There was so little I could do to help him except listen and try to be encouraging.

As I was walking back from class one day, I saw a tall young man standing on the steps in front of Ferrand Hall. Wearing tennis whites, with a white sweater draped over his shoulders, he had strawberry blonde hair and an appealing smile. A fifties movie could have starred him.

Asking around, I found out his name was John Haldeman. People called him Halde. He was six-foot-five, looked like Prince Philip, and was a great tennis player. A junior and a Chi Psi, he was very popular. I heard he was dating a well-endowed freshman from Minneapolis who was cheating on him. Everyone said he was one of the nicest guys around. They thought her behavior was terrible. Since his girlfriend lived in Ferrand Hall, I saw him often.

It had never occurred to me how different my dad was from other fathers until that first year of college. When Dad visited Boulder on his way home from Hong Kong, the aspen leaves were shimmering gold in late fall light. I was waiting outside for him, sitting on the steps in front of the dorm. An emerald green lawn stretched away for miles toward the Flatiron Mountains that erupted into a clear blue sky.

Right on time, my father drove up in a pink Cadillac. Set off by the green lawn, it looked huge. As I went out to meet him, kids bunched around the available windows in Ferrand Hall, trying to get a better look. My father had always driven Cadillacs, but for the first time it occurred to me, "Not *everyone's* father drives a Cadillac." As a matter of fact, no dad I'd ever known but mine drove a Cadillac, much less a pink one. For the first time, I felt a twinge of something…The car was so *big*. The pink was so *pink*.

Dad had brought me a present from Caracas, an eighteen-carat gold charm bracelet. From its large gold links dangled gold coins framed with gold scallops, gold mushrooms, and an engraved gold bell that tinkled every time it was touched by its blue sapphire clapper.

During his visit, Dad stayed at the Cosmopolitan Hotel in Denver. Patti had just been voted C.U.'s freshman queen, and Dad invited us to celebrate her victory by bringing dates and meeting him for dinner. Before dinner, we had drinks in his room; he'd rented the Presidential Suite, which occupied the entire top floor of the hotel.

I was impressed by the fact that the bedspread print—green leaves and little brown squirrels eating acorns—was repeated in the drapes and again in the gold statues beside the bed. Dad had stocked the bar with every kind of liquor imaginable, along with many soft drinks and mixes. We all had Cokes, except for dad, who fixed his usual pitcher of dry martinis.

He took the four of us out to dinner at Trader Vics in the Outrigger. My friends were visibly impressed. Dad made Patti and our dates feel like adults, putting his arm around them, telling his wonderful stories and laughing his wonderful laugh. When they were with him, I could see they felt as charming and elegant as he was. Everything bathed by sunlight glows.

As we left for our dorms that night, he said, "Now, you kids come back to the hotel next week after I've finished my business here."

"Why?" I asked.

"It's too bad to let this liquor go to waste," he said. "I'll leave it for you under my name at the front desk."

Two weeks later, a date and I stopped by the hotel where he'd stayed. My date waited in the car while I went to the front desk and asked for the liquor. The man behind the desk looked puzzled.

"Charlie Breckenridge?" he said, "Hmmm." He looked through

the desk ledger for a few moments, and then said, "I'm sorry. No one by that name has stayed here in the past two months. Could he have been registered under another name?"

"Charles?" I offered.

Wrinkling his forehead, he looked again, and then asked an associate if he recalled anyone by that name. No, the associate said, he didn't remember him either. They both looked hard at me.

"Forgive me," I said. "I must have made a mistake. "

Years later, I was still wondering if Dad was there under an assumed name, or if the hotel staff had appropriated the liquor themselves.

The leaves that year turned spectacular shades of orange and gold before falling one by one in lazy circles to the ground. Before long the snow had arrived to cover them. The first snows in Boulder drifted to the ground in fluffy, soft, flakes that melted quickly, but snowfalls held fast in the mountains. Soon groups began to gather on weekends at the dorms or the D.G. House, and then flock by the carload to Aspen or Steamboat Springs to ski. We went mainly to Aspen, with its incomparable mountains and cheap rooms.

My second trip there, I met Frank Guider. After making the lowest grades ever recorded at Dartmouth his freshman year, he joined the Army and became a member of their ski team. Frank was dark, of medium height, and good looking. We began to date, and I went to Aspen or Steamboat Springs several weekends to see him race slalom or downhill. Watching him weave down those steep hills was like seeing music translated into movement. He was my first intimate brush with a bad boy, only he was a different kind of bad boy—one from a privileged family.

Frank grew up in Vermont. His father, a prominent alum of Dartmouth, was a wealthy lawyer who had a vast estate. Frank showed me an aerial shot of a mansion centered on grounds as large and well groomed as a golf course. Mr. Guider's ambitions for his son were as vast as his property and investments, but Frank had thwarted those ambitions. He would evidently not be inheriting the estate.

After a couple of dates, it became clear that I needed to end the relationship with Frank. I thought I loved him, whatever that meant, but clearly, he didn't love me. He had dated an older woman with a child since he was in tenth grade. She had red hair, so I must have reminded him of her. Obviously still in love with her, he loved her little boy too. I never asked if the child was his.

The last time I saw Frank, I went to Steamboat Springs to tell him goodbye. I wanted to watch him race one more time, to stand at the bottom of a steep hill and sway to the rhythm of his body making tight turns around the flags, his skis cutting through powder snow and flinging it into the freezing air as it caught and reflected the light surrounding his moving body.

After I'd said goodbye to him over hot cider, I thought of the aerial shot of his father's estate in Vermont and felt a stab of pain. I'd never know that life. Frank walked me back to the bunkhouse where we college girls stayed. Large flakes of wet snow blanketed our shoulders and hair, and within a few blocks, we looked like snow creatures, cold as January, that had just come down from the mountains. Streetlights whirled around us, small white moons, welcoming us back to our separate lives in the world.

I started dating a boy from Colorado Springs who was a Chi Psi. He was smart, an English major, loved to read, and wanted to be a teacher. Witty, he had a great sense of humor, and we laughed a lot when we were together. He would probably have been a perfect match for me. But by that time I had also met John Haldeman for the first time at a Chi Psi party. The boy I was dating went home for the weekend and John called to ask me out, bringing the relationship with his fraternity brother to an abrupt end.

How governed by the rules of chance the process of mating is. We're directed by what adults have recommended—advice we probably scorned at the time, like my mother's about marrying a steady man, a good provider. Some girls replay a Cinderella escape from cold ashes. But most of our mating choices are happenstance—a mix of chemistry, human migratory patterns, song lyrics, and the weather.

John and I went out every weekend, mostly to frat parties. During the week, after a tennis match, he'd pick me up at the library in his car. We'd stop for a chocolate-peanut butter sundae at the

Dairy Queen on the way back to my dorm. John was easy to be with. Popular and honorable, he was different than many of the boys at C.U. who drank too much and acted beastly. He never pushed me farther than kissing, which was as far as I wanted to go.

Once I started dating John, Steve hung around the dorm even more. It frightened me. I finally called his college roommate from Pasadena, Jim Pomeroy, and asked him to tell Steve to quit following me. Jim tried to talk me into seeing Steve again, but I said it was over. I don't know what Jim said to Steve, but he stopped lurking around.

By the end of our freshman year, it was clear that none of the Pasadena kids would return to C.U. for sophomore year. Perhaps they'd partied too much, the biggest danger of going to a party school. But there were also outside activities to enjoy, miles of trails through the foothills to explore, and so many new people to meet, you could easily forget to study. Patti and I were the only ones left standing.

The two of us proudly flew home on United Airlines, both having maintained respectable 3.0 averages. Next year, we'd live in the D.G. House, which was beautiful, warm, and welcoming. I knew I wouldn't major in Home Ec, but I hadn't yet chosen an alternative. English had been my first choice until my disastrous freshman comp class.

Patti's parents met us at the plane and drove us to Pasadena. Chad was eight. He'd grown tall and handsome. Right away, the two of us went out and had an Orange Julius. He confided in me that girls were calling him—older girls in sixth grade. He looked embarrassed, but pleased. Although I didn't say anything, it horrified me. Mother and I were hardly civil to the little girls when they called, but our rudeness didn't stop them.

Poor Mother looked haggard and drawn. The weight of so many unpaid bills was pulling her down. When Dad arrived home a week later, he took one look at me, and with obvious disgust in his voice, said, "My God! How did you get so fat?!"

I was stung. It was the first time he'd ever criticized me. But my clothes were mighty snug. I didn't even have to try and lose weight that summer though. When Dad was home, he cooked only steak or chicken, and Mother's hamburger patty dinners didn't appeal to me.

Since neither of them fixed deserts, my extra weight fell away and I never gained it back.

John and I talked every week on the phone. Our relationship had become serious. In August, I visited Minneapolis to meet his parents. The Haldemans lived in a beautiful gray and white frame house in an older part of town near one of the city's many lakes. John's parents were friendly and welcoming. We had dinners on their screened-in side porch.

Often included in our gatherings were John's Aunt Genie and Uncle Lynn. Their warmth and sense of humor reminded me of Western people. But they were even better because they were sober.

One night, the Haldemans had a dinner party to introduce me to the rest of the family and some close friends. The meal was a marvelous spread of cold salmon, several exquisite salads, and fresh green beans. We were all trying too hard when Uncle Lynn said to me, loud enough for everyone to hear, "Now Jill, I'd recommend that you eat hearty, because it's wieners and buns from here on out." Our laughter made the rest of the party easy. I felt fortunate to be welcomed into the midst of such wonderful people.

John and I took walks around several lakes right in the center of town. The natural beauty of the lakes had been preserved by a wealthy philanthropist named Charles Loring. He bought all the property around the lakes before people could build on it. Then, he donated the land to the city for walkways, green borders, and parks. I warmed immediately to the agrarian-populist history of an area where people and parks took precedence over cars and freeways.

Although we never discussed it, John and I both knew we'd get married. The Midwest seemed like a good place to live and raise children. I would finally be part of a real family in a real community. Although I'd miss the western mountains, reaching like ancient gods into the sky, Minneapolis was a paradise of pristine lakes, green parks, and trees. It was what Boise had hoped to be with the addition of irrigation canals.

Life in the D.G. House my sophomore year was a giant step up from dorm life. The stucco-and-wood House was nicely decorated, and the food was even better than dorm food. Prepared in smaller amounts, it was more like home cooking. I was over my euphoric brownie-binging phase, but I still appreciated every good meal placed in front of me, which is just what our Frat servers, wearing white jackets, did.

Not long after my sophomore year began, John took me out to dinner at an elegant restaurant up in the Flatirons overlooking Boulder. With hundreds of lights twinkling below us, he formally asked me to marry him. Then, he presented me with a beautiful 1.5 carat emerald-cut diamond ring. His friends from the Chi Psi Lodge sang "The Girl That I Marry" under my window that night. Everyone in the D.G. House swooned.

Being engaged was a relief, since the prevailing myth at C.U. during the fifties was if you hadn't found your husband by the end of your sophomore year, you were doomed to be an Old Maid. Of course, it was still important for a girl to get a degree, "In case the husband dies." But people felt sorry for senior girls who didn't at least have engagement rings. Aunt Jo came out for the engagement party at The House, complete with hors d'oeuvres, white tablecloths, and candlelight.

One evening, a group of us watching the *Huntley-Brinkley News Report* were horrified to learn that President Eisenhower had been forced to send national troops to Little Rock to protect the "Little Rock Nine." They were black teenagers, not much younger than we were. White mobs were trying to keep them from entering the all-white Central High School.

Governor Orval Faubus had not only refused to protect them, but had sent out the Arkansas National Guard to keep the frightened looking black students from desegregating the school. Mobs of savage looking white people screamed at them. It was hard to believe that human beings could hate other human beings so much.

A sorority sister interrupted the show to hand me a letter. My name and address on the envelope was in Mother's handwriting, which surprised me because she never wrote letters, not even to her own parents. It was a short letter, and I read it quickly. Unable to hold back an outcry, I ran to my room where I read the letter two more times.

Mother wrote that Dad had been arrested. Although he was originally jailed in Spokane, Washington, he'd just been moved to The Tombs, a jail in New York City, awaiting trial. I sobbed softly, so no one would hear me. Although I felt numb, I knew Mother's letter was a forecast of disaster.

That night, for the first time since I was a child, I didn't end my prayers with, "And please let Dad's deal go through." One thing was clear now—his deal would never go through. I didn't know until years later that he'd been arrested for securities fraud.

Overnight, college life changed from a blessed escape to an endurance test. Aunt Jo called right away, furious at Dad, vowing she'd never speak to him again.

"Jill," she said, "your dad hasn't made your life any easier, but we Breckenridge women are strong. You'll get through this."

She offered to pay my tuition for the rest of the year, as well as my room and board. Any other living expenses would be mine, so I'd have to find part-time work.

I didn't tell anyone that Dad was in jail. Because of my dark secret, I began living a double life again. Although I was still one of the Delta Gamma sisters, known for having good personalities; for being peppy, accepting, and fair; for singing songs like, "Well, well, well, Hannah, my Delta Gamma...," my song had become a sad solo. It seemed to me that no Delta Gamma, Hannah or otherwise, would ever understand.

I went to the employment office at the college and found that the good jobs on The Hill, like working in the little clothing stores, were all filled by upper classmen or local people. The only jobs available were babysitting and cleaning. I signed up for as many of them as I could get.

When I walked past The Sink on Friday afternoons en route to a night of babysitting, I stared straight ahead. The place throbbed with music, noise, and kids. Long tables were packed with students playing Chug-A-Lug before they wove their way back to the houses for dinner. I didn't miss the beer drinking; I didn't even mind having to work; but I missed being young and carefree. Those days were gone.

Fortunately, like Grandmother Breckenridge, I knew how to

work. I got lots of babysitting jobs and enjoyed being in a real house where real people lived. There was always something make-believe about the dorm and the D.G. House. They were pretend families. These were real families. I enjoyed most of the kids, and I didn't mind doing the dishes or cleaning up.

But one of my regular jobs, although it was the easiest, tortured me. On Tuesday, after my only morning class, I took care of a baby named Timmy until dinnertime. His mother said not to touch him, not to raise the shades or turn on the light in his room, not to take him out of his crib. She gave no explanation for this procedure, but she was very firm about it.

We didn't know the word at the time, but the baby was probably autistic. I often found myself glancing over toward Timmy's door. When I listened outside it, I heard a repetitive banging sound. The only time I peeked into his room, his eyes, caught in the crack of light, glowed like the eyes of a night animal. Alone and wet, he stood in a yellow sleeper behind the bars of his crib, silently rocking himself back and forth, banging his chest against the bars.

Besides babysitting, I had two cleaning jobs on alternate Saturdays. One I hated and one I loved. I hated cleaning the apartment of Mrs. Future Faculty Wife in her cramped, crummy student housing. Since the apartment was small, it didn't take long.

While I was there, Mrs. Future ate lunch with her two little girls at the large kitchen table and fed me at the kitchen counter no more than four feet away. Neither she nor the little girls talked to me. If the girls looked my way or spoke to me, she scolded them.

I hardly touched her food, then went back to the D.G. House to eat. All of us girls sat around big tables covered with white cloths, everyone but me tipsy from Saturday afternoon parties at The Sink. The girls tried to act sober, occasionally collapsing into giggles or spitting mouthfuls of half-chewed food into cloth dinner napkins.

My favorite job was cleaning the huge house of the Goldthwaite family. I was a gift to Mrs. G. from her father-in-law. His son, The Reverend, was a grumpy minister. Mrs. G. was a big, loose-boned woman, who wore shoes as big as ponies, aptly called saddle shoes.

Mrs. G. always baked cookies for the church staff. She insisted we take a break every afternoon and sit down at the kitchen table, where she would serve us pots of freshly brewed tea and plates of warm sugar cookies sprinkled with cinnamon, or warm chocolate chip cookies.

When Mrs. G. sat down, she showed interest in each one of us. This was after she'd been up studying most of the night. Evidently, Mr. G. didn't approve of his wife finishing her college degree. He was even grumpier if she stayed up late. So she went to bed with him, waited until he was asleep, and then got up to study.

Her benefactor father-in-law paid for the classes, just as he paid for me to clean every other week. Because I admired Mrs. G. so much, I dusted as if her house were made of precious stones. I vacuumed every neglected stairway and closet of that huge parish house. In a fury of adoration and gratitude, I scrubbed every crusty corner and ledge with a toothbrush.

Mrs. G. meant as much to me as Mrs. Dedman had—even more because she never distanced herself from me. The time I spent in her house every other Saturday taught me something I've never forgotten. We can never know what burden another person is carrying. A genuine act of kindness has the power to save a life—or at least, to help make a life worth living.

When I told John about Dad, he didn't seem concerned, and he often took me to one of my jobs on his way to play tennis. He didn't study much, and got mediocre grades. I never saw him set foot in the library where I spent many afternoons and evenings. After graduation, he had a job waiting for him in his father's company, which did some manufacturing but mainly sold business storage and school lunchroom equipment. College was a recreational time-out for him before he went into the family business.

Already a senior, John was president of the Chi Psi Lodge and was busy with obligations there. The wild parties at The Lodge were legendary. At one event with a farm theme, straw was scattered across the floors of the party rooms. No large farm animals attended, but ten brown-and-black striped chickens wandered around, clucking and pecking at the straw.

I spent much of the evening trying to rescue them from a drunk college boy intent on twisting off their heads. I stuffed the threatened chickens into John's bedroom, which saved their lives for the moment, but didn't please him. He was extremely neat, and the chickens pooped on his rug. Then, they scratched and snagged his bedspread before shaping it into nests, pretending they were safely in their coop.

At another party, a frat boy carried around a bowl teeming with goldfish and tried to set up contests based on who could swallow the most. Nobody volunteered, so he began taking bets on how many fish *he* could swallow. Before the bowl was empty, I was ready to go home.

The crowning horror of those frat parties was always supplied by an extremely tall couple. The boy was over seven feet tall and the girl also cut a towering figure. Toward the end of every party, the same scene played itself out. In the boy's second-floor bedroom, the couple got so drunk the girl passed out. Her boyfriend had to get her downstairs to the living room, but she was too heavy for him to carry. So he laid her on her back, put one of her feet under each of his armpits, and dragged her down the stairs. Her head made a horrible cracking noise as it hit every step.

After Mother gave me Dad's prison address I wrote him several times. I said that I knew he was innocent. He wrote back once to thank me for writing. To his credit, he didn't agree with my statement about his innocence. He just wrote that he loved me and appreciated my letters.

One day, while I was vacuuming the living room at Goldthwaite's, Mrs. G. tapped me on the shoulder. John was on the phone. Mrs. G., looking embarrassed, mentioned he'd asked to talk to "the cleaning woman."

When he picked me up, I said, "Don't ever do that again."

"What do you mean?" he said, surprised that I didn't think it was funny.

"You know what I mean," I said, glaring at him. "You've never worked a day in your life. Cleaning is good, honest work. Unless you want to support me, don't do that again."

This episode wasn't my only concern about John. I'd recently noticed how demeaning and demanding he was to restaurant waitresses and hosts. The worst part was that the ruder he was, the more they toadied to him. Although I couldn't have named this uneasiness at the time, deep inside I knew it was a warning about privilege, about the exemption from sensitivity and empathy it can bestow. But at eighteen, I hadn't seen much of the world and John's background was so different from mine, it was like a foreign country.

I mulled over my concerns about him and concluded that, in spite of his remark, he was the nicest boy I'd met at C.U. He was a gentleman, always polite. And—the big *and*—he never got drunk. At the Chi Phi Lodge, he was a stabilizing influence, although he hadn't been able to save most of the party chickens. I shrugged off my uneasiness.

Mrs. G.'s father liked me and thought I was a good worker. He decided, because the house was so big, he'd pay for me to come every Saturday. This made it possible for me to quit the job cleaning for Mrs. Future Faculty Wife. On my last day there, I squatted down to the level of her little girls, looked directly at them one by one, and calling them by name, said goodbye. They smiled shyly, then glanced uneasily at their mother.

The next time I babysat with Timmy, the caged baby, after listening for hours to his chest banging against the crib rails, I couldn't take it any more. Although I was afraid to raise the shades, turn on the light, or take him out of his crib, I laid him down and changed his drenched diaper. I rinsed out the diaper and squeezed it as dry as possible. Then I wrapped it in waxed paper and put it in my purse. If I took the diaper with me, his mother might not know I had disobeyed her.

I sat down on the floor next to his crib and talked softly to him. He moved away like a wild animal if I tried to touch him, so I held onto the leg of the crib and gently rocked it. That seemed to soothe him. He stopped banging his chest against the bars. I didn't know any lullabies, but I softly sang every song I could think of.

After a while, he lay down and turned his head toward me, glazed eyes open wide. I sang the few songs I could remember, sang them soft and slow: "Happy Trails to You," "Home on the Range," and "My Funny Valentine." I was so desperate for songs I even sang toned-down versions of "Well, Well, Well, Hannah, My Delta Gamma" and Dad's Navy song, "Cocaine Bill and Morphine Sue." I stopped short of the cocaine sniffs because the sound might have alarmed him. His eyes finally closed, and he fell asleep.

I'd been worrying about Dad, worrying about what life was like for him in jail, what food he ate, and how he spent his days. One afternoon, I went to the most expensive grocery store in town and picked out the hors d'oeuvres he loved best. I chose three different kinds of crackers; sardines, plain and drenched with wine sauce; smoked oysters, curled up, tiny and succulent, in their silver king-size beds; the huge cocktail onions and hot peppers he enjoyed suffering through; a big square of aged cheddar cheese; and Limburger, the smelly cheese I was always such a baby about, screaming and running out of the room every time he ate it. To make him extra happy, I bought two big chunks of Limburger, feeling a little sick from the putrid smell drifting up through the clear cellophane wrap. I paid for all of it from an envelope of paper bills I'd earned babysitting,

After writing a jaunty note, I packed it along with the food. Then I stuffed newspaper around the bottles to avoid rattles or breaks, and shipped it off to Dad. In my mind's eye, I saw how pleased he'd be when he opened the box; how his face would brighten when he got a whiff of that Limburger cheese; how he'd gather his friends for a party; and how happily they'd pass the time, which they certainly had plenty of.

One night at the D.G. House, we were watching a special on Hula Hoops, the latest rage. A sorority sister handed me a slip to pick up a package at the Post Office. I knew it must be the clothes Aunt Jo said she'd send. Thinking the box might be too big for me to carry on foot, I asked John to drive me there. We stopped to look at the Wanted posters, and both agreed that criminals looked more like rats than human beings. They must have been part of an altogether different species.

When I gave my name at the window, the man behind the counter looked at me strangely. He disappeared for a moment, and then lowered his eyes as he shoved a package my way. Although it had been ripped apart and barely taped together again, I knew it was the box I'd sent to Dad. Stamped all over it, probably twenty times, and circled in red, were the red words, REJECTED BY THE WARDEN.

John and I left the post office with the taped-up box and walked into a haze of almost invisible crystalline flakes of snow. I asked him to take me back to the D.G. House. We rode silently, as if the snow were not only falling and freezing on the windshield of the car, but inside us, freezing our words. My future husband dropped me off at The House shortly before dinner.

When the dinner bell rang and we girls entered the dining room, I imagined a scene that played out like a movie in my mind. On a cloth-covered table, I served up the hors d'oeuvres—a colorful spread of crackers, oysters, sardines, hot peppers, cocktail onions, Cheddar, and Limburger cheese. One by one, the girls saw the food and rushed forward to take part in the celebration, until they smelled the Limburger. Then they wrinkled their noses and backed off.

As I stood alone at the table, my sorority sisters pushed past me into the dining room, and the frat servers pulled out their chairs. By myself, I ate the crackers, pasted dry as cotton to the roof of my mouth; ate the sardines, their soft little bones sticking in my throat; ate the sour onions, my lips puckering; ate the hot peppers that burned like bile all the way down; and ate the Limburger, inhaling, open-eyed, the fragrance of that soft rot.

The nearly invisible snow fell harder until everything beyond and within that house full of sisters blurred and blended into a blizzard of white, except for the small circle where I stood, smiling politely, eating the pungent cheese.

My last semester of college, I finally had a class I loved. It was an English elective that some of the older girls in The House recommended to me. The teacher, Mr. Smyth, was in love with literature and actually read poems out loud to the class, modern poems you could even understand. Some of the lines were beautiful, and I savored every delicious word. We read short stories and plays too. Mr. Smyth's lectures were outstanding, and he made every class discussion interesting.

I felt like a shipwrecked survivor crawling onto solid land. Not only was the landscape lush and friendly, but already prepared food and drink were there waiting for me. I spent hours on my class papers. Each one came back with many good comments and a large A+.

I had finally found my major, even though I wasn't able to complete it. With Dad in jail, finishing college was out of the question. Although Aunt Jo had paid for the remainder of my sophomore year, she'd offered no more. Even if she had, it probably wouldn't have mattered. John was a senior, and we were getting married the next December. This was my last semester of college. But it was still a comfort to know there was a subject I loved and excelled in.

Not long before the semester ended, Mr. Smyth called me in to his office.

"I wanted to talk to you, Jill, and encourage you to finish college. You have a lot of ability."

"Thank you," I said, "but this will be my last semester. I can't afford to stay."

"Isn't there any way you can do it? You should have a career in English literature. You could be a teacher or scholar--even a writer if you wanted to."

Stunned by his praise, I mumbled, "My father's in some trouble, and there's no money. My Aunt helped me finish this year."

Mr. Smyth paused a moment, then said, "The committee seldom offers scholarships to girls because they think girls will just get married. But you've shown such exceptional ability in my class, I know I could get you a full scholarship if you wanted to pursue a degree in English literature."

I was amazed by his perception that I had any special ability, touched he would go out of his way to help me. But he didn't understand. I was getting A grades because I had to—it was something I did to survive. In 1958, at nineteen, I had no career aspirations, no vision of my life more grandiose than that of a wife and mother.

Thanking him for his offer, I said that I was dropping out of college at the end of the year to get married. His face saddened when I showed him my ring. He said he liked it, but not as much, I sensed, as he liked Shakespeare's *The Taming of the Shrew*, which we'd just read in class.

I received a paper back from him that day. He'd given me an A+ on it. The paper was titled, "The Spirit of the Shrew." In it, I compared Kate favorably to strong-willed Western women.

I wrote that I'd learned one thing from my Western women ancestors, and those in my present life: a good offense is always better than a weak-kneed defense. These strong women taught me that even when you're flattened, you must peel yourself up off the floor and keep going, keep pushing forward, no matter how many times you're knocked down.

Paired with those beliefs, I added, I inherited something from my background that Kate didn't. Busts and booms, famine and feast have always punctuated Western history. From that history, and a similar trajectory in my own family's challenging existence, I inherited a deep, abiding faith in justice and the happy ending. But since faith didn't always pan out, I also inherited a dark sense of humor. I concluded my paper, "This faith has always comforted me as I was falling."

10

Prison Bars and Wedding Bells

After I got home that summer, a neighbor, the mother of one of Chad's friends, stopped by. She said Chad told her daughter his dad was rich, and he would get her an eighteen-carat gold bracelet in Caracas, just like the ones he bought for Mother and me.

When Mother returned from work, I said, "I hear you haven't told Chad about Dad yet." She looked sheepish and said, "No, I just can't."

"It's your responsibility, Mother, and you have to tell him, right away."

She wanted me to do it, but I held fast. Afterwards, she said it was very hard. He cried. I don't remember ever talking to Chad about Dad. I couldn't comfort myself. What could I say to him? Dad had taken away any small hope we had for a normal family life. Now, we'd have to go it alone.

Soon after I got home from college, Mother drove Chad and me to Boise to see her parents, John and Sarah St. Clair, who we kids called Nana and Papa John. Mother worried it would be the last time she'd see them alive. We visited them in their upstairs apartment. It smelled of musty furniture and moldy carpeting.

Papa John was still alert but Nana had lost her memory. She hadn't lost her sense of humor though, and when Papa John teased her because he'd had to take over the cleaning, she said, "Speak when you're spoken to, John!" We sat in their living room with glasses of lemonade that Papa John had passed around.

Nana said, "Josephine, where's Charles?"

"He couldn't come," Mother answered, not adding any details.

"Oh..." Nana said, but in five minutes, she asked again.

"Josephine, where's Charles?"

"He couldn't come with us this time," Mother said.

"Oh, I see."

After a few minutes, Nana asked once again, "Josephine, where's Charles?"

Exasperated, Mother said, "He's in the hoosegow, Mother! The clink! The jug, the slammer!"

"He's where, Josephine?"

"He's in jail, Mother!"

There was a long pause.

"Oh," Nana said, "well, good enough for him!"

That summer I worked at Haggarty's, a women's clothing store, and prepared for my wedding in December. Mother was too nervous to help. She was also grieving for her parents, who both died soon after our visit. Mother couldn't afford to go to either funeral.

Because of our unpaid storage bills in Boise, all of Baba's furniture was sold. I grieved for his platform rocker, which I'd hoped to rock my own children in. Mother must have asked for money from Aunt Jo, Uncle Jim, and anyone else she could, to help pay for our living expenses and the wedding.

I never told John any details about our life, so the Haldemans had no idea how desperate our situation was. Because of shock, tradition, or pride, it never occurred to me to ask them for help, or even to have the wedding in Minneapolis.

After work and on weekends, I tried to get the house fixed up for the coming event. Our front lawn was a dead yellow, and the entire house smelled of Lulu's lapses. I raked up the dry grass, bought grass seed, rented a heavy roller, and enlisted Mother to help me plant and roll the yard.

As I gave orders, she worked along with me. Her eyes were as dead and glassy as a poor man's mule. I watered the seed every day, and like a Biblical prophesy, it put down roots and rose up, lush and green, from the dead ground.

The pee smell was harder to remedy. Our housed reeked of it. I bought some rug shampoo. Every night after work, I tackled another room, scrubbing the carpet until my arms ached. But the addition of soapy water only acted like an odor enhancer. When the damp spots dried, the smell was even worse.

It was clear the entire carpet needed to be ripped up and replaced. We might have asked the landlord to do it, but since Mother was behind in the rent, we decided against it. I prayed we didn't get evicted before the wedding. After spraying room freshener around the house, I left the windows wide open, hoping the smell would abate.

One day we got a call from Ol' Mart, who'd returned from Montana. She was in a nearby hospital, dying of congestive heart failure. For two years, she'd worked as a House Mother for a Montana sorority. The girls loved her as much as we did, and the sorority management insisted she stay until she had to be hospitalized.

Mother went to the hospital almost every day. When Pat and I visited, Ol' Mart was pale and thin, but still vibrant. A constant line of doctors, nurses, friends, and hospital residents filed through the room while Ol' Mart held court and told her funny stories. I don't know what happened to her black Cadillac, Ol' Liz, or to her jew-els. But, even without them, she'd become a famous hospital celebrity. Soon after our visit, she died.

In the fall, I addressed the wedding invitations alone. Mother couldn't help because her hands shook too much. Soon after the invitations were sent out, gifts began arriving. The Haldeman's friends sent beautiful silver platters, crystal bowls, and a vast array of towels and linen.

Their closest friends got together and sent a twelve-plate pink dessert set with three standing compotes—antique Meissen china, circa 1820. Every plate and compote was hand-painted with different butterflies and birds.

On December 21, 1958, a week before the wedding, Dad wrote me from McNeil Island, Box #PMB. 27230, Steilacoom, Washington, where he was serving his prison term. It began, "My Dearest Jilly," then went on, "I have attempted to write you a number of times, but this is probably one of the most trying experiences I've ever had to accomplish, and especially almost on the eve of your wedding, which of course makes it much harder and sadder—of all things, your father in a position, where it is impossible for him to be there and at least see his only daughter married. I know it will be very hard for you to ever forget and I'll never forgive myself for it. Was called in Friday by the chaplain and had a good heart-to-heart talk with him regarding the situation, which of course made me feel better, but still doesn't alter the situation any. Nevertheless, Jilly, I'm very happy for you and John…"

John's older sister, Mary, and her husband, Doug Dayton, gave us an elegant pre-wedding dinner party at the Huntington Hotel. We were married in the San Marino Episcopal Church. I wore Aunt Jo's heirloom Brussels lace gown, with an Empire sash of peau de soie. Uncle Am gave me away. Cyndy was my Maid of Honor, and Pat Sheldon, Patti Fosdick, and one of my C.U. annex roommates were bridesmaids. Lucille had the reception on her lawn.

My wedding deal had gone through, but the whole event felt phony, like a layer of decorative frosting over a sad cardboard cake. However, I'd kept my promise to Ol' Mart, and didn't marry a gambling man. And I also kept my promise to Mother, and married a steady man who would be a good provider.

After we left on our honeymoon, Mother had a party at the house for the out-of-town family. She served her spaghetti casserole, which, besides bacon, was the only thing I knew how to cook when I was married.

The recipe was very straightforward. You fried one onion and a pound of hamburger together in a large fry pan. Then you added a small can of drained sliced mushrooms and a large can of Chef Boyardee Spaghetti. After seasoning it with salt and pepper, you sliced cold Velveeta Cheese (it had to be cold or it stuck to the knife) over the top and baked it at 350 degrees for forty-five minutes. While it was cooking, for the last thirty minutes, you popped your foil-wrapped loaf of sliced French bread, liberally spread with melted butter and garlic, into the oven. Mother served it with a green salad. She said that everyone raved about the meal.

We spent our honeymoon in Scottsdale, Arizona, at a motel with a pool. The thrill of this arrangement was lost on me because I didn't like the sun or the water. Nor did I read or have any other sedentary interests. Thus far in my life, I had ridden Lucky, babysat, cleaned houses, or read the books and studied the notes for my various classes. John played golf every day while I sat around the motel. It was very boring. Since I was only nineteen, we couldn't get into nightclubs. We ate most of our meals at fast-food restaurants.

Mother's sex-education talk to me before the wedding was, "Well sex isn't too bad at first, Jilly, but soon, you just pretend you're asleep." She didn't mention Bride's Disease, a severe urethral infection, which I probably got on our wedding night. It was very painful and made me pee with less control than LuLu. After a couple of days, whenever I peed, the water in the toilet turned blood red.

I was weak and scared, but I couldn't get John to call a doctor or take me to a hospital. Maybe he was scared too, and just wanted to get me home. Maybe he didn't want to spend the money. I thought, "I've made a terrible mistake. He doesn't have any better judgment than my parents." Fooled by appearances again…

When we arrived in Minneapolis, I was too weak to walk. John carried me into the house and up to the second-floor bedroom, where a doctor treated me. I stayed in bed for over a week while taking heavy doses of antibiotics.

John's parents were wonderful to me, treating me like a second daughter. They were critical of their own children, said they were spoiled from having been given too much. This comment puzzled me, since the Haldemans had done the giving. It seemed they admired me for being a self-made woman.

Although I'd worried about fitting into John's Midwestern Minneapolis world, it turned out to be easy. I enjoyed meeting new people, and it wasn't difficult to learn how the privileged lived. Mrs. Haldeman and her exceptional maid, Ruby, kindly coached me. I watched how people set their tables and entertained. When I needed to buy something like engraved note cards, the clerks at Dayton's Department Store advised me which ones were appropriate.

Members of the family took responsibility for different holidays. I fixed Christmas brunch, staying up most of Christmas Eve night to wrap gifts, make homemade cinnamon rolls, and get ready for company. John, always in bed by nine, didn't help with the preparation or cleanup. I soon realized that a good husband needed to be more than steady and a good provider. If you didn't happen to be rich, he had to help at home too. Slowly, I realized that in our family, I was the maid.

We ate the other major holiday meals at my sister-in-law's or one of the Haldeman's clubs, where John and his father played golf. The food was beyond my imagining. It was 1959. Everything but my marriage seemed perfect. When I became active in the Civil Rights movement a few years later, I discovered that these private clubs prohibited Jews, African Americans, and single women from membership. After that revelation, the food didn't taste as good.

One day, I received a manila envelope from Aunt Jo. Her accompanying letter said she'd thought long and hard about sending it. She knew how much I loved Dad, but she thought I should know some of the facts about his case.

In the envelope was a December 7, 1958, article from *The Spokesman-Review* in Spokane, Washington. It was their Sunday morning edition—the one that drew the largest readership. The story takes up the entire left half of the front page. What first pops out from the page is Dad's mug shot, with #26200 hanging around his neck. Wearing one of his nice shirts, he looks both handsome and angry.

The bold-faced headline reads, "High Living Ends in Prison for Handsome, Fast Talker." The subhead reads "Elegant Suites at Hotel Just Memory—Checks Bad." The article, written by Bill Boni, begins "The facts that are stranger than fiction abound in the story of Charles Corder Breckenridge. The fictions which also loom large in Charles Corder Breckenridge's story give the facts a hard run for their money.

"It is a story of a fantastically complex 'get-rich-quick' scheme involving refugee Chinese and untold millions which—at least by hindsight—would appear to have been too implausible to take in a schoolboy."

The article goes on to say that during the past January "a tall, handsomely dressed man and an expensively garbed attractive blonde woman checked in at the Davenport hotel in Spokane. The man signed the registry card in a bold flowing hand for Mr. and Mrs. C.C. Breckenridge from Reno, Nev."

Detective Elmer Meader, who arrested Dad on a charge of grand larceny for cashing bad checks, said, "...my, he was a smooth talker. If I hadn't had him so dead to rights especially with that information about New York wanting him, I would've been almost afraid to lock him up."

He said that many "good people, earnest people" showed up in the next few days to put up bond for him, until Detective Meader told them more about him. Then no one put up bond. Dad was in the Spokane jail until March 7, when two detectives took him to New York. By that time the

High Living Ends in Prison for Handsome, Fast Talker

Faces Police Camera

Charles C. Breckenridge, bold and colorful figure in a shady financial deal that involved hundreds of thousands of dollars, is shown being photographed for police files before he was convicted in federal court at Coeur d'Alene, Idaho, of check fraud.

Seattle office of the SEC had become involved. W. Forbes Webber, former FBI man and now an SEC attorney, said, "'What we found among his papers in Spokane just about wrapped up the case...'"

"'The vastness of it was probably the beauty of it,' Webber continued. 'It wasn't uncommon for Breckenridge to set a comparatively small figure as what was needed to start the project rolling—perhaps $100,000. Then, if he was trying to get $10,000 from a prospect, he could promise him 10 percent of the gross proceeds—in this case, $750,000.'"

Webber stated that at least 40 people, and probably more, had lost everything they invested.

The woman posing as Dad's wife was Marcelle "Mickey" Matney, a New Orleans nightclub hostess. Before the Davenport hotel, they'd stayed at another hotel nearby registered as Mr. and Mrs. C.C. Matney, New Orleans.

"Where did the $350,000 go, which the SEC estimates Breckenridge collected on these sales of stock and other interests?...Apparently $65,000 of it went to his land 'contact' in Venezuela. Of the remaining $285,000...no trace remains.

"'There's a lovely $800 fur coat, which that woman with him was wearing,' says manager Schilling. 'We're holding that, and a mink stole, and some other furs, and some dresses, and some clothes of his.... Not long after the New York police took him east, we heard from a store back there that the fur coat...hadn't been paid for.'"

The article ends with "What was it the late P. T. Barnum supposedly said? 'There's a sucker born every minute.' And what did posterity add to that phrase?... And two to take him.'"

Heartsick, I tucked the article away. Mentioning nothing to John or to Mr. and Mrs. Haldeman, I put it out of my mind until I began writing this book more than forty years later. For the fourteen years I was married to John Haldeman, I never told anyone, even my closest Minneapolis friends, about my parents. I buried the burden of them like a criminal burying a parcel of bloodstained clothing. Living the double life I'd become good at, I divorced my past from my present.

Dad was in McNeil Island Prison, Washington, for eighteen months, since he'd already spent ten months in Spokane, New York, and Idaho jails. His jail time in New York City's The Tombs was the darkest. Now torn down, The Tombs was considered the worst jail in the country. The only light note to his stay there was that his cellmate, the son of a well-known comedian, was very funny.

But humor couldn't make up for all the sleepless nights he endured. The Tombs held mainly addicts. After their arrest, they were thrown into jail without any medical help. Dad said that he and his cellmate were kept awake every night by the cacophonous pleading, cursing, and screaming from addicts going through drug withdrawal and the DTs.

But all aspects of his incarceration weren't that bad. At McNeil Island Prison, Dad began by dispensing uniforms to incoming white collar prisoners, which meant he had contact with all the new arrivals. I can only imagine what deals he set up there.

Dad and his cellmate kept a constant game of chess going. Although his cellmate was Jewish, he didn't practice strict dietary restrictions. But he claimed he did. That gave him access to the prison kitchen, where he prepared special food for every Jewish holiday. He always brought some food back to Dad, a welcome relief from the monotonous prison diet.

Later when Uncle Jim, who looked a lot like Dad, walked into the prison to visit him, the guard said, "You must be Charlie's brother. Come on, I'll take you back to his room." Dad's room was next to the kitchen. At that time, he cooked for the guards and other employees who worked in the prison. Dad always loved good food, and he couldn't have gotten closer to it.

When Dad was in prison, an SEC investigator interviewed Aunt Jo to determine if Dad was a good candidate for parole.

"Many fine families have one," he said. "I'm convinced they're born that way. They just keep going on the same fast track until somebody stops them."

For Dad, prison was long overdue. As a boy, his mother always rescued him, paying his jail fines right away. In trying to keep its good name, the family shoved his behavior under the rug, so he never suffered any real consequences for all his misdeeds.

During the hard times after Dad's arrest, Mother and Chad moved from our rented Pasadena house with its front yard of newly green grass, its roses and eucalyptus trees, and its foam-green shag rug carpeting, and moved into a little rented house.

At the time, my brother said the new place was nothing but a garage with a door and window cut out of the garage door. Its yard was a cement driveway. Now Chad says he never told me that. He didn't think it was so bad—just a smaller house. He thinks Mother must have said that, since she saw losing the house on Brigden Road as a total humiliation.

While Dad was serving his time, Mother told me she'd never take him back. One evening, he arrived at the front door in his prison suit—not striped pajamas with a number on the pocket as I'd imagined, but a real suit. Chad says Dad knocked on the door, walked in, and hugged Mother and him. He remembers that Mother didn't say much. No one cried.

Dad later told Chad and me that he attended AA in prison. He stopped drinking and smoking once and for all. The only person who helped him at McNeil Island was a Catholic priest. No other rehabilitation counseling was offered. Just lots of time to think about what a mess you'd made of your life.

This was the plan of the Quakers, who started the original prison system. Prison was to be a brief time-out, where those who'd erred could commune with themselves and with their God. Then, they'd return to the community and have another chance to get it right.

Dad was a successful graduate of the prison system. Chad said ex-cons from prison would occasionally call or stop by the house, trying to get him involved in something shady again. But Dad would have nothing to do with them. He was through with his old life forever.

In their post-prison years, although Mother was still drinking, my parents seemed quite content. Dad was patient about her alcoholism, and, while he was alive, Mother kept it in check. She continued working for the same insurance company, and Dad took a job selling Imperial Homes. People bought their own lots and then chose the design they wanted for a prefab house. One of Chad's friends said his uncle bought an Imperial Home from Dad, and thought "he was a fine man."

Mother finally got her wish. Dad had the steady job she'd always hoped for.

After three years with Imperial Homes, Dad started selling cars at a Lincoln Continental dealership, where he worked until he was in his early seventies. Nearly every year, he was voted "Salesman of the Year." Once, he won a trip for two to Hawaii.

My parents with my sons Chad and Michael, 1972.

Dad kept his promise to never smoke or drink again. He read the *Forward Day by Day* spiritual devotion books every morning. They were heavily underlined and dog-eared.

John and I had twin sons in 1960. Four years later, our third son was born. Although John didn't approve, the Haldemans encouraged me when I went back to college. The twins were a year old at the time. Mrs. Haldeman kept a guest bedroom in their house ready for me. I went there when I needed time alone to write papers or study for tests. On those days, Ruby, who worked for the Haldemans, fixed lunch for the three of us. I felt lucky to have received the gift of two more wonderful women like Mrs. Dedman and Mrs. G.

I'd also received a new benefactor in Mr. Haldeman. He paid the woman who worked for them to clean for me once a month. That gave me a little more time to study.

It took me ten years, but with money I earned babysitting a neighborhood boy, and with help from scholarships, I slowly finished my last two years of college. Then, I began teaching English and history to seventh graders in Edina, a wealthy suburb of Minneapolis.

After fourteen years of marriage, John and I divorced. When my sons were twelve, twelve, and eight, I joined forces with John Fenn, a playwright and teacher, and his two teenage children, thirteen and fourteen. We formed a challenging but largely successful blended family. By that time, my brother Chad, a social worker, and his wife, Sally Brown, a visual artist and teacher, lived in Minneapolis too.

One summer my parents visited us and the whole family took a trip to the North Shore of Lake Superior. At Gunderson's Resort in Schroeder, each family had its own cabin, and we met in the largest cabin for evening meals. It was the best time I'd ever had with my parents. I taped seven hours of interviews with Dad and three hours of interviews with Mother.

Dad was close-lipped about his collisions with the law, but at one point, he said, "Jilly, you know I've been no model of virtue, but your mother was the only woman I ever loved."

During Mother's interview, when I asked about her relationship with Dad, she said, "I never had an unhappy day in my life till the day I married your father." She sighed, and then continued, "I never wanted to marry him. The night before the wedding, I looked around my beautiful bedroom, and thought, "What have I done? I'm happy just the way I am."

"Why did you marry him, Mother?" I asked.

"I don't know," she replied. "He simply pestered me to death!"

Dad's stomach had been bothering him for some time. The doctor had brushed it off, and told him to take a few Tums. Only a good medical practitioner, by going down with a scope, could have caught his stomach cancer in time to save him. When my parents returned to California, the cancer was finally diagnosed, but it was too late. Dad worked for as long as he could at the car dealership. Every lunch hour, he came home to rest and put up his aching feet.

Writing to Aunt Jo, he tried to make amends before he died. She wrote back that he'd always "cared more about things than about people." She kept her vow, and never forgave him or spoke to him again. He grieved because he couldn't make it right with her before he died.

After Dad got too sick to work, he read all of Louis L'Amour's Western novels. The older women he'd sold cars to rallied around him. They mailed him cards and religious tracts. One sent an Oral Roberts' book; another, a plaque that read, "I Believe In Miracles." He received a letter from The Ladies of Lourdes, Iowa. Because of one woman's ten-dollar contribution, more than five thousand Capuchin monks prayed for him twice a day.

When Dad took his last communion from an Episcopal Priest in the hospital, he shushed Mother and me because we whispered. Getting right with his God was a serious matter to him. A year after his stomach cancer was diagnosed, he died at seventy-five.

The three of us—my mother, brother and I—put on our good clothes and conducted a memorial service for him on the patio of my parents' rented apartment. The Southern California air was dry and light; the dust-colored foothills were surprisingly smog-free. The gray stone patio was spotless from Dad's daily hosing. His clay pots ringing the patio held begonias, flush with orange and red blooms. Perfume from a neighbor's carnations hung in the air, thick as honey.

We set up the scratched TV tray he'd eaten on for over twenty years, put a white candle on it, and set the wick aflame. My brother read a prayer from the Episcopal service for the dead; my mother read Dad's favorite, the 23rd Psalm; and I read a poem about his being "Salesman of the Year" at the Lincoln Continental car lot. I wished the yellow-headed parrot he often saw in the trees would join us, but it didn't attend the service. A few house sparrows pecked for seeds around the edge of the patio. After our ceremony, we went out and ate Chinese food in his honor.

Dad left behind two closets full of silk shirts monogrammed CCB, seven cashmere sports jackets, and twenty pairs of elegant shoes, handmade in Hong Kong. He owned seventeen disposable razors and more pairs of fine socks than ten men could wear out in a lifetime.

Rather than stuff his beautiful clothes in plastic bags and give them to the Good Will, Mother called one of his friends to come and take what he wanted. That afternoon, a handsome black man who'd had business dealings with Dad arrived. He was Dad's size, and thrilled to have his elegant clothes.

"Your dad...I've never met a better front man! He could sell anything! Did you ever see that fake silver jewelry he was going to sell?"

I told him I'd seen it—glaringly fake silver set with globs of glaringly fake turquoise stones. I couldn't understand how a man who bought Mother exquisite bracelets of Navaho silver and turquoise could have liked it.

Dad's friend laughed and said, "I told him, 'Chaalie, that stuff is gaabage. It's simply gaabage, Chaalie,' but he thought it would sell like hotcakes."

For about a month, Mother felt relieved that Dad was no longer suffering. She wore his pajama top to bed because it smelled like him, which comforted her. Items Dad had ordered from mail order catalogues continued to arrive steadily: sheets and towel sets, Teflon fry pans, and several clocks. Mother wrote DECEASED in huge red letters on the outer wrappings and sent them back.

Although my grief for Dad felt clean, I was left with many unrevealed secrets and unanswered questions about our life together, about the kind of man he'd been. I gave up any hope of answering those questions.

Shortly after Dad died, Mother was fired from her job. When Mother was working, she drank and smoked just at night, taking little puffs of the cigarettes she never inhaled. Once she lost her job, she smoked and drank all day. By then, she was mad at Dad.

"It's just like him to die first and leave me alone to figure it out!" she said.

I visited Mother twice in California. Before I went the first time, alone, she agreed to stay sober. I said I'd have to leave if she started drinking. The first three days went well. Then Mother got drunk and abusive.

Now I had to follow through on my pledge to leave. This was complicated because I had no car, no place to stay, and not enough money for transportation or to change my return flight date. My friend, Pat, came to my rescue. Her parents were out of town at the time. She picked me up and took me to their house, where I slept in the double bed that smelled like them, hung my clothes in their full closet, and wandered through their house like a wraith until it was time to fly home.

I swore I'd never go back again, but Mother apologized and asked me to bring the twins out to see her the next summer. She'd rent a little house in Balboa. We'd all be together and the boys could play in the ocean. Again, she promised to stay sober. I should have known better, but I wanted it so badly—for myself and for the children.

As regular as clockwork, three days after we arrived, Mother started drinking again. That night, I tucked the five-year-old boys into their beds. Sunburned from their day at the beach, excited and happy, they had trouble falling asleep. In the universal way of children, they whispered and giggled.

Suddenly, Mother appeared in their doorway carrying a large metal spoon raised over her head. I was right behind her, but couldn't catch her before she lurched toward them yelling, "Shut up! You god-damn little sons-a-bitches!"

As she went for one of the children, she tripped over the end of his bed and tumbled to the floor. The boys, out of fear and embarrassment, giggled again.

On the way home on the plane, one of them asked, "Is that the way Nana acted when you were growing up?" I said yes, and their eyes grew large in solemn understanding.

I never visited Mother again. Out of a sense of duty and to assuage my own guilt, I called her once a week and got off the phone as quickly as possible.

A year later, her friend, Lucille said, "Josephine, what's that under your scarf?" As she pulled the scarf down from Mother's neck, she saw a large throat cancer that had metastasized out. Lucille insisted she see a doctor. It was too late to do much, but they gave her chemotherapy to shrink the tumor so she could breathe.

Chad visited her once during that time. In spite of being nauseated from the chemo treatments, she still drank. Adding more poison to her already poisoned system just made her sicker. Chad said she'd take a drink, and then vomit repeatedly.

After the chemo treatments were over, her neighbors in the downstairs apartment took her to weekly doctor appointments. Before every one, Mother asked them to stop at the bank. The husband finally wondered out loud why she went to the bank so often. Mother pulled rolls of quarters from her coat pockets.

"Those doctors hound me about losing weight," she said, "so I add a few more rolls of quarters every week. Then, when I get on the scales, they leave me alone."

On the phone, I asked Mother if prayer was as helpful to her during her illness as it had been for Dad.

"Are you kidding?!" she said. "When your dad and I were first married, I had a deep faith, but over the years, I lost mine. When your dad died, he was the devout one. Wouldn't you know it?!"

The cancer had spread to her liver, and Chad soon got a call from the hospital to come out. She was dying. When Chad and I got to the hospital, Mother, in full make-up and red lipstick, was sitting up in bed, prepared to meet her death. She could no longer speak. I was disappointed, but later realized it was probably a blessing. Who knows what she might have said?

When we went through Mother's clothes closet later, we found seven empty vodka bottles. Some were stashed against the wall behind her shoes, but most were tossed onto the purse shelf above her hanging clothes. Evidently, she kept hiding her empty bottles long after Chad and I left home, long after Dad died. By that time, there was no one to hide her drinking from but herself.

Mother, who claimed to have lost her faith, had her funeral at the

Episcopal Church in San Marino. It was a strange choice, but she was probably worried about the afterlife. Even though she'd lost her faith, perhaps she thought the service would give her a leg up to heaven.

The funeral was a poor affair. Only eight people attended. The Latter Day Saints didn't show up even though they'd been courting Mother since she got sick. While she could eat, she was happy to partake of their Sunday suppers that were offered free to the sick and suffering, but she had no money to leave them. Several of the people she'd worked with at the insurance company came, as did her old friend Lucille. The minister didn't know her and delivered a perfunctory eulogy.

Although Mother said nothing to me from her deathbed, she got the last word, going against what Dad set up for them before he died. He had taken out a $5,000 life insurance policy to be divided between Chad and me after Mother's death. They both decided I would get Mother's rough-cut diamond ring. The stones in this ring had once belonged to Papa John. Two of the diamonds were gifts from the Madam of the Silver City whorehouse who favored Papa John when he was a young man. The third diamond was from his stickpin. Chad would inherit Dad's star sapphire ring.

Shortly before she died, Mother wrote across the will in a wavering scrawl, "Since Jill's diamond ring is worth more than Chad's star sapphire ring, I leave the entire $5,000 to my son, Chad." He used the insurance money to send the few things we wanted to Minneapolis.

I didn't take any of my Mother's other personal belongings except one ring. She was a Leo, and the ring is a gold lion's head with small diamond eyes and a ruby in its open mouth. Whenever I wear it, I turn its fierce eyes and sharp teeth away from me.

At the time Mother died, I was experiencing boom and bust periods as a freelance teacher and writer. Four years later, when I needed money between jobs, I sold Mother's Silver City diamond ring.

There's no way to prepare for the death of parents. The night after a parent dies, nobody feels like sleeping. The mouth prevails.

Death crowds out everything but hunger and words. After both our parents' deaths, my brother and I were often ravenous, our bodies reacting, perhaps, to the inevitability of ultimate destruction. At other times we talked nonstop, a flood of feelings pouring forth into words. But we couldn't sleep.

Sometimes a death releases tears, and sometimes not. The day Dad died, neither Mother, Chad, nor I shed any tears. They were all swallowed by our grief. That night, Mother and Chad still hadn't cried, but I couldn't stop. All night long, I cried silent tears. Without a sob or a hiccup, tears spilled nonstop from my unblinking eyes and down my cheeks.

After my mother's death, not a noisy or silent tear fell from the eyes of my brother or me. I felt no release. Just a sadness so deep, my back teeth ached. At the same time, I felt an inappropriate sense of relief. I would never again have to pore over the Mothers' Day cards saying "To the best Mother in the world!" until I found one saying, "Thinking of you on this day."

I grieved about the relationship we never had. Then I pushed my mother's memory from my mind and buried it in the metal box with her ashes. But no box is strong enough to contain memory. Because none of the land mines strewn through our life together had been disarmed, I kept stepping on them. Every time one silently exploded, I thought, "I'll never escape this sorrow."

I continued to have a close relationship with Aunt Jo until she died. She was a great support while I wrote *Civil Blood*, my novel in poetry and prose about the Civil War. My interest in history had come from her, and I loved having her be part of that creation. Every week, I called and read her the newest sections. If they were sad, she wept.

When Milkweed Editions published *Civil Blood*, we had a staged publication reading at The Loft in Minneapolis. Actors read their parts from cuttings of the book that my partner, John, a playwright, had put together. Aunt Jo came out for the reading.

Once, I visited her and her second husband in Sequim, Washington. During those later years, she slowly finished telling me her life story.

She always began by recounting again her mother's egg money story. How she'd saved, and then lost the money for her children's college education during the Great Depression.

Then, Aunt Jo told me stories I hadn't heard. She said my grandmother, Anna Corder Breckenridge, had marched and demonstrated for women's suffrage. Since my grandfather, John G. Breckenridge, whom I called Baba, also believed women should have the vote, he supported her.

Aunt Jo showed me an old newspaper article about him, published in the *Idaho Statesman* on February 14, 1937, eight months before I was born. The paper was yellow and beginning to crumble.

It began, "No obstacle is too great—not even 20 miles a day over rough sagebrush roads—when a youth really hungers for an education." The article went on to say that my great-grandfather died in 1878, four years after the family arrived in the 100-wagon train from Missouri. At first, my grandfather, a 9-year-old boy, rode his pony 20 miles back and forth to school, often over snow-drifted roads.

Then, "…he found a true friend in Tom Ranahan, one of the early stage drivers…who was a member of the pony express carrying the mail as far as Salt Lake City.

"At Ranahan's invitation, when the stage stopped at the Tollgate (that his stepfather had run) each morning…young John crawled into the stage boot and rode inconspicuously to Boise, catching another stage back in the evening. But when John Boomer, owner of the line, discovered that Ranahan was hauling a free passenger almost daily, he threatened to discharge him.

"But big hearted Tom Ranahan, whose loyalty and fearlessness were bywords in the community, was not afraid to defend the little fatherless boy and told his boss to fire him if he wished, but by heck, he intended to befriend the plucky youngster who was willing to suffer privations for an education. It is related that Ranahan was not fired."

Aunt Jo said the article described, much better than she ever could, what we Breckenridges stood for. Although I was married, divorced, and a mother of three, Aunt Jo continued, through family stories, to educate me in all the ways not to be like my parents.

One day, I asked Aunt Jo to tell me about her gambling. Her game of choice was Black Jack. She said that after reading every book she could find on the game, she came up with a system. At first, when she and Uncle Am went to Reno or Las Vegas, they played golf during the day and gambled at night. But as she got older, she lost interest in golf.

After that, when they went to Reno or Las Vegas, she sat in the casino all day and gambled while Am traversed the golf course. Aunt Jo liked some dealers better than others. One Reno dealer finally asked her not to sit at his table any more. She was winning so much money, his boss thought he was cheating. The next day, when she came back to play, he was gone.

She had no illusions about beating the system. Over the years, she kept a running total of how she did. Even though she won or lost from five to ten thousand dollars on Black Jack during every trip to Nevada, after several decades, she came out a little ahead. That was enough profit, she said, for all the fun she'd had.

Aunt Jo invested in stocks the same systematic way she played Black Jack. Every day she read *The Wall Street Journal* from beginning to end. Using information gleaned from its pages, she carefully picked her stocks. Sometimes she waited years for the one she wanted. Gradually, she built a strong portfolio.

All the while, Uncle Am played his game too. After he died, Aunt Jo found a group of file folders in the bottom drawer of his desk. The folders were labeled, "Reno," "Las Vegas," and several other locations. In each folder were the names and phone numbers of the women he knew there.

In her later years, Aunt Jo was on the board of the bank in Boise, the first woman to hold that position. On one visit, she gave me two of her bracelets, which I treasure. She also gave me Grandmother Breckenridge's white Haviland bone china. After serving holiday dinners on it for years, I've passed it on to my youngest son and his family. Now, they set their table with it for our holiday meals.

When Aunt Jo died, her net worth was over four million dollars, a larger estate than her husband's. Another child of the Depression, she had closets full of barely worn clothing and shoes, plus five complete sets of make-up, four of them unopened.

I was relieved that Aunt Jo died before her diabetes made it necessary to amputate her feet and legs, one of her biggest worries. But her death left a black hole in my life. I still miss her living, breathing presence.

Many months after her death, my heart's dead flowers of despair were hauled away, and gratitude bloomed in their empty vases. My cousin Breck, Aunt Jo's son, did some research, and found that funds were being solicited for a new Japanese garden being built in Boise. After talking to the curator of the garden, Breck asked if I wanted to go in with him to create a monument for his mother.

I remembered her lush garden in Sequim, Washington, where she lived her last years. Her vegetable and flower beds, built up and logged in, afforded an older woman, who could no longer bend or kneel, the luxury of turning over the dirt and creating a constant panoply of food and flowers. How she loved flowers!

I couldn't match the amount of money that Breck put in, but together we donated a fountain in Aunt Jo's name. The image of that fountain's fluid music providing solace to garden visitors still gives me great pleasure.

When I visited Boise some time later, I went to the garden site, and saw that the Japanese Garden was built directly in front of the old Idaho State Prison, now a historical landmark. I knew that my father was never imprisoned there, but he'd been jailed more than once as a teenager. The prison's foreboding gray mask, molded from tons of poured concrete, was perforated only by the blind eyes of barred windows.

After taking a deep breath, I realized it was probably an apt juxtaposition.

The sadness and violence locked away in that prison for years could finally escape through its obstructed windows and seek refuge in the garden. There, the stone fountain, bubbling serenely, was surrounded by lovingly arranged dark stones, yellow, pink, and lavender flowers, and lacy trees sheltering chirping flocks of birds.

Still, the prison loomed ominously over all.

Epilogue

Forty-five years after my father's arrest in 1958, I finally realized there was no escaping my past through distance or achievement. Slowly, I worked up the courage to learn the truth about my father's last big deal.

I was able to attain his records through The Freedom of Information Act by paying only the cost of reproducing them. By early 2003, I'd received—in packets weighing five to fifteen pounds—nearly 2,000 pages documenting my father's arrest, trial, and ultimate sentencing. After totaling up the figures, the amount of money people lost was approximately $280,000,000 in 2011 dollars. On November 17, 1958, Dad was found guilty and sentenced to three years in prison at McNeil Island, Steilacoom, Washington.

Two pages of the U.S. District Court Records contain a reproduction of a letter my father wrote to the judge on January 10, 1959. In beautiful handwritten printing, the letter begins, "My Dear Judge Clark." Then, Dad reminds the judge that upon sentencing him, he had reserved the right, within sixty days, to change or modify the length of his sentence.

The letter goes on to say that Dad had already spent ten months in "Federal Detainment" in the Spokane, Washington jail and The Tombs in New York City. Dad presents his case, writing:

"I pray that you will consider it prudent to make a reduction in my sentence" for these reasons:

"Josephine, my wife, and Charles, Age 10, my son, (Jill, our daughter was married on December 27th to a very fine young man) have bravely weathered the storm and the reverses I have put upon them. Josephine has seen fit to stick by me, and they need me now very much. She is employed, but her income isn't enough to adequately support herself and our son. Neither is Mrs. Breckenridge in a condition, physically or emotionally, to bear up under the responsibility of making a livelihood, while, at the same time, trying to maintain our home.

"You found, on examination of my record, that I had no arrests prior to January, 1958. I have always been steadily employed, or in business for myself, outside of my Navy enlistment, and have always tried to maintain an honorable existence. My intentions now, and have always been, to make full restitution on all of the N.S.F. checks, some have already been taken up, and to do all in my power to salvage as much of the over-all venture as possible.

"In view of the above, I pray you will see fit to make a modification in my sentence so that my release can be hastened and I may be returned to my family.

"I have excellent assurance of steady employment upon release, and I feel I can conduct myself hereon in such a manner as to merit this further consideration on your part.

Respectfully yours,
Chas. Breckenridge"

On January 15, 1959, Judge Clark reduced my father's sentence from three years to eighteen months. This reduction meant he was imprisoned for a total of two years and four months.

My father's conviction and sentence were a victory for the SEC and their prosecution of criminal acts. However, there's no bureau in Washington that can undo the destruction to victim's lives. From the early 2000s on, many failed or fraudulent companies, banks, and Ponzi schemes have victimized both innocent employees and investors. These victims are the first ones I feel for. Nothing can make right their losses.

In most cases, I feel sorrow for the wives, often ignorant of what was going on. They tried to keep the family afloat, before and after the bomb dropped, but their family lives were ultimately destroyed.

In all cases, I feel for the children. Their loss isn't just a loss of security; it's also a loss of trust, and of normal family lives. Of course, every human being learns and grows from hard knocks. Tennyson once called experience "The dirty nurse…" But no one would wish this tragedy on innocent children.

Even though my father was a relatively small player in the fraud game, he introduced many people to tragedy. Trying to make sense of the case against him in non-legal terms, I remember saying once that my dad was the "horse thief" of the family. But the truth is more lethal than that flip statement.

Hidden by the mask of night, a horse thief gallops across your land and steals your horses. Probably, he doesn't know you, and you don't know him. He wants the horses. You have them. He takes them. It's an impersonal act.

My father, on the other hand, stole horses from people who trusted, respected—even loved him. He stole horses from close friends he'd known since childhood. And, worst of all, he stole them from his family. He told us he was just going to borrow the horses for a while. Then, he'd return them. In fact, he'd return two or three times the number of horses he'd taken—maybe even more. And if any horses were lost, his huge backup herd would cover them.

I knew all along that my father was a man who cut corners. The childhood story about him putting dirt clods under the strawberries was evidence enough about his character. An SEC investigator, interviewing family members before his trial, said to my Aunt Jo, "You'll never really understand these guys. They're not like you and me."

But I need to understand. To look, unflinchingly, at the facts and the damage my father did to all of us. It's clear that he was a gambler. Yet he never pulled down the handle of a slot machine or stacked up a pile of colored chips and shoved them across a green tabletop. He knew the odds.

He was willing to work for his money, and he worked hard to strike it rich. He worked as hard as the 49-ers. Worked as hard as the big land speculators, the railroad builders, and the timber barons. These men dealt millions of acres of land, dealt millions of trees, millions of miles of railroad line.

In May of 1862, President Abraham Lincoln signed The Homestead Act into law, which helped settle the American West. It allowed heads of households to claim 160 acres of land if they would agree to live on it for five years. By 1900, over 500,000 claims had been filed for

80 million acres of land. My grandfather's stepfather traveled from Missouri to Idaho and began ranching there because of this act. Both the myth and the reality of discovering and settling new land were as ingrained in my father as the rags to riches stories of his childhood.

But even if his big deal had gone through and we'd migrated to Venezuela, would it have been a break for us? Jonathan Raban states that if the land to be settled is less than fertile—in other words, dry and rocky, or "jungle" land—farmers and ranchers need over 3,000 acres to do even a small amount of farming and to run 150 head of cattle without overgrazing the land.

The early Plains States homesteaders were doomed from the beginning because their land grants were simply too small. Even if they'd known about crop rotation, they didn't have enough acreage to rotate crops, much less graze cattle without depleting and destroying the land. And even with 3,000 acres, it would have been hard to make a go of it.

Perhaps Dad could have eked out a living in Venezuela because he would have had more land, but the Chinese, who were going to get five acres apiece, didn't stand a chance. They would have been, at best, sharecroppers; at worst, indentured servants.

Charlie Breckenridge was the manifest in Manifest Destiny—a true Westerner. It was his destiny to explore, to expand, and to bring new settlers into unsettled land. His settlers were Chinese farmers escaping a tyrannical government and looking for a better life—the same goals as many of our early pioneers. He would bring them over—not on the Oregon Trail in covered wagons, but across the ocean in boats and planes. He, the New West Prophet, would lead the way. And this time, he'd make it all the way to Oregon.

Dad was offering people "the World's Greatest Opportunity for Successful FARMING and CATTLE RAISING VENTURES in BOOMING VENEZUELA." His sales material—the copy and the photographs—are as fictionalized as any pamphlets given to settlers throughout Europe and the Eastern United States, enticing them to settle the West, the Great Plains, or the Midwest.

Dad not only believed it was possible to successfully farm the

Venezuelan land, he also believed he could foster and build a community where all people—including his family—would live and work together in harmony. Unlike the original settling of America, "all nationalities" would prosper in Venezuela.

For Dad, who wanted it so badly, believing it made it so. He was like many early pioneers. First, they wanted to believe. Then, they believed. Then, they lost the money they'd invested, lost the years and labor they'd expended, lost even their land—with nothing to show for it but a hard lesson learned.

So, as one of the victims of my father's failed big dreams, what have I learned? I've always known that, although Dad was far from perfect, he loved me unconditionally. Today I carry on his laugh, his sense of humor, his penchant for storytelling, and his love of good food and fine clothes. What Dad gave me was imperfect love—imperfect love from an imperfect man. That was what he had to give.

This morning, I showered and stood in front of the bathroom mirror. With my feet spread apart, I rocked back and forth while I blow-dried my short red hair, streaked with blonde as it turns gray. My mother's eyes stare back at me from the mirror, eyes that look green when I wear green, and blue when I wear blue.

I've inherited her small bones supporting my fragile tent of flesh, bones becoming more brittle with the onslaught of scoliosis and osteoporosis. To offset this fragility, I've inherited Grandmother Breckenridge and Aunt Jo's broad shoulders, their determination and strong will.

In the years since Mother's death, I've often thought sadly about our relationship. I originally felt I'd lost her when violence stole my childhood, thought she'd walked out of my life arm-in-arm with trouble and a bottle. I couldn't forgive her bouts of ambivalence and meanness magnified by alcohol. But that's only half the story. Her half.

To be fair, I have to examine my half. With my self-righteous indignation, I was an active participant in the ongoing warfare. My half is that I walked Mother to the front door of my self, pushed her out the door, and locked it. Whenever she tried to come back in;

whenever she knocked guiltily, hat in hand; whenever she was sober and tried to make up to me with a hug or a pat on the back, I slammed the door in her face.

At the time, I hated her—an overreaction toward a flawed alcoholic parent. Anger wagged me like a vestigial tail. I hated her for not being the mother I wanted and needed. Hated the child she remained and the life she delivered me into. I needed to have someone to blame, just as I needed to uncritically adore my father—the guiltier party—for the damage that became our lives together.

I realize now that even though I was often the recipient of my mother's anger, her actions weren't totally about me. But I took them personally. Love and hate are the related passions of a two-sided coin. If you let it, hatred can eclipse the light of love.

I remembered how much she did for me when I was young. She taught me to look up toward something larger than the chaos around us. She took pride in all my accomplishments, encouraged me to explore my creativity through lessons she miraculously paid for and ferried me to. She started me on the path that led from painter to cowgirl to poet.

Looking through family memorabilia for this book, I found that she'd saved almost every picture taken of me; saved my childhood drawings; saved newspaper articles I'd appeared in; and even saved my grade school report cards, their construction paper covers crumbling into dust.

But no matter how hard I tried, how much I prayed about it, I couldn't forgive her. I wanted to forgive, not just for her sake, but for the sake of my own soul. Yet every time I thought of her, something tightened, grew hard and brittle inside me. Cold, cold as walking across the face of the moon alone.

After struggling for years trying to understand the nature of forgiveness, I reluctantly came to the conclusion that I'd probably never be able to forgive my mother—at least, not in this lifetime. Then, I heard Yale theologian, Miroslov Volff, discussing his book, *Exclusion and Embrace* on Minnesota Public Radio's "Speaking of Faith." I copied down some of his quotes, and was repeatedly drawn back to them, reading them every night before falling asleep.

Volff said, "We are always in relationship—even with our enemies." He continued, "Embrace is a recognition of the Other who is
part of who I am." And finally, "You begin with the Will to forgive.
You embrace an act of vulnerability—every step of Grace is stepping
into an unknown land."

The next morning, about five, I awoke after having a dream. In
the dream, I lived in a huge house I was about to sell, so I'd hired
three women to clean for me. They arrived just after sunset and began cleaning without turning on the lights. The house was in good
shape except for the basement, which was in total disarray.

I went to sleep and woke in the middle of the night because the
three women were standing by my bed in the dark waiting to be
paid. Neither before nor after they cleaned had I actually seen them,
but I knew they were there, sensed their presence. I got up and paid
them several thousand dollars for completing the job, an amount
that didn't surprise or upset me. Whatever they had done seemed
well worth it.

When I heard drums, I went to the basement. It was filled with
Native Americans—men, women, and children. Windowpanes had
been taken out of the two high windows in the basement, and Native Americans, in a continuous stream, flowed inside through those
windows. The basement was full of people, and a long line of mostly
children waited to use the downstairs bathroom.

I had two immediate thoughts. The first was, "How am I going
to feed all these people?" and the second was, "I've just gotten this
house cleaned, and they're making a terrible mess!"

The drummers, along with a few ancient elders, sat in the middle
of the room. They'd built a fire in a fireplace that hadn't existed before. Around them, The People were dancing and chanting. It was a
healing ceremony. A beautiful young woman was in charge. I wanted
to join them and dance, but since I wasn't one of them, she didn't approve. So I stood outside the circle.

I was sad because the young woman was a shaman, who works
between the visible and the spirit worlds, and I wanted to be healed.
In the unarguable logic of dreams, her great powers were proven to
me. As she was dancing, she had to pee, but the line to the bathroom

was long, and she didn't want to stop the ceremony. So she pulled out one of the pointed pockets in her full-length Native skirt, and when she danced by the fireplace, she peed through her pocket into the fire. The flames hissed, flared up red, blue and yellow, to burn brighter than before.

It was then I noticed that one of the seated elders, a tiny ancient woman, had fallen over, curled up on her side, and died. The others continued dancing, but they kept glancing toward her, upset about losing her. I walked into the circle, knelt beside her, and felt her wrist. Although her skin was warm, she had no pulse.

Filled with sorrow and loss, I picked her up and put her over my left shoulder as you would a small child. She fit perfectly there, and felt warm above my heart. Holding her, I began to dance with The People. The beautiful young woman in charge held out her hand to me, welcoming me into the healing circle. At that point, I woke up.

Forcing myself to get up, I groggily wrote down the dream in my journal: "This dream is about taking up my little child mother, my old woman mother and holding her in my arms, embracing her, and never shoving her away again, this old woman, this child, this mother, who was and is herself, separate from me, but half of me, who first gave me life and did what she could, in the only way she could—the imperfect way of all damaged humans—to sustain and nourish my life.

"This is my beautiful little mother who I welcome back into my open arms and embrace into my self, never putting her down, never pushing her away, never ripping her out of my self again, for she is an essential part of the whole self I must again become...the whole self I have again become..."

Twenty-four years after my mother's death, I experienced what has been called the bliss that follows the dying, when some age-old problem has been resolved and put to rest. I wondered if this ecstasy would last, this bliss of reuniting with the other, who is also my self.

And it did. It lasted. For the next day and the next. Not as passionate in memory as the actual experience, but solid, more like fact than dream—and larger. Instead of a single Monarch butterfly, the memory is a whole tree of Monarchs, after a long impossible journey, alive and fluttering.

ACKNOWLEDGMENTS

My deepest thanks go to my parents, who gave me life, along with this tale to tell. Thanks, as well, to the Ragdale Foundation, the Norcroft Foundation, and The Dwelling in the Woods where much of this book was written. I'm also indebted to Pat Sheldon, who shared her home with me, and tirelessly gave her time as the first editor of this book.

For the people who generously read, or gave me the crucial support, information, or inspiration that helped me write, complete, and publish my book, I'm grateful beyond words. This list includes, among many others not mentioned by name: my agent, Marly Rusoff; John W. Fenn; Chad and Sally Brown-Breckenridge; Phebe Hanson; Joan Drury; Julie Landsman; Pat Francisco; Patricia Hampl; Paulette Bates Alden; Deborah Keenan; Patricia Hoolihan; Chris Porter; Lisel Mueller; Jackson Petersburg; Wendy Watson; and Carol Mockovak.

I'm indebted to Richard White for his lucid explanation of the streams of Western emigration in his *A New History of the American West.* For the needed help I received in describing and confirming historical events and dates, I'm grateful to the Time-Life *This Fabulous Century* volumes that covered 1900 through 1960; the Time-Life *The Old West: The Ranchers*; the Beaulieu *Encyclopedeia of the Automobile, Vol. 1,* edited by Nick Georgano; the *Encyclopedia of American Cars: 1940-1970,* by Richard M. Langworth and The Editors of Consumer Guide; Irving Howe's *Men to Match My Mountains*; Sally Denton's *American Massacre: The Tragedy of Mountain Meadows, September 1857*; Jonathan Raban's *Badland: A Romance*; Walter A. Friedman's *Birth of a Salesman: The Transformation of Selling in America*; Miroslov Volff's *Exclusion and Embrace*; the web sites and staffs at The Tournament of Roses, the Idaho Historical Society, and the Boise Convention and Visitors Bureau; the staffs at the SEC/FOIA, The Justice Department, the Washington Federal Court System; and to the *Idaho Statesman,* Boise, Idaho; and *The Spokesman-Review,* Spokane, Washington.

I deeply appreciate the excellent work done to restore and reproduce my old photographs and newspaper articles by Mark A. Sanders and his staff at the Imaging Center, College of Biological Sciences, at the University of Minnesota.

Finally, working with Nodin Press publisher, Norton Stillman; and bookmaker, John Toren, has been a great pleasure. My thanks to them both.

ABOUT THE AUTHOR

Poet and memoirist Jill Breckenridge was born and raised in
the West, where she tried her
hand as a cowgirl, accordion
player, babysitter, model, and
(almost) chicken plucker. She
later taught English, history,
business, and creative writ-
ing, edited a newspaper, and counseled blocked writers. As a former
director of The Loft, a center for writers in Minneapolis, she origi-
nated the Mentor Series, a program connecting national and local
writers.

photo: Jackie Odermann

Jill won The Bluestem Award, judged by William Stafford, for
her book of poems, *How to be Lucky*. Her sequence of poetry and
prose about the Civil War, *Civil Blood*, was published by Milkweed
Editions. The book was nominated for the American Library
Association's Notable Books of 1986. Jill's latest book of poems, *The
Gravity of Flesh*, won a Northeastern Minnesota Book Award.

Her honors include a Bush Foundation Fellowship, two Minnesota
Arts Board grants, and Loft-McKnight Awards in both poetry and
prose. Jill holds an MFA in creative writing and a master's degree in
counseling psychology with an emphasis on creativity.